THE CHESSBOARD OF WAR

GREAT CAMPAIGNS OF THE CIVIL WAR

SERIES EDITORS

Anne J. Bailey
Georgia College &
State University

Brooks D. Simpson
Arizona State University

ANNE J. BAILEY

The Chessboard of War

Sherman and Hood in the Autumn Campaigns of 1864

University of Nebraska Press
Lincoln and London

∞

Library of Congress
Cataloging-in-Publication Data
Bailey, Anne J.
The chessboard of war : Sherman and Hood
in the autumn campaigns of 1864 / Anne J. Bailey.
p.   cm.—(Great campaigns of the Civil War)
Includes bibliographical references (p.   ) and index.
ISBN 0-8032-1273-9 (cl. : alk. paper)
1. United States—History—Civil War,
1861–1865—Campaigns.
2. Georgia—History—Civil War,
1861–1865—Campaigns.   3. Sherman's
March to the Sea.
4. Tennessee—History—Civil War,
1861–1865—Campaigns.
5. Sherman, William T. (William Tecumseh), 1820–1891.
6. Hood, John Bell, 1831–1879.   I. Title.   II. Series.
E476.69.B35   2000
973.7′3–dc21
99-39771
CIP

In memory of
Mildred Padon and
Mabel McCall

Contents

Illustrations

Maps

Series Editors' Introduction

Americans remain fascinated by the Civil War. Movies, television, and video—even computer software—have augmented the ever-expanding list of books on the war. Although it stands to reason that a large portion of recent work concentrates on military aspects of the conflict, historians have expanded our scope of inquiry to include civilians, especially women; the destruction of slavery and the evolving understanding of what freedom meant to millions of former slaves; and an even greater emphasis on the experiences of the common soldier on both sides. Other studies have demonstrated the interrelationships of war, politics, and policy and how civilians' concerns back home influenced both soldiers and politicians. Although one cannot fully comprehend this central event in American history without understanding that military operations were fundamental in determining the course and outcome of the war, it is time for students of battles and campaigns to incorporate nonmilitary themes in their accounts. The most pressing challenge facing Civil War scholarship today is the integration of various perspectives and emphases into a new narrative that explains not only what happened, why, and how, but also why it mattered.

The series Great Campaigns of the Civil War offers readers concise syntheses of the major campaigns of the war, reflecting the findings of recent scholarship. The series points to new ways of viewing military campaigns by looking beyond the battlefield and the headquarters tent to the wider political and social context within which these campaigns unfolded; it also shows how campaigns and battles left their imprint on many Americans, from presidents and generals down to privates and civilians. The ends and means of waging war reflect larger political objectives and priorities as well as social values. Historians may continue to debate among themselves as to which of these campaigns constituted true turning points, but each of the campaigns treated in this series contributed to shaping the course of the conflict, opening opportunities, and eliminating alternatives.

Series co-editor Anne J. Bailey's examination of William T. Sherman's march from Atlanta to Savannah and John Bell Hood's invasion of Tennessee in the fall of 1864 reminds us of the close relationship between these two campaigns. For though the fall of Atlanta may have brightened Abraham Lincoln's prospects for reelection, it presented both commanders with troublesome challenges. Frustrated in his attempts to cut Sherman off from his lines of supply and communication, Hood decided to strike northward; at the same time, Sherman, realizing that Atlanta had become something of an albatross, chose to move south. His target was not an army but the hearts and souls of Confederate supporters and the logistical infrastructure of the Confederate heartland. That he succeeded is evident in the stories that persist to this day of the terror and destruction surrounding the March to the Sea. Yet as even Sherman realized, the Union triumph would be far from complete unless Hood's Army of Tennessee was put out of action. Thwarted from intercepting retreating Union forces at Spring Hill, Hood threw his men at the Yankee defenses at Franklin, incurring tremendous losses. It was left to George H. Thomas to deliver a death blow to what remained of Hood's army south of Nashville but only after delays and bad weather nearly cost him his command at the hands of an impatient Ulysses S. Grant.

By January 1865 Grant and Sherman could turn to Virginia and the Carolinas and prepare to crush the core of Confederate resistance east of the Mississippi. In retrospect, the result might seem preordained, but Bailey reminds us of the importance of contingency and command decisions in shaping the result.

Preface

History records many unusual events during the American Civil War, but none are more fascinating than the two major campaigns that took place in the western theater late in 1864. The opposing generals, William Tecumseh Sherman and John Bell Hood, took armies that had been fighting for months and headed them in completely opposite directions. The curious phenomenon of armies turning away from each other to enter enemy territory had happened in earlier wars, but never in the American Civil War. Yet in the autumn of 1864 that was the strategy the two men adopted when Hood marched north into Union-controlled Tennessee and Sherman moved south into Confederate Georgia. The two commanders delegated the job of facing the invader to subordinates, while they led the main columns another way. Hood could have dogged Sherman as the soldiers in blue marched to the sea, but he decided instead to leave that task to Rebel cavalry. He embarked on his own sweeping campaign, a march through Tennessee that he hoped would carry him to the Ohio River and beyond. Sherman left the job of dealing with Hood to George Thomas in Nashville. "Thus were two opposing Armies destined to move in opposite directions," Hood later wrote, "each hoping to achieve glorious results." Both Hood and Sherman longed to make a decisive strike that would help end the war, and both thought that what they were doing in the West was important. Still, both men had the same long-range goal, to reinforce one of the two opposing armies in Virginia, for most Americans believed that the war would be won or lost in the eastern theater, where Robert E. Lee confronted Ulysses S. Grant. Neither could know that their actions, not those of Lee and Grant, would hasten the war's end.[1]

This book covers four months of the war, from September through December 1864. It is not a detailed tactical account of the Tennessee campaign, for many fine historians have already analyzed the battles at Spring Hill, Franklin, and Nashville. Nor will the reader find a comprehensive study of what occurred during Sherman's March to the Sea. Rather, I have tried to assess how military events in Georgia and Tennessee intertwined and how they affected the political, social, and economic conditions of people in those areas and in the nation. Numerous books deal with either Sherman's march through Georgia or Hood's Tennessee campaign, yet no recent volume looks at the two together, even though they unfolded simultaneously and concluded the main fighting in the western theater.

Important issues emerged during these two campaigns. Sherman's successful march across Georgia meant that his name would forever be linked with the change in warfare that made civilians fair game, but the two campaigns also introduced another question, that of the viability of African American soldiers actually fighting in the Union's western armies. Lincoln supported this radical measure, but Sherman did not. Therefore, most soldiers in the Confederate Army of Tennessee had never fought former slaves in Union blue. Those circumstances changed during the last months of 1864. While Sherman continued to thwart Lincoln's efforts to use blacks in combat, the Confederacy's principal western army faced African American soldiers on several occasions in the autumn, a milestone of no small proportions to many Southerners. Black units played a significant role at Nashville, a major battle in the western theater.

Yet the main concern in the autumn of 1864 was the Northern presidential election. Atlanta fell two months before that important second Tuesday in November, and the Confederates needed a military success to offset Sherman's victory. Throughout September and October, Hood's army had the potential to affect the vote, but after the November election assured Abraham Lincoln four more years in office, the Confederacy had no alternative but to achieve independence on the battlefield. Most modern historians tend to dismiss events of the weeks between the fall of Atlanta and the election as inconsequential to the outcome, but at the time Lincoln worried that a military mistake in September or October might cost him the White House. Moreover, many Northerners as well as Southerners had tired of the war and hoped for a negotiated peace that would end the struggle. But Hood was a fighter, not a politician. Sherman recognized the connection between politics and war, but Hood did not. In the weeks before the Northern election, Hood seemed oblivious to the political consequences of his actions. Whether Lincoln's defeat in the presidential race would have made a difference in the outcome of the war is less important than that many Northerners and Southerners thought the results of the vote would be pivotal in determining the future course of events. Any military action in the weeks before the election could have significant consequences for the prospects of peace, whereas what happened after the election could affect morale, particularly Southern morale. Sherman, counseled by Grant, understood that he could not implement his strategy, a march to the coast, until after election day. Hood, on the other hand, believed his only recourse was to end the war on the battlefield. More by coincidence than design, it was after that Tuesday in November that Hood marched north while Sherman turned south.

I have looked at these campaigns as two halves of a whole, just as Americans both North and South did that autumn. Certainly Abraham Lincoln could not rest easy until he knew that he had received the approval of the people to lead the nation for another term; nor could he relax until the situation in the western theater was resolved. There is no denying that the fall of Atlanta in early September was crucial in the political campaign, but even Lincoln recognized that with several weeks to go before the election, he could take nothing for granted. For that reason, he would suffer some anxiety over the course of events in the West. The day after Christmas, the president wrote Sherman to say how pleased he was that the Georgia plan had succeeded while Hood's invasion of Tennessee had not. Lincoln saw these twin campaigns as inherently connected. He told Sherman that after "taking the work of General Thomas into the count, as it should be taken," the Union strategy was "indeed a great success. Not only does it afford the obvious and immediate military advantages, but, in showing to the world that your army could be divided, putting the stronger part to an important new service, and yet leaving enough to vanquish the old opposing force of the whole—Hood's army—it brings those who sat in darkness to see a great light."[2]

The title of this book does not include Thomas's name although he also deserves credit for the Union success. Sherman and Hood were the two commanding generals in the western theater and ultimately responsible for the success or failure of the twin campaigns. Warfare is like a game of chess, a test of skill and nerve. Both Hood and Sherman wanted to make the right move, one that would win the game. The failure of either man would determine the victor as well as the outcome of the war in the West.[3]

The reader should also be aware that I have used Southerner and Southern to refer to Confederates and the Confederacy. While I understand that these two terms can also apply to Unionists, I have chosen the traditional meaning in this work.

Acknowledgments

Many kind and generous people helped me with this book. Several read the manuscript, including Larry Daniel, Nat Hughes, John Marszalek, Richard McMurry, Brooks Simpson, Daniel Sutherland, and Steven Woodworth. They made suggestions and pointed out errors, but they should not be held accountable for the final product of my many revisions. I especially appreciate the helpful suggestions of editor Trudie Calvert. My thanks go to the University of Nebraska Press for conceiving the idea for this series and to Brooks Simpson, who serves with me as co-editor. I modestly add my name to the list of authors who have agreed to write books for the Great Campaigns series and only hope that this effort will be worthy of such fine company.

This work is a result of a long fascination with the battle of Franklin, and I owe a special debt to Mildred Padon and Mabel McCall at the Layland Museum in Cleburne, Texas, where Pat Cleburne's pistol resides. As a native of Cleburne and a volunteer at the museum in my younger days, I learned to love the town's history as much as they did, and I heard from them the story of its founding by veterans of Cleburne's division in 1867. My father's family lived in the old Johnson County seat of Buchanan during the war and later moved to nearby Granbury (where Hiram Granbury is buried) in Hood County, named, of course, for John Bell Hood. It was impossible to separate my childhood from the battle of Franklin, and it is to the memory of these two special people that I dedicate this book. I also want to thank my family and friends, Shawn and Shana Bailey, Lyndal Wilkerson, Michelle, Gregg, and Stefan Morse, Anastatia Sims, Carolyn Malone, and Dan and Chris

Sutherland, for their help in many small ways. I also owe a debt of gratitude to Norman D. Brown, who shares an equal fascination with General Cleburne and has always given me encouragement. And, of course, I thank Grady McWhiney, who is more than a mentor. His guidance and never-failing support have been invaluable throughout my career.

THE CHESSBOARD OF WAR

CHAPTER ONE

Sherman and Hood

A smoky haze blanketed the depot of the Georgia Railroad as the petite dark-haired woman nudged her way through the crowd to the waiting train. After settling in a packed coach, she turned to gaze out the window at the bustle around the station before arranging the baskets of bread, pies, and cakes; sacks of potatoes, onions, and peppers; and assorted articles of clothing where she could watch them. It had taken several days to prepare for this trip, and she wanted to safeguard her treasures. Mary Gay was on her way to Dalton in the north Georgia mountains to visit her brother, an officer in the Confederate Army of Tennessee.

When she arrived at Atlanta, where she switched to the Western & Atlantic line, she found the terminal even more congested than the one she had left near her home in Decatur, just a few miles away. Yet she had little difficulty locating the train for the second leg of her trip. The cars were crowded with other travelers on similar missions: young wives with squirming children, anxious to see their husbands and fathers; mothers and fathers tending precious supplies carefully prepared for sons at the front. Occupants in the crammed cars soon began chatting, for rich and poor found common ground; they all carried items destined for loved ones with the army. In the spring of 1864 travel was slow, for many local residents cluttered stops along the way. It had become difficult to survive on farms around the military camps, where thousands of horses and mules and huge herds of cattle had grazed the countryside bare, forcing entire families to migrate south. Even so, Gay arrived safely, enjoyed a brief visit with her brother, and, on April 26, departed. Less than two weeks later Maj. Gen. William T. Sherman opened his spring campaign, turning the Rebels' left flank and forcing them to abandon the Dalton stronghold in early May. The fight for Atlanta had begun.[1]

More than four months would pass before Mary Gay visited the army again. Those would be anxious months for Gay and her mother; her only brother, Thomas Stokes, belonged to Hiram Granbury's brigade in Patrick Cleburne's division, one of the finest bunch of fighters in the entire Rebel army and a unit that won praise for its bravery during the army's withdrawal through north Georgia. That summer was a hard one for families in the Northern states too. It was the fourth summer of the war, and the fighting had taken a great emotional and physical toll on both sides. Many Americans, grown weary of war, hoped the summer campaigns would end the nation's great conflict. From June through August, Yankees and Rebels alike watched the events unfold.

By mid-1864 neither the Union nor the Confederacy had secured a military advantage. The North had a new general in chief, Lt. Gen. Ulysses S. Grant, and he had launched his strategy of moving Union armies simultaneously in May. Although it prevented Confederates from shifting large numbers of reinforcements between theaters by applying pressure on all fronts at once, it increased the number of casualties and did not promise an end to the fighting. In the eastern theater, Grant, commanding George Meade's Army of the Potomac, had not defeated Robert E. Lee, and the two sides extended their bloodbath into the early summer. As the Army of Northern Virginia held its own against the larger Federal army, Abraham Lincoln began to question his chances for reelection in November. He recognized that his bid for a second term in the White House ebbed and flowed with battlefield victories and defeats, and his chances faded as the number of Northern deaths multiplied.

Politics weighed heavily on Lincoln's mind, for the prospects of the Republican Party fluctuated with battlefield fortunes. The question was not whether Grant would eventually lead the nation to victory but whether he could do it before the November election. After weeks of bloody fighting and staggering casualties at the Wilderness, Spotsylvania, and Cold Harbor, the campaign in Virginia settled into a stalemate around Richmond and Petersburg, and Lincoln's chances for reelection dropped. Grant's strategy brought no immediate results, but both he and Lincoln were heartened when Sherman drove Gen. Joseph E. Johnston's Confederates toward the industrial heart of Georgia. Although Grant could not defeat Lee and the Army of Northern Virginia, Sherman faced not only a different foe but also a very different situation. Except for the battle of Chickamauga, the Army

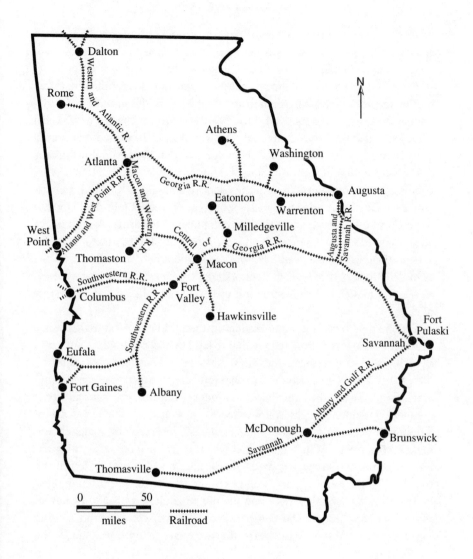

N

Dalton

Rome

Western and Atlantic R.

Athens

Washington

Atlanta

Georgia R.R.

Augusta

Macon and Western R.R.

Eatonton

Milledgeville

Warrenton

West
Point

Atlanta and West Point R.R.

Central

of

Georgia R.R.

Augusta and Savannah R.R.

Thomaston

Southwestern R.R.

Macon

Columbus

Southwestern R.R.

Fort
Valley

Hawkinsville

Fort
Pulaski

Savannah

Eufala

Albany and Gulf R.R.

Fort Gaines

Albany

McDonough

Brunswick

Savannah

Thomasville

0   50

miles   Railroad

1. Georgia in 1861

of Tennessee had suffered too many defeats without offsetting victories, and the interminable dissension within the officer corps had exhausted morale. The rank and file might be just as courageous and determined as other Rebel soldiers, but many general officers exhibited only mediocre military skill.

The inability to stop Sherman throughout May and June frustrated many men in the Confederate ranks, for the Rebels steadily fell back. "If we had a good general at the head of our army, we would have the bulk of Sherman's army in twenty days," judged a Rebel soldier. "I don't believe Johnston ever did or ever will fight." Many soldiers thought that Johnston had not done enough to stave off Sherman, and President Jefferson Davis agreed. In mid-July Davis finally decided to remove Johnston, promoted John Bell Hood to temporary full general, and gave him command of the army. Although not all soldiers liked the change, one man confessed, "I am not as much of a Johnston man as I have been." He was too cautious and not willing to risk a fight until he was sure he could win. Another Rebel simply told his family, "They hav made old J. Johnston quit us because he falls back. I am sorrow of it."[2]

Davis knew replacing commanders in the middle of a campaign was a gamble, but he was willing to take that risk if Hood could hold Atlanta and, by doing so, boost war-weariness in the North. A Northern politician predicted that if the South remained defiant until election day, the Peace Democrats "would sweep the Lincoln dynasty out of political existence" and a negotiated settlement might follow. Scores of songs reflected the earnest longing for peace among soldiers and civilians. Northern despondency propelled the popular "When This Cruel War Is Over" to a bestseller, and parlors across the nation reverberated with the haunting melody of "Tenting on the Old Camp Ground." The sad lyrics of the latter ballad, written in 1863, betrayed the melancholy sweeping the nation as the number of casualties rose. Both Northerners and Southerners lifted their voices in this moving plea for peace: "Many are the hearts that are weary tonight, wishing for the war to cease."[3]

Lincoln was a realist, and he knew he needed a military victory somewhere to counter unpopular political measures. As the reality of Grant's high casualty count from the late spring and early summer touched households of average voters, however, even the Northern president expressed doubts about his chances for reelection. His lenient blueprint for reconstruction, which he had announced in December 1863, had brought criticism from the extremists in Congress, and they had countered in early July by passing the Wade-Davis Bill, a punitive measure that would have given the Radicals control of the South. When Lincoln refused to sign the legislation, the Radicals denounced him in the Wade-Davis Manifesto. With just months to go before the election, Lincoln had outraged a powerful faction of his party. Hostile opposition among some Republicans had swelled; Salmon Chase, the Radical secretary of the treasury, had resigned in late June.

Other controversial actions also jeopardized Lincoln's chances for reelection. When he called for five hundred thousand new volunteers in July with deficiencies to be filled by a draft in September, a newspaper declared, "Lincoln is deader that dead." Moreover, his decision to support the unpopular policy of refusing to exchange prisoners, proposed by Secretary of War Edwin Stanton early in the year, appeared heartless to the average voter. Likewise, his stand on emancipation was controversial in the North and remained a sensitive issue. "I am going to be beaten," he told a soldier, "and unless some great change takes place *badly* beaten." In August he wrote that it seemed "exceedingly probable" he would not win the election.[4]

When Atlanta did not fall right away, talk of peace spread. Confederate chief of ordnance Josiah Gorgas commented in August that people spoke of peace "very openly." Confederate Vice President Alexander H. Stephens told his brother that he was confident that if the army made "no blunders" and the South could hold on for ten weeks Lincoln would lose. Yet if Lee stumbled at Petersburg or Atlanta fell, observed the *Richmond Examiner*, then all the calls for peace would end up "where last year's snow is, and last night's moonshine"—only a faded memory. A Rebel who deserted to the Federals outside Savannah summed up the situation when he claimed that the "whole dependence of the South is upon the election, in the success of a man of peace principles."[5]

Most Confederates recognized the importance of the Northern election. An Augusta, Georgia, newspaper plainly stated what many Southerners firmly believed—it was critical to sway Northern voters to unseat the Republican administration. Southerners desperately wanted to believe that the war might end if an antiwar Democrat won the election. "It is unquestionably our policy to do everything in our power to increase the number of unconditional peace men at the North," declared the press. "We believe this can be done by carrying the sword in one hand and the olive branch in the other."[6]

To carry the sword, Davis had turned to Hood. Born in 1831 to Kentucky parents with Virginia roots, Hood grew up in Bluegrass society. When he was seventeen years old, he left for the United States Military Academy at West Point with an appointment secured for him by a relative who served in

Congress. It did not take him long to discover how woefully ill-prepared he was to meet the academic standards expected of cadets; in his plebe year he ranked forty-fifth in mathematics, sixty-first in French, and even lower in English. When his studies failed to improve and he was publicly reprimanded for his conduct, he considered resigning. An Illinois classmate, John M. Schofield, encouraged Hood to stay, and in 1853 he graduated, forty-fourth out of fifty-two.

Despite his academic shortcomings, Hood, known to his friends as Sam, was popular. One cadet recalled that he was "a jolly good fellow" who enjoyed life. Yet the West Point experience had a profound influence on his future. It was there that he met Robert E. Lee, who became superintendent of the academy in 1852, and George Thomas, who was the young Kentuckian's instructor in artillery and cavalry. Hood's graduating class included some future stars: Schofield, James M. McPherson, and Philip H. Sheridan. McPherson, who often helped Hood with his lessons, was an outstanding student, graduating at the top of his class.[7]

After leaving West Point, Hood had a respectable though unremarkable military career. In the mid-1850s he was among those picked to join a new command, the Second United States Cavalry, which Secretary of War Jefferson Davis convinced Congress to authorize for duty on the Texas frontier. Since the secretary also played a prominent role in determining many of those assigned to this regiment, it became known as "Jeff Davis's Own." Several men who would earn fame in the Civil War served as officers in this unit, including Albert Sidney Johnston, Robert E. Lee, George H. Thomas, William J. Hardee, Edmund Kirby Smith, Earl Van Dorn, Fitzhugh Lee, and, Hood, at the time just a lieutenant. Of these, only Thomas remained loyal to the Union in 1861, and an early biographer claimed that Thomas always thought Davis organized the Second U.S. Cavalry because he believed there might someday be a war between the North and South. Indeed, four of the regiment's officers, Johnston, Lee, Hood, and Smith, eventually became full generals in the Confederate army, providing half of the South's eight full generals. Moreover, Hood's Texas experience also made a lasting impression on the young soldier, for when Kentucky did not secede, he adopted the Lone Star State as his home.[8]

At the time Davis turned to Hood in the summer of 1864, the Texan's Old Army service was not widely known, but his Civil War record was impressive. He had risen rapidly from regimental, to brigade, to division commander, and his wounds testified to his bravery. He had lost the use of his left hand while leading his Texas brigade at Gettysburg, and another wound at Chickamauga had required the amputation of his right leg in the upper part of the thigh. While recuperating from the loss of his leg in the winter of 1863–64, he was a frequent guest in Richmond society, and it was during that time that he caught the eye of the Confederate president. Promoted to lieutenant general in the spring of 1864, he was given command of a corps in the Army of Tennessee.

Davis knew Hood was a fighter when he selected him to replace Johnston outside Atlanta. Without question, the Texan was one of the Confederacy's war heroes, but that reputation had been won on fields where he commanded a brigade, division, or corps, not the entire army. He had no experience for the task Davis asked of him. And the situation outside Atlanta was critical; only a miracle could change the fate of the city. Hood's success hinged on skillful subordinates, but that characteristic was not a trait associated with the factional officer corps of the Army of Tennessee.

Even though Hood had no experience at such a high level of command, he quickly demonstrated that his reputation as a fighter was deserved when he struck Sherman three times in just over a week, on July 20, 22, and 28. He had done what Davis had wanted of Johnston—he had attacked—but like his predecessor, he was unable to stop Sherman. Just as Lee had earlier moved into the trenches protecting Richmond, Hood now settled into the earthworks around Atlanta. Unlike Grant, who had moved into the lines at Petersburg, Sherman did not have the patience or the time to starve the Confederates out. As Sherman's frustration mounted throughout August, so did Lincoln's anxiety.

At the first of the month, a Republican leader announced that Lincoln's reelection was "an impossibility" because the voters were "wild for peace." That was particularly true in the states bordering the Great Lakes, where Canadian-based Rebel agents were stirring up antiwar unrest. Although talk of conspiracies, particularly among Copperheads in the Midwest who wished to establish a separate peace with the Confederacy, may have been exaggerated or even fabricated by Republicans, it could not be totally ignored in Washington. When the Democrats met to select their candidate for the coming election, the Republican Party needed some positive action on the battlefield, and if Grant could not deliver a victory, then Sherman must. Six hundred miles south of the Democratic gathering in Chicago, where the politicians flailed away at Lincoln's unsuccessful war policy, Sherman's soldiers did just that. The outnumbered Confederates could do little to counter the relentless pressure, and although Hood tried to stop the Federal drive around Atlanta in late August, he failed.[9]

The fighting at the end of August and the beginning of September concluded the Union campaign that had begun in May. For almost four months the Confederates had steadily retreated, and by the end of the summer Hood's depleted army was no match for Sherman's growing numbers. The fighting at Jonesboro on August 31 and September 1 only verified what the soldiers already suspected—the Army of Tennessee was not strong enough to hold Atlanta any longer.

Hood had no choice but to evacuate the city. Soldiers packed the streets as the army departed, and when the state militia followed, Atlanta's despondent occupants knew that the long fight was over. Hood refused to leave any supplies and ordered that all the locomotives and ammunition cars, along with all the military stores he could not take with him, be moved to the railroad yard and destroyed. At midnight on September 1, Confederate cavalry carried out his instructions, and for several hours the fires that resulted could be seen for miles. Violent explosions rocked houses and terrified the few remaining residents. The night of horror ended as the last Rebel horseman fled south leaving behind only dusty, vacant streets to greet the invader. No one could deny that Hood was an aggressive fighter, but he was not Robert E. Lee, and though Lee would keep Grant at bay for months, Hood, placed in an impossible situation, only managed to hold out for only a few weeks. Hood informed Davis that his army was "much mortified at the feeble resistance" it had made against Sherman, but he was certain that the men would "fight better the next time." Still, Hood's audacity, patterned on the months spent watching Lee command, had cost the army a quarter of its strength in the six weeks he had been in command. More important, after 128 days of fighting, Sherman could wire Washington, "Atlanta is ours, and fairly won."[10]

When Sherman marched into the city on a clear September day, Lincoln appreciated that he had just received a gift that might rescue his dimming prospects for four more years in the White House. He knew that this success, combined with David G. Farragut's earlier triumph at Mobile Bay and Philip Sheridan's victories in the Shenandoah Valley later in the month, would stop the Democrats from claiming that the war was a failure. "Union men!" wrote the editor of the *Chicago Tribune*, the "dark days are over. We see our way out. . . . Thanks be to God! The Republic is safe." With the luck of the North rising, many veterans, whose three-year commitments had ended, elected to reenlist and see the fighting to its conclusion. Perhaps, they reasoned, Lincoln could end the war by fighting rather than through negotiations. With renewed confidence, a Republican campaign slogan advised, "Don't swap horses in the middle of the stream."[11]

Both Northerners and Southerners recognized that Sherman's military victory had far-reaching consequences. "The political skies," reported a New York newspaper, "begin to brighten" for the clouds over the Republican Party had started to evaporate. Even Republican newspaper editor Horace Greeley, who had initially hoped to see Lincoln replaced, proclaimed, "Henceforth, we fly the banner of ABRAHAM LINCOLN for our next President." Republican hopeful John C. Frémont read the writing on the wall and withdrew from the race. On the other side, Southerners recognized that any chance for a negotiated settlement had taken a serious blow. The Charleston press reported that the outlook for antiwar Democrats had darkened, and in Richmond the *Examiner* observed that the fall of Atlanta came in the nick of time to save the Republicans from "irretrievable ruin." This unsettling military disaster would certainly "obscure the prospect of peace, late so bright." Still, many hopeful Confederates clung to the illusion that the Democrats could win in November, even though they knew that the Confederacy would need a miracle to offset the fall of Atlanta. With little chance of the stalemate in Virginia being broken, those Southerners anxious for the war to end fastened their hope on Hood's army in Georgia.[12]

Realistically, Atlanta was more of a symbolic victory than one that produced significant military results. "All Yankeedoodledom is clapping hands," reported one newspaper when the city fell, and Northerners were "huzzaing and flinging up caps, as though there was no longer a 'live rebel' in all America." Although Sherman had won a clear tactical victory over one of the two major Confederate armies and fulfilled his assignment in Grant's strategy of coordinated offensives, the surrender of Atlanta did not significantly cripple Confederate resources. Even though it was a railway hub and supply depot, Atlanta's importance had diminished throughout the summer as the fighting neared. Still, the city's capture produced enormous political results far beyond its military significance.[13]

Since Hood could not influence any political repercusions from his recent loss, he turned instead to the problems at hand. If he did not address the army's needs, including raising its spirits, there would be no Rebel army facing Sherman when Northerners went to the polls in November. A Rebel soldier admitted that the morale of the army had dropped after leaving Atlanta, but it had improved in the camps around Palmetto, where Hood bivouacked his army in late September. What the men needed most was rest.

The soldiers in both armies were weary, for the long, hard push toward Atlanta had taken a heavy toll. From the time Sherman's army group had opened the campaign in May until the blue columns marched into the Gate City of the South almost four months later, there had been almost constant fighting. Now, for the first time since the campaign began, there was no sound from cannon or musket. The men were "enjoying a good, old fashioned, genuine *rest*," one soldier informed his wife. "No one in the world can appreciate better than the tired & war-worn soldiers the meaning of that little word, *rest*." With Atlanta in Federal hands, Sherman could consider his immediate goal accomplished, and he settled into a temporary understanding with Hood that amounted to a cease-fire.[14]

While the soldiers relaxed, politicians pondered the future. Northern Democrats knew they were in trouble. When their convention opened in Chicago at the end of August, they tried to appease opposing factions by nominating a war candidate, George B. McClellan, while allowing the proponents of a negotiated peace to write the platform. McClellan overwhelmed his nearest opponent, but the convention nominated Ohio representative and Peace Democrat George H. Pendleton for vice president. With a supporter of the war as the presidential nominee and a vice presidential choice known for his opposition, the divided party struggled to attract voters. Democrats confused the electorate even more when McClellan repudiated the peace plank. As he wrote his letter accepting the nomination, McClellan had pondered how the fall of Atlanta would affect his campaign. Early drafts of his message supported an armistice but insisted that the fighting be renewed if negotiations failed to achieve a reunion. His final version, released a week after Hood abandoned Atlanta, backed away from talk of peace. Even though it was not clear how McClellan and the party would settle their differences, a popular campaign rhyme promised, "Mac Will Win the Union Back."[15]

Many Southern soldiers still continued to hope that Northern war-weariness would bring the Confederacy independence through the ballot box. In Virginia, Grant observed that the Rebels were determined to hold out until after the presidential election. "Deserters come into our lines daily who tell us that the men are nearly universally tired of the war," he informed the secretary of war, "and that desertions would be much more frequent, but they believe peace will be negotiated after the fall elections." A Vermont cavalryman in the Rebel prison at Andersonville recalled that Confederate officers told him they were confident the Democrats would elect a president who would help the South. A Lincoln victory seemed "so unlikely an event to them that its discussion will not be tolerated." One of Hood's Confederates reflected in his diary, "I see where old McClellan has been nominated by the Chicago convention which I suppose is all right as he is in favor of the cessation of hostilities."[16]

Northern soldiers also studied the political waters. "McClellan is fast losing what friends he had in the army," wrote Pennsylvanian Alfred Hough, "and I have no doubt Lincoln will have a large majority of the army vote." New Yorker John Gourlie told his brother about a comrade who had previously been a stalwart McClellan man and had sworn he would "see Old Abe d——d before he would vote for him," but after being captured in Virginia he had spent time in a Rebel prison before escaping back to his command, now camped at Atlanta. During his months as a prisoner he had listened to his guards boast that a McClellan victory would save the Confederacy. That, decided Gourlie, was "pretty plain talk" to a McClellanite who was fighting to put the rebellion down, and the Union prisoner soon switched sides, becoming a "Lincoln man to the backbone." Hough concluded that if more of McClellan's followers "could be placed under the Rebs care for about two months, it would cure them." The Confederacy was "about gone up," he believed, and to watch Northern men keep it alive by backing McClellan was "shameful."[17]

Although the fall of the Georgia citadel hurt the Democratic Party and erased some of Lincoln's concerns, he knew that in the mercurial game of politics nothing was ever certain. When he told Sherman that the Indiana state elections would occur on October II and the loss of Indiana "to the friends of the Government, will go far toward losing the whole Union cause," he revealed that he was not totally confident of victory. He needed to have Governor Oliver P. Morton, a staunch Republican, reelected and cautioned that losing Indiana was "too much to risk" if it could be prevented. The campaign for Atlanta might be over, but Lincoln's political battle was not yet resolved.[18]

In the Confederate states, discontented civilians, politicians, and soldiers blamed Davis for the current crisis. The general feeling, wrote a Rebel in Georgia, was that the president bore the responsibility for the "present state of affairs." Most Confederates recognized the implications of Atlanta's surrender on the Democrats' chances to remove Lincoln. If the army had held Atlanta, speculated a soldier, there would probably be "peace by Spring." In Richmond, a war clerk observed that everybody was abusing Davis for removing Johnston, and many Rebel soldiers agreed that elevating the Texan had been a mistake. There was even talk of a new commander for the

Army of Tennessee, admitted one Confederate, "as Hood, though an able man, has been unsuccessful & cannot command the entire confidence of the army."[19]

Hood's ability to maintain the respect of his troops fell correspondingly. Some people thought his impetuosity and eagerness to attack rash, even extreme. When he failed to save Atlanta, he had sought scapegoats, blaming his own soldiers for their failure to storm breastworks. He refused to concede his own shortcomings, and many soldiers, although sympathetic to him personally, judged him harshly. "Sherman is more than a match for Hood, & has completely out-generaled him," a Rebel surgeon unequivocally concluded. "If President Davis could have been content to throw aside his personal prejudices & let Joe Johnston remain in command of this army we would still be in possession of Atlanta & Sherman with his disheartened troops falling back towards Chattanooga." Hood, he decided, did not understand Sherman's strategy until it was too late to counter it successfully. Although it is true that Hood abandoned the city to Sherman's armies just days before the surgeon wrote this letter, a debate began (one that continues to the present) over whether Johnston could have done better. Nonetheless, Johnston certainly could not have pushed Sherman back to Tennessee as the doctor suggested. "Old Joe" had retreated before McClellan on the Virginia peninsula in 1862 and had called for the evacuation of Vicksburg in 1863. Yet in the Rebel camps southwest of Atlanta, many soldiers voiced their displeasure with Hood's failure. One of the Confederacy's two main armies was in serious trouble.[20]

Thus as the fourth summer of fighting drew to a close, many loyal Confederates pondered God's mysterious design for the future. More than forty months of war had brought occasional military setbacks, but never had the South seemed more abandoned by providence than after Atlanta fell. Even the losses at Vicksburg and Gettysburg the previous year had not discouraged the optimists, for reversals on the battlefield could be countered. Many Southerners had hoped that if Lincoln failed in his bid for reelection in November 1864 and the Peace Democrats gained power, a negotiated settlement would deliver the independence that the fighting had not. But as the autumn of 1864 approached, the prospect of a compromise that would stop the bloodshed slowly faded. Sherman, Sheridan, and Farragut had produced victories that boosted Lincoln's likelihood of reelection. To counter, Confederates who longed for a negotiated settlement focused their hope on their own military leaders. With Lee deadlocked in Virginia, all eyes turned to Georgia.

CHAPTER TWO

After Atlanta

The surrender of Atlanta left the Army of Tennessee in shambles both physically and mentally. Once again the Confederacy's second largest army had suffered a stinging defeat. Moreover, a Union army, not dependent on waterways or aided by the navy, had penetrated the Lower South. There had been occasional incursions across the Deep South from Alabama to South Carolina, but this was the first time such a huge Federal presence set up housekeeping deep in Georgia. The situation required the personal attention of the Confederate president, and he made plans to make his third trip to the western theater during the last week of September. Soldiers who had never seen Jefferson Davis were excited about his visit, but some veterans of the campaigns with the Army of Tennessee were apprehensive. Two years before, Davis had met with Braxton Bragg just before the battle at Murfreesboro. "The result was our army was defeated, and fell back to Tullahoma," recalled a Texas soldier. The previous October "Jeff Davis came around again," he added, and the army faltered at Chattanooga, then retreated to Dalton. He reasoned that if the future could be judged by the past, the army was going to do something wrong or would undertake some move that would not be successful. This cynical soldier feared that Davis's third visit to the Army of Tennessee portended another setback. Even the Northern press picked up on this odd coincidence. "The annual visit of Jeff. Davis to the Western department of the rebel confederacy," reported a New York newspaper, usually presaged some "startling movement," for "these annual visits are generally followed by some disaster."[1]

Confederates critical of Davis's military policies thought he did not pay enough attention to the West. Both of his previous trips to the western theater had resulted from reports of friction among army officers as well as poor morale among the soldiers. This third trip was no different, although this time he would see an army unlike any he had seen before, an army disintegrating before his eyes. Desertion was high, and many of the men who remained were despondent. A Louisiana soldier recorded in his diary earlier in the month that thousands were heading home. "It is a disastrous affair," he concluded, "and I think this army is so weakened and demoralized that it will never be worth a curse again." On the day Davis arrived, men trudged through wet red Georgia clay without shoes. Never before had the president faced such a test of his ability to bolster morale for the Confederate cause.[2]

The condition of Union soldiers was very different. After Sherman won Atlanta, vast quantities of supplies arrived by rail from Tennessee. While the Confederates suffered shortages, the Federal soldiers lived comfortably. "It is a pleasant, breezy afternoon," a Union major told his wife in mid-September, and as he sat in his tent he could admire Old Glory defiantly floating over the Rebel city. New Yorker John Gourlie told his brother that morale improved soon after tobacco and cigars arrived. After going without for months, "some of the boys got as much as 150 lbs of Tobacco." To his sister he wrote that the army was in "splendid condition and spirits & with Crasy Bill Sherman to command us will accomplish all we undertake."[3]

Soldiers could joke about "Crasy Bill" now, but that had not always been the case. In fact, Sherman had been pronounced incompetent by the press and he had asked to be relieved from command of the Department of the Cumberland in 1861. Even the assistant secretary of war, Thomas W. Scott, had bluntly announced that "Sherman's gone in the head, he's luny," after the general claimed he would need two hundred thousand men to take the offensive. But with the military clamoring for experienced officers early in the war, it was hard to ignore Sherman for long. He was a West Pointer, having graduated sixth in a class of forty-two in 1840. Even though Sherman had left the army in 1853 and was head of the Louisiana Military Seminary when the war began (where his students had included sons of his Southern friends from the Old Army), he had military experience. Sherman, known as Cump to family and friends, also had strong allies in Washington, including his brother John, an influential Republican senator. Additionally, Sherman had grown up in the house of Thomas Ewing, another powerful figure in prewar politics. Ewing had taken the nine-year-old boy to live in his home after Tecumseh's father died in 1829, and Sherman later strengthened the relationship with the Ewing family by marrying his stepsister Ellen.[4]

Much had happened to Sherman since that humiliating experience in Kentucky early in the war; he had proven his worth in battle time and time again and had cemented his position in the army through his close friendship with Grant. Thus, in the camps outside Atlanta few still considered him genuinely crazy, and with supplies pouring into the city, it seemed he was wasting no time in preparing his army for the next campaign. Vast stores of goods steamed in along the Western & Atlantic Railroad, which connected Atlanta with depots in Union-held Tennessee. Sherman knew he could not stay in Atlanta long, for his line of communication, which stretched back to Louisville, left him vulnerable. The Confederate cavalry had done little significant damage to the rails thus far, but Sherman knew that would not last indefinitely. His greatest fear was that Nathan Bedford Forrest might join Hood, and he had good reason to be concerned if Forrest was set loose in his rear. Sherman needed to eliminate his dependence on the railroad for as many men were needed to protect the tracks as he had at the front. Throughout September he formulated an idea that would allow him to break away from his supply line and head for the coast. He decided to make Atlanta a true military camp, and toward that end, he ordered all civilians, both Union and Confederate, to pack their belongings and leave.

Although the city's small number of noncombatants presented no military threat, Sherman had ample precedent for the decision, and he had used similarly harsh measures before, although not on such a large scale. His brother-in-law Thomas Ewing Jr. had also removed civilians, primarily women and children, from their homes in western Missouri the previous year because they had aided Rebel guerrillas. Sherman did not fear that Atlanta's Confederates would assist Hood's army, but he wanted nothing to hamper his men as they readied for the next campaign. He wired Henry Halleck that he did not intend to have his preparations hindered by the families of the enemy; he foresaw "a pure Gibraltar." Nor did Sherman want to worry about the safety of women and children in the midst of thousands of Union soldiers. So over seven hundred adults, with more than eight hundred children tagging along, exited the city scarcely a week after its surrender. Seventy-nine slaves also chose to accompany their owners rather than enjoy the freedom of a liberated Atlanta.[5]

Both the city's mayor, James Calhoun, and Hood protested. "War is cruelty," Sherman admonished the mayor, "and you can not refine it." Calhoun continued to appeal to Sherman's conscience, pointing out that the consequences would be not only appalling but also heartrending. Still, Sherman remained inflexible. He agreed to furnish transportation, but the refugees would be escorted south only as far as Rough and Ready, where Hood had to assume responsibility for them. Mary Gay, who visited the camps of Granbury's brigade to see her brother, recalled bitterly that most residents of Atlanta "were dumped out upon the cold ground without shelter and without any of the comforts of home. The order was merciless, she added, for all were suddenly thrown upon the "cold charity of the world."[6]

Southerners universally criticized Sherman while Northerners generally applauded his actions. Ellen Sherman, who had given birth to a son just weeks before, wrote her husband that she was "charmed" with his order expelling the inhabitants because it had seemed to her "preposterous to have our Government feeding so many of their people." She judged that "their insolent women particularly" should be punished, for they were responsible for the war and should be made to feel that it existed in "sternest reality." From Washington, Henry Halleck concurred. An authority on the laws of war, he assured Sherman that his actions had the full support of the administration. "We have tried three years of conciliation and kindness without any reciprocation," he concluded. Believing that war must be brought home to the women and children, he told Sherman, "I have endeavored to impress these views upon our commanders for the last two years. You are almost the only one who has properly applied them." He softened his harsh tone slightly when he admitted that he did not condone destroying homes or private property, for that was "barbarous." Nonetheless, he did approve of taking or destroying anything that might benefit the enemy armies.[7]

Sherman also hoped to exploit a political rift in Georgia. The state's irascible governor, Joseph E. Brown, had maintained a turbulent relationship with Confederate authorities on a variety of issues. Most notably, Brown's objections to conscription and his creation of a state militia had long troubled Richmond. Opponents referred to the Georgia militia as "Joe Brown's Pets" for his habit of periodically disbanding and reorganizing the men to circumvent changing provisions in the conscription laws. Most recently— shortly after the surrender of Atlanta—he had recalled the militia on the pretext that the men needed to harvest their crops. Brown knew his constituency. North Georgia farmers had first elected Brown governor in 1857 and then reelected him for three more terms; in November 1863, he had received over half of the votes cast. Sherman thought he might be able to lure Brown back int⌐ the Union; he was wrong. The general also told Lincoln that Vice President Alexander H. Stephens was "a Union man at heart" and might be willing to talk. He was wrong again. But when Sherman told Lincoln that Davis had arrived in Georgia, Lincoln commented, "I judge that Brown and Stephens are the objects of his visit."[8]

Davis reached Hood's headquarters at Palmetto on a rainy Sabbath in late

September. Certainly he was concerned about Brown and Stephens, but he also had the important mission of inspiring the army and convincing Georgians to rededicate themselves to the Confederate cause. To Georgian Herschel V. Johnson, who had been the Southern Democratic vice presidential nominee in 1860 and was now a Confederate senator, Davis confided that he still believed the state could be saved if all the soldiers absent without leave returned and those Georgians exempt from military service would temporarily enlist. The Army of Tennessee was not only demoralized after its recent losses, it also needed men. Davis knew he would encounter some resentment because of the army's current condition, but he was not ready for the shower of cries, "Johnston! Give us Johnston!" amid the soldier's cheers. One veteran understood the reason for the outburst: "The troops do not like Hood."[9]

Discontent was evident everywhere. Veterans remembered that when "Old Joe" commanded, shortages of food and supplies disappeared; when Hood came, they reappeared. Many soldiers suffered without shoes, food arrived slowly, and the call for gunpowder and other military necessities seemed unending. Just a few days before Davis arrived, Hood had reported less than forty thousand enlisted men and officers present for duty as the number of absentees continued to rise, reaching 53 percent by the year's end. To complicate matters, those men who remained had not been paid for ten months. Confidence in Hood reached a critical level, and the soldiers were quick to voice their disapproval. "My own opinion," wrote a Confederate soldier, "is that Hood was completely out-generaled."[10]

Some officers agreed. Just before Davis left for Georgia he had received a note from Maj. Gen. Samuel G. French at Lovejoy's Station outside of Atlanta. The two men had met in a hospital during the Mexican War when both were recovering from wounds. They had renewed that acquaintance when French, after resigning from the army, moved to Mississippi in the mid-1850s. "Several officers have asked me to write to you in regard to a feeling of depression more or less apparent in parts of this army," French told his friend. Perhaps it would be a good idea to send someone west to see "if that spirit of confidence so necessary for success has or has not been impaired within the past month or two. They might further inquire into the cause if they find in this army any want of enthusiasm."[11]

One officer who was exasperated with the situation was Lt. Gen. William J. Hardee, the commander of one of Hood's three corps. Hardee had asked for a transfer early in August, but Davis had discouraged him from leaving the army at such a critical time. After Hood laid the blame for the loss of Atlanta at Hardee's door, the Georgia-born general grumbled again. "It is well known that I felt unwilling to serve under General Hood," wrote Hardee, "because I believed him, though a tried and gallant officer, to be unequal in both experience and natural ability to so important a command." Davis had tried to pacify the feelings of both Hood and Hardee without success. He could not understand officers who did not have the self-discipline to put aside personal feelings. He patiently listened to the grievances of the two men, but when Hardee insisted that either he or Hood had to go, Davis refused to consider that he had made a mistake in his decision to promote Hood. He might have his own concerns about Hood's aggressive style of fighting, but he thought that with a face-to-face meeting, he could impress upon Hood the need for prudent, not impetuous, action. Therefore, to foster harmony within the army's high command, Davis relieved the Georgian. Hardee, who became commander of the Department of South Carolina, Georgia, and Florida, was replaced by Benjamin F. Cheatham.[12]

Cheatham was a Tennessean, having been born near Nashville, and reclaiming his home state was dear to his heart. He was not a military man although he served in the Mexican War before heading to California to pan for gold. When the war came, his Democratic connections gained him an appointment as brigadier general in the Provisional Army of Tennessee. He kept this rank when he joined the Confederate army and, after the fighting at Belmont, Missouri, earned promotion to major general. He led a division through the bloody battles at Shiloh, Perryville, Murfreesboro, Chickamauga, Missionary Ridge, and the Atlanta campaign. He was popular with his troops, although he often drank to excess and one private commented he was "one of the wickedest men I ever heard speak." Just five feet nine inches tall, with sun-roughened skin, he looked every inch the general and, commented a soldier, was "quite commanding in his appearance." He was not a man to keep emotions to himself, for he had threatened to resign after an altercation with Braxton Bragg in 1863. The hard-fighting Cheatham would be forty-four years old on October 20.[13]

Although the oldest of Hood's corps commanders, Cheatham was only a major general, while Hood's other two, Alexander P. Stewart and Stephen D. Lee, were lieutenant generals. Like Cheatham, Stewart was a Tennessean. Unlike Cheatham, he was a West Pointer, graduating a respectable twelfth out of fifty-six in 1842. After resigning from the Old Army three years later, he had become a professor at Cumberland University in Lebanon and at Nashville University. Although an antisecessionist Whig, he had joined the Confederate army, eventually taking command of a corps after the death of Leonidas Polk in June 1864. Known as "Old Straight" by his men, Stewart was, at the time Davis visited in the Rebel camps, just a week shy of his forty-third birthday.[14]

The third of Hood's corps commanders, Stephen D. Lee, also celebrated his birthday in the early autumn. He turned thirty-one years old just days before the president arrived, the youngest lieutenant general in the Rebel army. He had also attended West Point, where he had excelled in artillery and cavalry under Professor George Thomas, graduating seventeenth out of forty-six in 1854. Lee remained in the Old Army and did not resign his commission until February 1861, even though his home state, South Carolina, had seceded in December. For so young a man in such a high rank, he possessed an air of self-confidence that translated into a "dashing and inspiring" demeanor. On the whole, he was a competent soldier, although he had been known to order an occasional costly frontal assault. He served with the artillery in the Army of Northern Virginia, at Vicksburg, and as a departmental cavalry commander in the West before being summoned to Georgia when he replaced Hood as corps commander in July 1864. So as Davis and Hood settled down to discuss strategy, they had to consider that all three corps commanders were relatively new in that position. Whatever the two men decided needed to take into account that Cheatham, Stewart, and Lee had not operated together before in this capacity.[15]

The strategy that Davis and Hood developed was not complicated, and it allowed the army time to become familiar with the new chain of command before entering battle. Davis thought Hood should force Sherman to abandon Atlanta by hitting his supply line. Sherman's armies relied on provisions coming down the track from Chattanooga, and without food for his men or forage for the animals, the Federals would have to abandon the city. A strike against the railroad would compel Sherman either to withdraw north to protect his communications or to head south to open up a new line from the Atlantic or the Gulf of Mexico. Sherman's Achilles' heel was the railroad in northeast Alabama near where the Nashville & Chattanooga line joined the Memphis & Charleston at Stevenson, Alabama, for ten miles to the north the tracks crossed the river at Bridgeport on a mile-long bridge. But destroying that bridge would be difficult, if not impossible. Instead, if Hood headed directly north along the Western & Atlantic, Sherman would have to follow to protect his communications. If need be, Hood could fall back to Gadsden, Alabama, to secure his own supply line while still remaining a threat to the Federals. In any case, after the two men discussed all their options, Davis left believing that Hood understood that he should remain near Sherman.

When the subject of reinforcements came up, the Confederate president was optimistic. He felt confident that Governor Brown would return the ten thousand state militiamen he had recently recalled and consider making available another fifteen thousand that Brown protected as state officials. Davis also toyed with the idea of bringing reinforcements from the Trans-Mississippi but had to abandon that idea when Confederate soldiers in that department threatened to mutiny rather than cross the river. Hood had persuaded Sherman to exchange some of the men captured at Atlanta for healthy soldiers from Andersonville, but the number did not make a significant difference to Confederate rolls. Hood told Braxton Bragg just days before Davis arrived, "Sherman is weaker now than he will be in future, and I as strong as I can expect to be." He also tactfully asked Bragg for advice about the future operations of the army. Clearly the Army of Tennessee suffered from a numerical disadvantage that was bound to hamper almost any strategy Davis and Hood concocted, but the one agreed upon was probably the best they could have devised. It would, however, require fate to favor the Rebels and nearly flawless performance from both the soldiers and their generals. If the future was judged by the past, the campaign held little promise, for the Army of Tennessee had never turned in a faultless performance.[16]

Davis had also come south with a sensitive subject to discuss with Hood, the business of overall command. Hood had been a brilliant commander at a lower rank, but doubts about his ability to lead an army continued to trouble the president. Hood was young, only thirty-three, the youngest man to head a major Confederate army (Lee, by contrast, was fifty-seven). He had risen from a lieutenant in the Old Army to become a full Confederate general in less than four years; he was equal to Lee in grade if not in wisdom. The Texan had been in charge for forty-five days when forced to abandon the city he had been entrusted to protect, and even though Johnston had already retreated so far as to make Atlanta untenable, the responsibility for that loss still weighed heavily on him. Perhaps feeling concern about Hood's audacity, perhaps thinking that Hood needed supervision, Davis, for whatever reason, decided to pull in the reins on his commander. He would resurrect the old super command used (unsuccessfully) during the Vicksburg campaign when he had created a vast department under Joseph E. Johnston.

This reorganization would serve several purposes. Hood would report to a departmental commander, and a unified command would also have the advantage of coordinating the movements of Hood's army with those of Lt.

Gen. Richard Taylor's troops in Mississippi. Davis and Lee had discussed the problems of command in the West before the president left Virginia, and the two considered Johnston and Pierre G. T. Beauregard as possible candidates for the new position. Davis opposed returning Johnston to command, but he was willing to consider Beauregard. The surrender of Atlanta had been a political disaster for Davis, and he had suffered widespread criticism for not replacing Johnston with Beauregard in July. Now he had a chance to rectify that decision. Since Davis and Beauregard had not been on good terms for some time, the president asked Lee to intercede and ask if Beauregard would leave Virginia. Lee was more than happy to offer Beauregard's services and agreed to convince the Creole to accept. Like Lee, Beauregard was a full general, and as long as he stayed in Virginia, Lee would have trouble finding an assignment that was worthy of Beauregard's national renown. Beauregard, for his part, was eager to increase his authority and anxious to leave Virginia. Besides, many people thought Beauregard, the hero of First Manassas, deserved a more prominent position. At any rate, it was unlikely that Beauregard could make the situation in Georgia any worse. He would not have direct control of an army, and he might actually be able to smooth coordination between Taylor and Hood. Davis had already decided to unify his western command when he arrived in Georgia. Hood offered no objections.

After discussing strategy and command, Davis turned to yet another reason for visiting the army. He hoped that his own presence would go far toward raising morale, but, leaving nothing to chance, he had brought along two popular political figures, Howell Cobb of Georgia and Tennessee's governor, Isham Harris. Davis told the army that the coming campaign would force Sherman into a retreat "more disastrous than that of Napoleon from Moscow." His speeches were so successful that when he reviewed the troops, the cries for Johnston generally subsided, and most soldiers greeted him with enthusiasm. Davis promised the men of the First Tennessee Infantry that the coming campaign would be "the grand crowning stroke for our independence" and bring about a conclusion to the war. Besides speaking at Palmetto, Davis stopped at Macon, Georgia, and Montgomery, Alabama, before swinging back to Augusta, Georgia, where he met with Beauregard, and then to Columbia, South Carolina. At Macon the president addressed a gathering at a Baptist church, where he reminded an enthusiastic audience that he was the son of a Georgian who had fought in the American Revolution. More than that, he proclaimed, "I would be untrue to myself if I

should forget the State in her day of peril." His speech, frequently inter-
rupted by bursts of applause, had all the elements needed to bolster spirits.[17]

In these speeches Davis attacked Joseph Johnston, Governor Brown, and
others he perceived as political enemies and discussed his plans for the
army. At Augusta, Davis declared that to beat Sherman the army must
march into Tennessee. At Columbia, he revealed that Hood hoped soon "to
have his hand upon Sherman's line of communications" and that within
thirty days the army would be "in search of a crossing on the Tennessee
river." Both Grant and Sherman read newspaper accounts of the speeches,
and when Grant saw the comment about Napoleon, he remarked: "Mr.
Davis has not made it quite plain who is to furnish the snow for this Moscow
retreat through Georgia and Tennessee. However, he has rendered us one
good service at least in notifying us of Hood's intended plan of campaign."
Sherman observed in his memoirs that the Confederate president gave away
vital information. "To be forewarned was to be forearmed," he later wrote.
The *New York Herald* reported, "Old Abe will chuckle over this Macon
speech as something more refreshing than a joke, and Grant and Sherman
will find in it more useful information than could be gathered by all the
scouts of the Union armies in a month." To be fair, Davis probably did not
give away any strategy that was not already obvious, but the Northern press
used his comments to ridicule the Confederate president's lack of tact.[18]

While at Augusta, Davis met with Beauregard and finalized plans for the
newly created Military Division of the West. This was a distinguished title,
but Beauregard had little real power. By the time Beauregard assumed command, Hood's army had already embarked on the fall campaign. Since the
president had approved Hood's movements, Beauregard could do little but
acquiesce and offer suggestions. Yet his appointment was a popular move,
and when Beauregard took to the stump to address the people in Augusta,
he drew loud applause when he reminded them that he had fired the first
gun at Fort Sumter and hoped to live to fire the last shot of the war.[19]

After consulting with Beauregard, Davis started back to Richmond. He
had done all he could to stabilize the situation in the West, and he seemed
pleased with the results. Davis was not a quitter, and he still radiated confidence that the Confederacy could win on the battlefield instead of depending on the ballot box. At Columbia, he stopped at the home of his friend and
aide Senator James Chesnut. The local newspaper reported that a band,
along with the Arsenal Cadets, welcomed the nation's "honored leader" by
gathering in front of Chesnut's home. Again Davis felt obligated to give an
impromptu address. One more time he referred to Hood's future plans, in-

sisting that success lay just over the Tennessee line. "I believe," proclaimed Davis, "it is in the power of the men of the Confederacy to plant our banners on the banks of the Ohio," and in "the next thirty days much is to be done." Once again he told listeners that Hood intended to disrupt Sherman's line of communications, then march north and cross the Tennessee River. After a long speech, punctuated by enthusiastic applause, Davis was drained, and he accepted the hospitality of James and Mary Chesnut before continuing his trip home. He was satisfied that matters in the West were settled and that Hood knew what was expected of him and his army.[20]

Among those present at the Chesnut mansion that day was Sally Buchanan Campbell Preston, a distant relative of Patrick Henry. Known as "Buck," she was an eighteen-year-old sophisticated belle who could be "capricious, coquettish, and moody." She had added Hood to her list of admirers when they first met at the Chesnuts' Richmond home early in 1862, and he later confessed that he had "surrendered at first sight." Hood had impressed all the women "with his sad Quixote face, the face of an old crusader who believed in his cause, his cross, his crown," recalled Mary Chesnut. "We were not prepared for that type exactly as a beau idéal of wild Texans. Tall—thin—shy. Blue eyes and light hair, tawny beard and a vast amount of it covering the lower part of his face—an appearance of awkward strength." Hood proposed to Buck in September 1863 as James Longstreet's corps left Virginia for Georgia to reinforce Bragg's army. Hood later confided to Mary Chesnut that Buck had promised to consider the offer. She did not say yes, but she did not say no, so he had departed with the announcement, "I am engaged to you," to which Buck answered, "I am not engaged to you." Mrs. Chesnut observed: "Buck, the very sweetest woman I ever knew, had a knack of being 'fallen in love with' at sight and of never being 'fallen out of love with.' But then," she continued, "there seemed a spell upon her lovers—so many were killed or died of the effects of their wounds. . . . 'They say So-and-So is awfully in love with Miss S. P. Then I say, look out! You will see his name next in the list of killed and wounded.'"[21]

If Hood had been superstitious, he might have steered clear of Buck Preston, particularly after he was seriously wounded for a second time in the battle of Chickamauga. Returning to Virginia to recuperate from the loss of his leg, he was an instant celebrity. Richmond society, observed Mary Chesnut, idolized war heroes, particularly maimed ones, for mutilations were evidence of physical courage. Buck pointed out that Hood's injuries were "an honor" for "the cause glorifies such wounds." Mrs. Chesnut believed the young belle did not really love Hood but only felt sympathy because he was a wounded soldier. Yet Buck, she added, "must flirt." Although Hood had given up any hope of marrying Buck after losing his leg, the weeks spent in Richmond brought back his old desire, and Buck did not discourage his suit. Mary Chesnut, who listened to Hood's apprehensions concerning her young friend, believed that his courtship of Buck was probably the hardest battle he ever fought. As his physical wounds healed, the Confederate Senate began to consider him for a promotion, and Buck softened; she apparently agreed to marry him. Word of their engagement swept Richmond, and as Hood left to join the army in Georgia in the winter of 1864, he reveled in his newfound happiness.[22]

During the months of the Atlanta campaign, Hood corresponded faithfully with his fiancée. When he assumed command of the army in July, Buck told Mrs. Chesnut: "Things are so bad out there. They cannot be worse, you know. And so they have saved Johnston from the responsibility of his own blunders—and have put Sam in. Poor Sam!" Not only did Hood take command of the army in a terrible crisis, but disaster struck the Preston family under his leadership when Buck's brother Maj. William C. Preston was killed at Peachtree Creek. Buck's family had never blessed the engagement, and William's death could only have hardened their hearts toward the Texan. The Prestons had always had trouble with Hood's lack of refinement, and after Atlanta fell, his credibility suffered, a point Buck's parents never failed to mention. Thus as the fall campaign in 1864 opened, Hood's concern over his engagement often troubled his mind.[23]

Hood's fragile emotional state was matched by his equally infirm body. Campaigning was physically demanding even under the best circumstances, but it had been only a year since Hood had suffered two serious wounds in a three-month time span. The Gettysburg injury kept him from using his left hand, probably a result of nerve damage to the elbow. More serious was the loss of his leg, which had been amputated in the upper part of the thigh. Although the Texas brigade, which he had commanded in those battles, raised $3,100 in a single day for a cork leg, Hood was never able to wear an artificial limb comfortably. It is not known what psychological effects the injuries might have produced, but it was obvious that the wounds prevented him from moving easily, particularly when mounting and riding a horse.[24]

So as Hood set his army in motion late in September, ready to strike Sherman's line of communications, he had more on his mind than just military matters. A Union captive described him "as a thin, stooping man" with "a wooden leg and a wilted arm." The "baleful expression" in his gray eyes told of "overwrought nerves, sleepless nights and settled melancholy." Yet Hood's own discomfort was shared by his men. The temporary truce with Sherman that had allowed the Atlanta refugees to flee the city had further reduced Hood's already strained supplies. Hood had never been much good at logistics or administration, and as he prepared for the coming campaign, his chief of staff resigned. Hood did not replace him, choosing to leave most of the tedious administrative and logistical details to an assistant adjutant general. He ordered the railroad torn up west of Atlanta so that Sherman could not use it but doing so disrupted his own supply line. In early October, a Louisiana soldier recorded in his diary: "Nothing works right. The trains are all mixed pell-mell. Nobody knows where to find anything or anybody. There are no bread rations. We now miss the master hand of Gen. Johnston," he concluded. "Nothing worked wrong while he had command." As Hood began the march that he hoped would draw Sherman away from Atlanta, he demonstrated a disastrous flaw in his ability to lead an army. By failing to grasp the importance of logistics, he ensured a precarious beginning for his fall campaign.[25]

The time Hood's army spent in camp gave many soldiers one last chance to see family living in the area. Mary Gay, who had not seen her brother since April, was one of those to make a brief trip to the army. Her purpose was to return overcoats, blankets, and other articles entrusted to her safekeeping before the campaign opened in May. At great personal risk, she had kept the Rebel articles safely hidden for four months. Although she was happy to see her brother, she was equally saddened by the condition of the army. Still, she tried not to let her feelings show, and she listened as her brother talked of his wife in Texas and showed her the impression of the foot and hand of his only child, a boy he had never seen. The young woman managed to remain optimistic in his presence, but after the two parted, she "gave way to pent-up sorrow, and cried as one without hope—unreservedly."[26]

Gay had seen the Union army in Atlanta and could contrast it with the Rebel army she had just left. She had watched the Northern armies grow stronger each day. Sherman's soldiers knew it too, and a New Yorker predicted; "When we move again Johnnie Hood must look out for himself." Moreover, Union soldiers thought they detected a connection between the Rebel movement and the coming presidential election. An Ohio infantryman told his sister: "It is generally believed that the rebels are making the raid only for political influence in the north. They know that their only hope is in the northern copperheads and they want to encourage them all they can about the time of [the] election."[27]

CHAPTER THREE

Hood's March North

Although Southerners disagreed about the significance of the Northern election on the Confederacy's future, all realized that it presented a unique opportunity to upset the Republican Party. Even those people who wanted to see a battlefield victory understood that Lincoln's defeat could rejuvenate the Southern war effort and boost sagging morale. Thus Hood had a slim chance to disrupt Northern politics—very slim certainly, but a possibility. "After fighting four months to get into Atlanta," wrote the *Richmond Enquirer*, "Sherman is compelled to begin a new campaign to get out of the city." Sherman's capture of the industrial center had given the Republicans reason to claim the war was not a failure, but if Hood could neutralize that victory somehow, he could supply Democrats with ammunition for a new attack on the Lincoln administration. "The best policy of Hood is to avoid a fight," warned the armchair observer in Richmond, "and to harass the enemy, exhaust his supplies, and demoralize his army . . . for no general can keep a starving army together." If Hood could manage to keep Sherman off balance for just one month, it would be "a very healthy state of mind to go to the November polls in."[1]

It was a gamble, to be sure, but the Confederacy had few options left. Hood, of course, did not see his forthcoming campaign in political terms. He was a soldier: he believed that Confederates could preserve their honor and their independence only on the field of battle. By heading north, Hood could taunt Sherman and force him to retrace his steps or find his men cut off deep in Rebel territory. How much this would affect Northern morale depended on Hood's skill and the efficiency of his officer corps. Success or failure in this fall campaign rested firmly on the Texan's competence and ability to command, but he also needed capable subordinates.

Although Hood's decision to attack Sherman's line of communication carried risks, it seemed the only alternative in a desperate situation. Hood was outnumbered, but that made him more mobile than his opponent, and if he could entice Sherman back into north Georgia, or even Alabama, he could select the battlefield. He knew it was possible to divide and defeat a larger force. Lee had demonstrated that on several occasions, and Braxton Bragg had not won at Chickamauga because he was a brilliant battlefield commander. Good fortune, combined with Federal mistakes, had granted Bragg a victory. Even if Hood did not seek battle, he could prevent Sherman from moving east, toward the important powder works at Augusta, or south, toward the industrial city of Macon. Hood needed an opportunity like the one that brought Bragg victory in the Georgia mountains. More than that, Hood needed for Sherman to make a mistake that would leave the Federal army vulnerable to attack. Hood would also have to demonstrate the kind of leadership skill that separated Lee from other generals, and he would have to prove he was capable of planning an imaginative strategy that could offset overwhelming odds.

Rebel soldiers hoped that Hood was equal to the task when they crossed the Chattahoochee River at the end of September. "The whole Army is on the move," a Texan confided to his diary, "but no one knows where." Although the men might not know exactly what the plan was, they had an idea. Rebel officers confirmed those suspicions when they announced that Hood intended to flank Sherman out of Atlanta. Davis and Hood, the soldiers learned, had agreed on a bold turning movement to threaten the railroad to Tennessee, thus keeping Sherman from exploiting his possession of Atlanta. Hood had nothing to lose, for the city was in Union hands, but if Sherman followed the Confederates, he would be covering ground he had already battled for and won.[2]

Hood, it seems, never planned to fight, and the area he traversed was so large he could easily avoid battle. His movement became more of a raid than the shifting of a major army. By the first of October the Rebels reached the railroad, in spite of heavy rain that left the road muddy. Two days later they struck the tracks at Acworth and Big Shanty, where they captured one hundred prisoners. Although elated at heading north, the soldiers could not help but feel ominous foreboding when the weather failed to cooperate. "Rain, Rain, Mud Mud, March, March, is all we see, hear feel and do now," complained a soldier, while another recalled "a severe & disgreeable march of five days through the rain & mud." On October 9, a Rebel recorded in his

2. Georgia Theater of Operations, September–October 1864

diary a forewarning of the winter weather to come: "We had frost & cold whether."[3]

When Hood put his army in motion, Sherman was forced to consider his options. He asked Grant for permission to leave Thomas in charge of the defense of Tennessee while he marched through Georgia to Savannah or Charleston, destroying the railroads and inflicting "irreparable damage." The army should not, he cautioned, "remain on the defensive." When this message leaked to Henry Halleck, a surprised chief of staff immediately questioned Grant about Sherman's apparent change of plan. Sherman had previously suggested operating toward Montgomery and Selma before heading down the Alabama River, where he would unite with Union forces near Mobile. The administrative paperwork had already begun for a massive requisition of supplies to be directed to Mobile and Pensacola to accommodate this change of base. While Halleck made it clear that he did not intend to interfere with any of Grant's decisions, he personally thought that the move west was best.

Halleck meticulously explained his reasoning. The Alabama route was the shortest and most direct way to the coast, and it was not so directly exposed to a Rebel attack in the rear. Moreover, it did not leave Tennessee or Kentucky as open to Rebel raids, an important consideration in Washington. Halleck pointed out that the Alabama River was more navigable for Union gunboats than the Savannah River, and the route was more defensible for Union forces already in the state. Halleck also believed that Montgomery, Selma, and Mobile were, from a military standpoint, more useful than Augusta, Millen, and Savannah. Most important, Halleck observed, it would be easier to capture Mobile, and this movement would bring under Union control a valuable region of the Confederacy. In a confidential response, Grant admitted that Sherman's initial intention had been to take Mobile, but since Farragut had closed the port to Rebel traffic, it was no longer an attractive option. He favored moving on Savannah. "This is my view," Grant modestly offered, "but before giving positive orders I want to make a visit to Washington and consult a little on the subject."[4]

Meanwhile, Sherman took every opportunity to promote his scheme. He wanted to eliminate his dependence on the railroad. "It will be a physical impossibility to protect the roads, now that Hood, Forrest, and Wheeler, and the whole batch of devils, are turned loose without home or habitation," he argued. Sherman hoped that if he continued to push for his proposal, he would eventually wear down any opposition. Lincoln, however, was cautious; he told the secretary of war that a "misstep" by Sherman "might be fatal to his army." Grant, also hesitant, finally admitted, "If there is any way of getting at Hood's army, I would prefer that, but I must trust to your own judgment." Sherman shrugged off any threat that Hood might offer. "Instead of being on the defensive, I would be on the offensive," he pointed out, "instead of guessing at what he means to do, he would have to guess at my plans. The difference in war is full 25 per cent."[5]

Scarcely a week after Hood took the offensive, Sherman received permission from Washington to proceed with his plan to head for Savannah. "If you are satisfied the trip to the sea-coast can be made, holding the line of the Tennessee firmly, you may make it," Grant wired on October 11. Unfortunately, the telegraph lines were down, and Sherman never received this dispatch and did not know for over two weeks that he had Grant's approval. That did not stop Sherman from making preparations, however, and he requested that Halleck furnish Thomas at Nashville with all the troops he could spare. Sherman estimated he would be out of contact for about ninety days.[6]

Having made provisions for Thomas, Sherman turned to other matters. Caught in the tide of Northern politics, the general needed to clarify his stance. He wrote to the chief of staff rebutting a flood of rumors about his disloyalty to the Lincoln administration; one newspaper claimed that Sherman had pledged ninety-nine out of every one hundred army votes to McClellan. The recent stories were, Sherman assured Washington, "pure fabrication." He was not a voter, he pointed out, and he abstained from airing his political beliefs. In fact, he naively complained, "I cannot conceive how my opinion is pertinent to the occasion." Angered, he told Halleck to be sure Lincoln did not question his loyalty: "Show this to the President, except this conclusion: Damn the mischievous newspapers." Still, with gossip circulating that Sherman might speak publicly in support of McClellan, Lincoln certainly felt concerned. In mid-September the president told Sherman that he had contemplated visiting Georgia, a visit, following so soon after the surrender of Atlanta, that also undoubtedly would have enhanced Lincoln's public image.[7]

Yet Sherman avoided direct involvement in politics, and even those around him had no idea how he stood on the issues. Henry Hitchcock, who joined Sherman as military secretary in late October, canvassed the staff about the general's position. No one knew, he told his wife, "he has never said, and quietly ignores all discussion of either." But Sherman had told Hitchcock in private what he thought about the two presidential candidates, and Hitchcock reported to his wife that he felt confident that Sherman was not a McClellan man. Hitchcock was right, for Sherman had told Ellen that he preferred Lincoln. Although he called McClellan an able man, the Young Napoleon had annoyed Sherman early in the war. "When I was in Kentucky he would not heed my counsels and never wrote me once," Sherman recalled petulantly, "but since I have gained some notoriety at Atlanta and the papers announced, as usual falsely, that I was for him, he has written me twice and that has depreciated him more in my estimation than all else." No matter, Sherman continued: "He cannot be elected. Mr. Lincoln will be, but I hope it will be done quick, that voters may come to their regiments and not give the Rebs the advantage they know so well to take."[8]

At the time Sherman wrote this letter the Confederates were indeed trying to seize an advantage west of the Mississippi River. A Rebel army under Maj. Gen. Sterling Price invaded Missouri in September in one last effort to win that state for the Confederacy. Sherman was forced to commit some of his favorite units to stopping the Rebel columns. He told his old friend Maj. Gen. Andrew Jackson Smith, who commanded a detachment from the Army of the Tennessee, that he had tried, without success, to have Smith's troops transferred to Georgia. "General Halleck asks for you to clean out Price," Sherman complained. "Can't you make a quick job of it and then get to me?" But it would be over two weeks before Smith finished off Price, and by the time he marched east, it was too late for him to join Sherman. The delay in transferring Smith's troops across the river would have a profound effect on Hood's future. Smith did not accompany Sherman on his march; instead, his ten thousand battle-hardened veterans reported to Thomas at Nashville.[9]

The autumn raids by Hood and Price followed a pattern Union authorities could have predicted. War had a traditional seasonal rhythm, and October was customarily the last month suitable for active campaigning. Two factors, the weather and the crops, dictated these rules. The condition of the roads affected movement, for the heavy, cumbersome artillery left ruts, and even a minimal number of baggage wagons moved slowly. In autumn, a raiding army could depend on the fall harvest for food, and there was still enough green grass for the horses. By November, when the frost appeared, campaigning would become harder, particularly to the north. These rules, of course, had been broken frequently during the war, but Hood would soon experience the wisdom behind them. Sherman, whose columns would move south, where the climate generally remained moderate even in the winter, had less reason to heed custom.

Hood's October raid frustrated Sherman, for he had trouble determining the Texan's immediate goal. He grumbled to a fellow officer that Hood was "eccentric," and he could not predict his movements as he could those of Johnston, "who was a sensible man and only did sensible things." In an effort to find out more, Sherman employed numerous spies, including some women. "I have ordered one of my female scouts from New Orleans to Augusta," he wrote Halleck, "and will send some out from here and give you prompt notice of any of Hood's army going East."[10]

The woman he requested from Louisiana was Nora Winder. Traveling with her twelve-year-old son, Winder spent several weeks in the Augusta area and at the state capital of Milledgeville before heading for Savannah. She gathered information from Rebel friends and was paid through Union contacts. When one of those connections failed to provide her with money for travel at Milledgeville, she told the general: "I had to work my way a part of the time. Weaving pays well in the Confederacy, and I am a splendid weaver." Without sufficient funds, the mother and child "had to walk; though if we had been riding we would have been suspected by the pickets, and as we were walking we were never suspected to be going farther than five or seven miles." Although her intelligence would have given Sherman useful information about the defensive works at Augusta, he did not receive her dispatch until too late to affect his plans.[11]

In any case, before Sherman could put his own program in motion he had to take care of Hood. He had no choice but to follow the Rebel trail, for public opinion would not abide Hood wandering about Georgia unopposed. Leaving one corps to guard Atlanta, Sherman took forty thousand men after the Confederates. Hood, however, moved rapidly and erratically. After destroying about ten miles of track near Acworth and Big Shanty, one of his divisions reached the little town of Allatoona. Hood needed rations, and he had heard that the storehouses there held enough food for his entire army.

The responsibility for leading the attack at Allatoona fell to one of the few Northern-born generals in the Confederate army, forty-five-year-old Maj. Gen. Samuel G. French. The New Jersey native had earned two brevets for bravery in the Mexican War, and, although he had a promising military career, he had left the army in 1856, married into a prominent Southern family, and became a Mississippi planter. Despite being out of the army for several years before the war, the old soldier in French often surfaced, and he did not always agree with his young commander. In fact, French had asked to be relieved over a command controversy in August. Hood, willing to see French go, had approved, but President Davis, French's longtime friend, had not. So French headed a division even though he personally harbored doubts about Hood's competence. Although Davis allowed Robert E. Lee in Virginia to handpick his subordinates, the Confederate president continued to meddle in the officer corps of the Army of Tennessee. As in the past, when he had forced Bragg and Johnston to accept men they did not want, Davis now did so to Hood.[12]

Whatever French might think of Hood, he had orders to take Allatoona. But the Federal soldiers there had other plans and defiantly refused French's demand that they surrender. Brig. Gen. John M. Corse had instructions to march from Rome to Allatoona and hold on there until reinforcements arrived. Throughout the day on October 4 and into the following morning, Sherman sent wigwag signals exhorting the blue-clad troops at Allatoona to hold fast for he was coming. This was not exactly true, but it gave the defenders needed confidence. Sherman was, in fact, on top of Kennesaw Mountain some distance away watching the smoke from the skirmishing around Allatoona and listening to the echo of the cannon. He translated the letters C-R-S-E-H-E-R, glimpsed faintly from a signal flag, to "Corse here," meaning Corse had safely arrived from Rome. Sherman soon learned from another signal that the Confederates had given up the assault. Allatoona was safe. After the battle, Sherman received a dispatch from Corse that confirmed the garrison had not surrendered. "I am short a cheek bone and one ear," he bragged, exaggerating his injuries, "but am able to whip all hell yet."[13]

French's Confederates had retreated, fearing they would be caught between Allatoona and Sherman's army. Before withdrawing, French had tried to burn the rations to prevent them from reaching Atlanta, but when the Confederates tried to set the storehouses on fire, the matches refused to ignite. Disappointed, the Rebels had to leave the supplies. A Federal major told his wife that he heard rumors that the Confederates suffered heavy losses, and that, he added, was "first rate." Newspaper accounts praised Corse and changed Sherman's "hold fast, we are coming" to the more dramatic "hold the fort, for I am coming." After the war, an Illinois evangelist used these words as a basis for the hymn "Hold the Fort," which later became a gospel standard.[14]

Although the battle at Allatoona received notice in the Northern press, the Southern public knew little of Hood's progress. A journalist complained that Hood had closed the usual channels of communication between the army and the people. The *Charleston Mercury* noted, "There is a degree of secrecy observed about this movement of ours which has not characterized former movements in this army." Yet all agreed that morale was high, and

the soldiers felt confident they could force Sherman to withdraw from Atlanta. "What a glorious result if it can only be achieved!" a Rebel soldier told
his wife. The men were in fine health and even finer spirits. "I have scarcely
ever seen a greater change that has taken place in the Army since the visit of
President Davis. Gen'l. Hood has published his plans to the whole army &
by this course has gained the confidence of the men. I believe they will fight
for him now as well as they would for Joe Johnston." A reporter related,
"Our army is said to be improving daily, and are anxious to get a fair show at
the vandals, who have hitherto had the game in their own hands."[15]

For the first time in weeks, Hood had seized the initiative. Beauregard,
who ostensibly controlled the army, had little influence over its movements.
He caught up with the rapidly moving columns at Cave Springs, a spa located in the mountains near the Alabama border, but since he would not actually assume command of the Military Division of the West for another
week, he only offered advice. Hood had already resolved to continue his
raid. He would tear up the tracks between Kingston and Resaca, then turn
for Dalton, where the Confederate army had wintered the previous year.
Hood pointed out that each mile Sherman followed put more distance between the Union army and Atlanta. He told Bragg on October 8 that this
strategy would force Sherman either to fall back to Chattanooga or move
south. "If the latter, I shall move on his rear," he promised, "if the former, I
shall move to the Tennessee River via La Fayette and Gadsden." After listening to the Texan's intentions, Beauregard left believing that Hood would
strike the rail line but still remain glued to the Union army.[16]

As Hood marched north, his men began to feel the results of moving so
fast. The troops, ill equipped at the beginning of the campaign, experienced
increasing shortages. The scarcity of shoes remained a problem so Hood ordered his corps commanders to have moccasins fashioned from fresh
rawhide for the barefoot men. He needed other supplies too, including at
least three hundred additional wagons and tents. Nonetheless, upon reaching Resaca, Hood demanded the surrender of its seven-hundred-man garrison but declined the Federals' dare, "If you want it come and take it." He
contented himself with destroying the railroad instead. The weather
seemed to reflect Hood's changing fortunes, for as the Rebels headed for
Dalton, about fifteen miles north of Resaca, the skies darkened. When the
rain came, the weather turned cold and miserable. Hood seemed oblivious
to the changing season, and upon arriving at Dalton he issued a demand for
the troops to surrender.[17]

But this garrison was different. The men at Dalton were not the same Northern soldiers the Army of Tennessee fought through the spring and summer. Three-quarters of the town's nearly eight hundred defenders belonged to the Forty-fourth U.S. Colored Troops (generally known as USCT), an infantry unit organized at Chattanooga the previous April. The blacks found themselves at Dalton as a result of the ongoing debate between Sherman and Lincoln. The president wanted to use black soldiers in combat, while Sherman resisted this experiment. In fact, Sherman refused, and Lincoln, who was politically astute enough to recognize that the general's recent military successes gave him an advantage, dared not order his commander. While Sherman was willing to give blacks a try in menial positions and garrison duty, he defied adding black regiments to his white army, a stand that was popular with his men. "I prefer some negroes as pioneers, teamsters, cooks, and servants," he had written in late July, "others gradually to experiment in the art of the soldier, beginning with the duties of local garrison, such as we had at Memphis, Vicksburg, Natchez, Nashville, and Chattanooga." Sherman would go only this far to appease his president, and this experiment now placed these black soldiers in jeopardy.[18]

The idea of African Americans wearing the uniforms of the United States armed forces touched nerves in both North and South. A law in 1862 had provided for the enlistment of black soldiers, but even Lincoln had been hesitant to implement it at that early stage in the war. After the Emancipation Proclamation took effect in January 1863, he had encouraged the enrollment of blacks. Although most served on garrison duty in occupied areas or performed manual labor with white armies, they did occasionally engage in battle. After white Confederates faced black soldiers at Port Hudson and Milliken's Bend, Louisiana, and Fort Wagner, South Carolina, in the summer of 1863 a growing controversy assumed greater proportions. The Confederate Congress had ruled that captured black soldiers would be treated as escaped slaves and not as prisoners of war, and the debate erupted into a heated exchange of communications between Washington and Richmond. After Union authorities charged Nathan Bedford Forrest with the massacre of black soldiers at Fort Pillow, Tennessee, the previous April, the treatment of black prisoners took on added significance among most Republicans in Congress. When Grant approved the construction of a tunnel that would enable his men to explode a powder charge directly under the Rebel line at Petersburg in the summer, Meade intervened after he discovered that black soldiers were scheduled to lead the attack. To prevent any possible charges that he was using African American soldiers as cannon fodder, Meade ordered the substitution of white troops in the initial assault. Grant concurred.[19]

On the Southern side, soldiers loathed the idea of fighting former slaves, black men now armed with weapons denied them before the war. This had been a white man's war for the Army of Tennessee; Sherman had seen to that in recent months. So as the Rebel army approached Dalton, many Confederates faced their first prospect of an integrated battle. Well aware of the feelings among his own soldiers, Hood sent Union colonel Lewis Johnson a communication that offered paroles for all the white officers and soldiers, but cautioned him that if he had to assault Dalton, he would take no prisoners. An Indiana soldier translated this to mean, "All Dark soldiers would be shott or Hung."[20]

The colonel declined to surrender. Johnson, a German who had joined the Union army as a private in the Tenth Indiana Infantry, had decided only weeks before that being colonel of a black regiment was preferable to remaining a captain in a white regiment, a position he had held for the previous two years. He took his new responsibilities seriously, but when one of his cavalrymen returned from a reconnaissance and reported that the Rebels "had men enough to eat us up," Johnson agreed to negotiate.[21]

Hood and Johnson talked under a flag of truce. The Confederates had already inflicted casualties, and Hood warned that "he could not restrain his men, and would not if he could." The colonel, he warned, could choose between death and surrender. The threat to take no prisoners weighed heavily on Johnson. He believed the Rebel soldiers, particularly the men of Cleburne's division, who were standing right behind Hood and his staff during the negotiations, were "over anxious" to fight for they continually violated the flag of truce. Up and down the line, the Rebels taunted the black troops and their white officers and shouted, "Kill every damn one of them." Facing growing hostility, Johnson finally agreed to terms after he received assurances that the enlisted men would be "treated humanely."[22]

Few African Americans expected lenient treatment at the hands of their captors. Lt. Morris S. Hall of the Forty-fourth USCT noted: "As soon as the terms of surrender were made known my men flocked around me and asked if I thought their lives would be spared or [if] they would be murdered as some they knew at Fort Pillow. Of course I could not answer them positively but quieted their fears as much as possible." Yet when the white officers asked to remain with their men to guarantee that the Rebels upheld their part of the bargain, Hood refused. He told the colonel that the black captives were not prisoners of war; they were runaway slaves and would be returned to their owners. Johnson, of course, protested and pointed out that his government would retaliate.[23]

This was only one of Johnson's grievances. He claimed that in spite of the agreement that promised decent treatment, the Rebels robbed and abused the prisoners in a "terrible manner." He singled out Maj. Gen. William B. Bate, a Mississippian with a reputation as a fighter, for his "meanness and beastly conduct." A Cincinnati paper labeled Bate a "brute" and claimed that he had grown truculent when he heard an agreement had been made to parole the white officers. He wanted to "dispose" of any men who willingly commanded African American troops. Although Johnson had harsh words for the Confederates, he praised his own command. The African American soldiers had wanted to fight, he noted, and he commended them for their "spirit and bravery" in the initial skirmishing, for the newly minted soldiers of the Forty-fourth USCT had contested the ground "as stubbornly as old troops."[24]

To no one's surprise, the black soldiers faced a different future than the white prisoners. Hood turned a large number of the six hundred blacks over to men claiming to be their owners, but about half were sent to Mississippi. A Charleston newspaper reported, "The negro soldiers were at once divested of their blankets, overcoats, shoes, hats, and in many cases, their breeches." While a barefoot Rebel admitted that the Confederates relieved the captives of their footwear, he disputed the rest. "We would wear their shoes," he claimed, but "we would not wear their *headgear* or *clothes*." After the captives were stripped, they were put to work tearing up the railroad. When a black sergeant complained, "he paid the penalty for disobeying orders"—probably meaning he was shot—and "the rest tore up the road readily," wrote an Arkansas soldier. One who refused to obey instructions, recalled Colonel Johnson, "was shot on the spot, as were also five others shortly after surrender, who, having been sick, were unable to keep up with the rest on the march."[25]

Although the ultimate fate of the captured African Americans is unknown, some were still prisoners several weeks later. A Southerner who saw them in Alabama noted that the majority of the blacks were very young. "A man with any humanity could not look upon them with any other than feelings of the deepest pity; not on account of any lack of clothes," he observed in late October, but because "all the peculiarities, of right belonging to the race, especially when assembled together in a crowd, were gone. No songs, nor dancing, nor any sign of mirth or gladness, and their manner of getting along in camp showed their utter lack of contrivance peculiar to soldiers." Beauregard even inquired officially about the condition of the prisoners when he asked if the blacks working on the railroad and fortifications around Corinth, Mississippi, were the same ones captured in Georgia. If they were, then Beauregard wanted to know if they had received medical attention. There is no record of Hood's reply, but a Charleston newspaper speculated that few blacks had survived after Dalton. "As a general thing, the men of the army were in favor of hanging the last one of them on the nearest limbs," the paper declared, and it was "very questionable" if many were carried far as prisoners of war. A Confederate chaplain who saw the captives at a train station in Mississippi observed that the blacks were "in the most distressing condition—evidently dying."[26]

The question of using African Americans as soldiers was not only controversial in the Confederate ranks, it was divisive. During the months when the army wintered at Dalton in early 1864, Maj. Gen. Patrick R. Cleburne had proposed enlisting slaves in the Confederate army in return for their freedom. The benefits seemed obvious to him. It would increase the number of eligible fighting men at a time when desertion was becoming a problem, and it would eliminate one objection that England and France used as a basis for refusing to recognize the Confederate nation. His proposal, carefully thought out and presented, met with vehement opposition in a closed meeting of the general officers. The harshest criticism came from Maj. Gen. William H. T. Walker, a temperamental Georgian who would later die in the battle of Atlanta. Walker, who asked Cleburne for a copy of the "incendiary" proposal, canvassed the division commanders looking for those who condoned the suggestion. He then sent the whole package of correspondence to Davis by special messenger. The president responded by telling Walker that he had decided the best policy would be to avoid publicity and bury the recommendation.[27]

So early in the year the general officers had drawn lines in the sand over the issue of black soldiers, and the old factions that had divided them under Braxton Bragg resurfaced. Yet as Cleburne waited with his men outside of Dalton in October, he had no way to know that he had scored a victory in the debate. Although the general public knew nothing of Cleburne's proposal, if the Irishman read any local papers in the autumn, he would have seen Davis's tentative suggestion that slaves be used in the army. The general would have seen irony in the fact that when the last session of the Confederate Congress convened on November 7, Davis, still personally voicing opposition to arming blacks, warned that "should the alternative ever be presented of subjugation or of the employment of the slave as a soldier, there seems to be no reason to doubt what should then be our decision."[28]

While both sides debated the merits of African American soldiers, Hood had to consider his next move. He had few options. He could not stay where he was, for the fields in north Georgia were exhausted. The Federal garrison in Chattanooga prevented a further move in that direction; by mid-October the city held about fifteen thousand Federal troops. Hood could turn directly west toward Alabama, but he would have to cross through mountain passes, and even if he did reach the great bridge near where the railroad from Nashville joined the Memphis & Charleston line, the Federals could pull together scattered outposts for a stout defense. John Schofield, Hood's old friend from West Point days and now a Union major general of volunteers, had already asked if he should cover the road from Chattanooga to Bridgeport. As Hood studied the map, he realized that Federal troops stationed along the Tennessee River created a formidable barrier. The growing number of enemy soldiers to his north also prevented him from doing any more significant damage to Sherman's line of supply. Therefore, Hood grasped the only alternative he saw. He moved away from both Sherman and the rail line, heading southwest into Alabama. After all, Davis had earlier approved a withdrawal to Gadsden. Sherman had hoped Hood would turn toward the Tennessee River because he had prepared for that possibility. Sherman later admitted, "Hood's movements and strategy had demonstrated that he had an army capable of endangering at all times my communications, but unable to meet me in open fight."[29]

While military events consumed Sherman's time, he could not ignore politics. Since several states held elections in October, the timing of Atlanta's fall had been particularly crucial. Sherman knew that Lincoln kept a close watch on public opinion, and a major problem was that not all Northern states allowed soldiers in the field to vote. Indiana was one of those states that required soldiers to return home to cast a ballot, and its Republican governor asked Lincoln to do what he could to have that state's soldiers furloughed so that they could legally vote in their home districts. Lincoln turned to Sherman, whose armies contained a large number of Indiana soldiers, and, in a letter sent by special messenger, reminded Sherman that the loss of the election could be disastrous for the Union. He feared that ceding Indiana "to those who will oppose the war in every possible way" might have a "bad effect upon the November election."[30]

Lincoln believed that a victory for the Republican Indiana governor in October probably assured a Lincoln victory in November, and he feared the unpopular draft might cause him to lose the state. He told Sherman that he would greatly appreciate anything the general could do to send the soldiers home. He emphasized that the men did not need to remain until the November election but could return to their units right away. In typical Lincoln fashion, he added, "This is in no sense an order, but is merely intended to impress you with the importance, to the army itself, of your doing all you safely can, yourself being the judge of what you can safely do."[31]

Sherman agreed to the War Department's request to release Indiana soldiers who were hospitalized, but when Forrest threatened the railroad in mid-Tennessee, Chattanooga filled with men unable to reach Nashville. On September 30, Sherman notified his commanders to halt furloughs. When Brig. Gen. Jacob Cox asked for clarification, he was told the measure was "temporary" and depended on the condition of the track. Lincoln informed Indiana's governor that he could not "press the General on this point. All that the Secretary of War and General Sherman feel they can safely do, I, however, shall be glad of." Indeed, Lincoln was heartened when Ohio and Indiana voted Republican. Nonetheless, many Democrats questioned the soldier vote and some even suggested fraud. Men of the Sixtieth Massachusetts Infantry received invitations to participate in the Indiana election, and Republican officials exerted little effort to oversee how many times each man voted. A letter written by a New Englander read: "Yesterday was the State election here, and most of our regiment went down to the city and voted. Some of the boys voted twenty-five times each. . . . Governor Morton, the Republican candidate, was elected by a large majority. So the Massachusetts men helped elect him."[32]

Pennsylvania was a different matter. Results in the state stayed undecided for much of the month while the soldier vote was counted, and although it went Republican, the state still remained uncertain for the November presidential election. Yet when a Confederate War Department official observed that the October vote had gone for Lincoln's party, he wrote, "This foreshadows Lincoln's re-election, and admonishes us to prepare for other campaigns, though languishing for peace."[33]

Northern politics did not influence Hood as he formulated his latest plan. He could not sway voters in the October elections, although preventing furloughed soldiers from reaching the Midwest might have made a very slight difference. There is no record that Hood gave any thought to the impact his future movements might have on the November presidential election.

Beauregard, who joined Hood in Alabama, also did not seem concerned. Although the Creole now officially commanded the department, he held a title with little real power, and Hood did not ask Beauregard's permission to alter his strategy, which now called for a march into Tennessee: he had completely revised the plan he and Davis had agreed on in September. In fact, Hood had already wired Richmond of his intentions. He would tempt Sherman no longer; he would initiate a campaign into Union-held Tennessee.

Beauregard, who recognized that his position was little more than that of an adviser, acquiesced. He pointed out practical considerations and observed that Hood's major problem would be logistical. The army needed a new supply line, not an easy task in the exhausted regions that Hood must cross. Hood asserted that he could find plenty of provisions in the fertile area of mid-Tennessee, and his army would doubtless capture some supplies from the enemy. The first of Hood's arguments demands further consideration. Certainly Hood needed to leave north Georgia, for that area had been bled dry by the recent campaigns and nothing remained to feed either side. But much of mid-Tennessee had suffered too, for Federal garrisons dotted the landscape and Union foraging parties frequently visited the farms. Hood needed to time his invasion carefully, for once the crops from the fall harvest went to market, there would not be much readily available in the barns. To realize the maximum yield from local farms, Hood needed to be in Tennessee before November.

Beauregard and Hood had to rethink the mechanics for carrying out this new strategy. The two men pored over maps, trying to decide the best route to follow. Friction developed when Beauregard insisted that Joseph Wheeler's cavalry remain in Georgia to oppose Sherman. Hood gave in when Beauregard promised that Forrest, then in Mississippi under Richard Taylor, would join the Army of Tennessee. The plan was a good one, Beauregard later wrote, "but success depended upon the manner in which it should be carried out." Taylor, in whom Beauregard confided, thought the Creole declined to interfere because the plan had the approval of the president, and Hood seemed confident of success. Taylor concluded in his postwar writing: "I could not blame Beauregard; for it was putting a cruel responsibility on him to supersede a gallant veteran, to whom fortune had been adverse. There was nothing to be said, and nothing to be done, saving to discharge one's duty to the bitter end."[34]

Hood, who had waged a fairly successful campaign in Georgia in early October, now became indecisive and vacillating. The next few weeks would be as confusing to his own soldiers as they were to the enemy. Even a Federal general admitted that Hood's October raid was "brilliantly executed" and that the Texan had not only perplexed Sherman's commanders but had given "hope to the insurgents." This pattern changed rapidly. To begin with, Hood did not cross the Tennessee River at Guntersville, thirty miles above Gadsden, as he had told Beauregard he would. Instead, he changed directions and headed west. Beauregard did not catch up with the army until Hood was more than one hundred miles from the rail line that brought supplies to Sherman's army in Atlanta. Not only was Hood moving away from Georgia, he continued to increase the distance between his army and Sherman.[35]

When the Rebels approached Decatur, Alabama, a possible river crossing, they found the garrison stronger than anticipated. One of the units hurried from Chattanooga to prevent the Confederates from fording the Tennessee was the Fourteenth U.S. Colored Troops. This regiment, composed of former slaves, had been organized by Col. Thomas J. Morgan at Gallatin, Tennessee, in late 1863. Many of the recruits Morgan accepted were men already working for the army in menial positions as wagon drivers and cooks. The colonel handpicked them according to their motivation to fight for freedom and then tried to instill a sense of pride that would help them become examples to other black units. Strict discipline was necessary if he ever hoped to see his regiment selected for battle.

Morgan had worked hard to have his black regiment recognized. One of the ways he made his unit stand out was to organize the companies according to height. "When the regiment was full," he observed, "the four center companies were all composed of tall men, the flanking companies of men of medium height, while the little men were sandwiched between." He was proud of his accomplishments and even bragged that his men "drill well, and go through the evolutions with as much grace and ease as any regiment in the service." As a result, he had finally seen his men selected for an active role in the war, for they had successfully defended Dalton against a Rebel cavalry raid in the late summer. Now, in October, Morgan had received orders to reinforce the threatened garrison in northern Alabama.[36]

The fighting at Decatur was not much of a contest because after some heavy skirmishing Hood quickly decided the garrison was too heavily defended and moved on west. But the black troops of the Fourteenth USCT distinguished themselves by charging a Rebel position. "The affair did not last much more than 20 minutes," recalled a Union soldier, "and the colored boys had to fall down along the water's edge under the bank of the river, while the enemy ran along above them, and shot down on them." Still, Morgan heaped praise on the men for their determined assault, and as the regiment returned to the Union lines, the white officers "mounted the parapet and gave it three rousing cheers." A black sergeant turned to a white superior and said, "Captain, we've got it at last."[37]

After bypassing Decatur, Hood found many reasons to justify his decision to continue toward Mississippi. Clearly he wanted a river crossing that was not guarded at all, and Tuscumbia, near where Alabama, Tennessee, and Mississippi join, seemed ideal. It would be easier for Forrest, who was still in Mississippi, to join him. The Rebel army still needed supplies, especially shoes, and at Tuscumbia Hood would be closer to the terminus of the Memphis & Charleston line. Unfortunately, Hood's failure to inform Beauregard of his plans earlier meant that the railroad, which brought the army provisions, was not running. Underbrush needed to be cleared away from more than thirty miles of abandoned track before he could receive supplies. A Georgian who rejoined his division in the Alabama camps recalled that it took him twenty-eight hours to travel thirty miles because the train broke down so often.[38]

Hood's men might want to reclaim Tennessee, but the army was tired and footsore. The march west, in a cold rain, proved particularly hard for those without shoes. "The road was full of water and mud," wrote a Texan. In "some places the mud and water would be knee deep." As October ended, the soldier grumbled, "Every body wet and muddy. . . . We are living on parched corn. Have had no meat for several days." Moreover, the region offered little forage. Samuel French noted that the Tennessee river valley was beautiful and the soil rich, "but what a desolation everywhere." All he saw were fallow fields and downed fences, for raiding parties roamed freely and almost every means of subsistence had been consumed or destroyed. It was not until the army reached Tuscumbia that the troops rested, and a Texan observed: "We get some shoes and clothing while here, preparing to go into Tenn. The supposition is now that we will go up in[to] middle Tenn. and go into winter quarters." A Georgian echoed this prediction when he told his mother that Hood intended to strike the Federals before the winter set in, but then the army would camp until time for the spring campaigns. Most soldiers believed that it was too late in the season for a major campaign.[39]

By moving into western Alabama, Hood completely departed from the strategy he and Davis had agreed on. Hood had drawn Sherman out of Atlanta just as Davis hoped, but when Hood turned west, Sherman balked. He refused to let Hood tempt him into Alabama. From this point, Sherman and Hood went separate ways, each with his own agenda. On October 19 Sherman wrote his wife, Ellen, that Hood was "afraid to fight me on open ground" and instead had tried to destroy the railroad that supplied the army. Two days later he told her that Hood had escaped into Alabama and probably aimed to invade Tennessee in an effort to disrupt the Union supply line. "Maybe he will and maybe he won't," scoffed Sherman. "If a reasonable number of the drafted men reached me, I think he won't." In any case, pursuing "Hood is folly," he announced to Thomas, "for he can twist and turn like a fox and wear out any army in pursuit." So instead of allowing Hood to lure him west, Sherman began preparations for his march south.[40]

Hood had a scheme. He intended to march toward the Ohio River and, if successful, to Lee in Virginia. Unfortunately, there were too many variables in this scheme. Hood's failure to inform the authorities of his constantly changing plan was not much different from Johnston's refusal to keep the Confederate president updated during the early summer. Even Lee had not marched into Pennsylvania without the blessing of the Confederate cabinet. That neglect was "inexcusable," charges Hood's biographer Richard McMurry. Hood's plan, "at least in his view of its ultimate possibilities, was a wild dream."[41]

This campaign was the first real test of the Texan's mettle as a commander. Unlike Atlanta, where he had to react to a situation he had not created, he would now bear the full responsibility for his strategic decisions. Any chance for success depended on speed, but the army seemed to be moving in slow motion, and the autumn weather, chilly and interspersed with rain, would make movement difficult at best. On November 4, Hood telegraphed Beauregard that his supplies had not arrived, forcing him to delay his departure into Tennessee. Although the weather cooperated early in the month, by mid-November the heavens opened and the river rose almost twenty feet. The muck and mire that had once been hard ground stopped repairs on the railroad and made the movement of supplies by wagon almost hopeless. The pontoon bridge that the Confederates had strung across the Tennessee River, useless in the high water, broke at one point. To make matters worse, Forrest had not arrived.[42]

Each day Hood delayed was critical. The army marched into Tuscumbia at the end of October; it would march out three weeks later. Although many reasons for the holdup were not Hood's fault, the next twenty-one days would make the difference in the subsequent campaign. Hood later claimed he failed to move because Forrest had not arrived, and he blamed Beauregard for not shifting the cavalry rapidly enough. But at the time, neither man seemed concerned whether Forrest joined Hood in Alabama; both appeared content to have Forrest meet Hood in Tennessee. The two generals finally reached a point where they were unable to communicate productively. When Beauregard arrived at Tuscumbia, Hood moved his headquarters across the swollen river to Florence. Everyone seemed ready to shift the responsibility for future operations on someone else—Hood blamed Forrest, and by extension Beauregard, for the delays, and Beauregard distanced himself from the whole operation. Moreover, Hood's neglect of logistics was conspicuous. Samuel French challenged Hood at a meeting of the general officers on November 1 about the advisability of taking so many pieces of artillery into Tennessee unless the army had a full supply of horses. Hood countered unrealistically that, once in Tennessee, "men would join us, horses could be obtained, and the men be supplied with shoes and clothing." This simple statement reveals how out of touch with reality Hood had become, for the lack of proper arrangements for his artillery indicates that the army was in no condition to invade hostile territory.[43]

Meanwhile, Grant had second thoughts about Sherman's intention to move away from the Confederate army. He was concerned about Smith's slow progress from Missouri to join Thomas in Tennessee and knew that both Lincoln and Stanton had reservations about Sherman's campaign. "Do you not think it advisable, now that Hood has gone so far north to entirely settle him before starting on your proposed campaign?" he asked Sherman. "Now that he is so far away," added Grant, he might "go in one direction while you are pushing the other." Well aware of what effect such a move by the Rebel army might have on Northern voters if it were successful, Grant concluded, "If you can see the chance for destroying Hood's army, attend to that first, and make your other move secondary." Sherman responded by pointing out that Hood was too mobile to destroy. Moreover, he argued that if he could march his army across Georgia, it would demonstrate to the world "that we have a power which Davis cannot resist. This may not be war, but rather statesmanship." Accordingly, Sherman saw his raid and the presidential election as two sides of the same coin. "Mr. Lincoln's election (which is assured,) coupled with the conclusion thus reached," he decided, "makes a complete logical whole."[44]

Sherman had seized the initiative, and President Davis could do little but admonish Hood for failing to follow the original plan. "The policy of taking advantage of the reported division of Sherman's forces by attacking him

where (or *when*) he cannot reunite his army is too obvious to have been overlooked by you," he lectured on November 7. "I therefore take it for granted
that you have not been able to avail yourself of that advantage during his
march northward from Atlanta, and hope the opportunity will be offered
before he is extensively recruited." Nonetheless, Davis was not immune to
the temptation of a drive into Tennessee. If Sherman moved the main army
south, he told Hood, "you may first beat him in detail and subsequently
without serious obstruction or danger to the country in your rear advance to
the Ohio River." Yet Hood apparently interpreted this telegram as Richmond's approval for his new plan.[45]

The Army of Tennessee abandoned any chance of protecting Georgians
from Sherman's armies. As a result of miscommunications, misconcep-
tions, and simple errors, the army had moved too far west to be of any use.
When Beauregard talked with Hood in northwest Alabama, the two had
considered the possibility of returning to Georgia, but by then some two
hundred miles separated Hood from Sherman, an impossible distance for
an army short on shoes, food, and transportation to cover quickly. In addition, when Beauregard had met with Governor Brown in October, Georgia's
chief executive had assured the general he could raise thirty thousand men
to fight with Wheeler's cavalry, an unreasonable boast and one that Beauregard should have ignored. Samuel French concluded on November 20:
"Here are two armies that have been fighting each other from about the first
of May to the first of November, six months—parted—the one heading for
the Atlantic ocean, two hundred and ten miles from Atlanta, and the other
marching from Tuscumbia, Ala., for Nashville, Tenn., one hundred and fifteen miles distant."[46]

Each man hoped that his strike would help end the war. While Confederates tried to overcome multitudinous problems, Sherman efficiently completed arrangements to leave Atlanta. As he readied his armies, Sherman
never overlooked the political consequences of his actions, and he carefully
timed his departure with the election. He anticipated that his preparations
would be complete by November 10, his troops paid, and "the Presidential
election over and out of our way." His march across Georgia was only the beginning of his plan to make the Southern people feel the hard hand of war.
He told one of his officers that he proposed to abandon Atlanta "and sally
forth to ruin Georgia." He intended to show that "war and individual ruin
are synonymous terms."[47]

The noted Southern author and South Carolina native William Gilmore
Simms wrote on November 20 that "when Hood removed from Sherman's

front, I then declared my opinion that if Sherman had the requisite audacity—it did not need Genius,—he would achieve the greatest of his successes, by turning his back on the enemy in his rear, & march boldly forward towards the Atlantic coast. I fear that such is his purpose. If so,—what have we to oppose him?"[48]

CHAPTER FOUR

Sherman's March South

On the Tuesday that Northerners went to the polls, a Georgia woman predicted, "To day will probably decide the fate of this confederacy if Lincoln is reelected I think our fate is a hard one." Many Southerners agreed, for they saw four more years of Republican rule as four more years of war. In the western theater, as the crisp nights announced the change of seasons, both sides prepared for autumn campaigns that might change the course of the war. While Hood had dreams of reaching the Ohio River and winning a great victory on enemy soil, Sherman wanted to prove to Southerners the futility of continuing the struggle against Northern might. He intended to dispense that "hard hand" on the South by traversing the heart of the Confederacy. Just days before Hood crossed into Tennessee, Sherman started south. "It surely was a strange event," Sherman later reflected, "two hostile armies marching in opposite directions, each in the full belief that it was achieving a final and conclusive result in a great war." Both Hood and Sherman had faced skeptics when they proposed their respective plans, and Hood had eventually put his into motion without the explicit approval of either his superior or the Confederate Cabinet. Sherman, on the other hand, had worked to sell his, first to his friend and chief, Ulysses Grant, and then to his president, Abraham Lincoln. On Wednesday, November 16, as the Confederacy came to a standstill to observe the day of prayer declared by the president, Sherman's wagons rumbled out of Atlanta.[1]

Sherman had spent ten weeks in the city, and during that time he had carefully pondered his options. Hood's move through north Georgia could have caused him serious problems in implementing his own plan, but once Hood was out of picture, Sherman could proceed. On September 20, Sherman had told Grant he would not hesitate to cross Georgia with sixty thousand men, for where a million people live "my army won't starve." Unlike Hood, who intended to push into Tennessee, where near blizzard conditions would torment his poorly clad soldiers, Sherman would march south, where the temperature rarely fell below freezing for very long. "This campaign," he pointed out, "could be made in winter." Sherman thought that humbling Georgians was psychologically important, perhaps even more important than defeating Lee in Virginia. Southerners "may stand the fall of Richmond," he judged, "but not of all Georgia." He had told Grant, "If you can whip Lee and I can march to the Atlantic I think Uncle Abe will give us a twenty days' leave of absence to see the young folks."[2]

From the day Sherman rode into Atlanta, he knew he could not remain there indefinitely. Feeding his army required huge quantities of provisions, and any disruption along the railroad was a nuisance. To repair just eight miles of track destroyed by the Rebels, for example, the work parties needed thirty-five thousand new ties and six miles of iron. Although restoring service took only about a week, it required ten thousand men. A clerk in the Richmond War Department noted, "The armies are equidistant from Nashville, and if Sherman's supplies fail, his condition becomes desperate." Sherman knew this too, and he was anxious to be out of Atlanta. "Until we can repopulate Georgia, it is useless to occupy it, but the utter destruction of its roads, houses, and people will cripple their military resources," he told Grant. Protecting the roads would cost a thousand lives each month and gain no result. "I can make the march, and make Georgia howl," he confidently announced.[3]

Sherman's plan depended on only two variables: the Rebel response and the fickle fall weather. Sherman guessed corrrectly when he predicted that Hood would not be a factor. Indeed, when he told Grant that Hood probably thought "by going north he could inflict greater damage upon us than we could upon the rebels by going south," he was right on the mark. The weather, however, could be less easily forecast. Sherman, of course, wanted dry roads for rain or snow could make navigating Georgia's thoroughfares arduous. He hoped that the autumn rains would come before he left, and when thundershowers began the first week of November he telegraphed Grant that this was the rain he had been waiting for and promised that as soon as it ended, he would be off. Henry Hitchcock confided in his diary, "We hope this means just what the General has been desiring,—that the fall rains should come all together, early in November, and give us fine weather for some weeks, which is what we want *now*."[4]

Anticipation rose as the date for departure neared. Sherman diverted the

mail to Nashville in an effort to make the Confederates think he might return to Tennessee. He also ordered surplus supplies there and instructed
men to reduce their belongings to the bare necessities. Unlike Hood, Sherman understood the importance of logistics, and he made careful plans to
acquire supplies while out of touch with his base. He studied his maps carefully and knew that he would cross through Georgia's rich agricultural belt,
a region heretofore untouched by either side. He also recognized that the
timing of his march coincided with the fall harvests. To make his force mobile, he reduced the amount of artillery, sending the excess to Chattanooga.
Men found unfit for strenuous duty also headed back to Tennessee along
with any cavalrymen without horses. "If the rains clear away I will not delay
for any cause," he proclaimed. "The sick must march or fall into the hands
of the enemy."[5]

As part of his preparation, Sherman reorganized the army. John Schofield had gone to Knoxville, and his command fell to Jacob Cox, while
Thomas, who was now at Nashville awaiting Hood, was replaced by Maj.
Gen. David S. Stanley, an Ohio native who had turned down a Confederate
commission in 1861. The XVI Corps was broken up and scattered between
the XV and XVII Corps as Maj. Gen. John A. (Black Jack) Logan and Maj.
Gen. Francis P. Blair, both political generals, returned home to rally sup-
port for Lincoln. Sherman kept four veteran corps with him (XIV, XV,
XVII, and XX) while he ordered the IV Corps from the Department of the
Cumberland and the XXIII Corps from the Department of the Ohio to join
Thomas.

Perhaps the most significant switch came in the cavalry. Grant sent James
H. Wilson, recently promoted to major general, from the Army of the Potomac to take command of Sherman's horsemen, and the twenty-seven-year-
old Illinois native, who had graduated sixth in his class at West Point, would
make dramatic changes. Under Wilson, Union cavalrymen would emerge
from the shadow of their Confederate counterparts and become a viable arm
in the fighting. Sherman, however, opted to send Wilson to Thomas in Tennessee and kept with him only a small force under Brig. Gen. Judson
Kilpatrick. Controversy followed this New Jersey-born West Point graduate, and Sherman had commented, "I know that Kilpatrick is a hell of a
damned fool, but I want just that sort of man to command my cavalry in this
expedition."[6]

Apprehension about Sherman's plans made some soldiers uneasy. "A
great many officers are resigning to avoid the coming campaign, and a great
many others are trying to resign but cannot," remarked one soldier. "They

are being laughed at by the whole army here, and by their present conduct they are losing such soldierly reputation as they have made. I can't see why they are so much afraid of this campaign, for I regard it as one of the easiest campaigns I have engaged in." Rumors circulated that Sherman intended to head into hostile country in the face of unknown opposition, which some men thought was too risky, and as terms of enlistment expired, many Union soldiers elected to return home.[7]

By November, suppositions turned to reality when the army learned more about the coming expedition. Although some soldiers left the army, most had confidence in Sherman's abilities and made preparations for the coming campaign. "It is now certain that we are to march to Atlanta destroying the R. R. as we go, burn that city, and then strike boldly through the heart of Georgia to Savannah, if we can get there, and if not, then to any other seaport," wrote Maj. James Connolly. Exhilarated at the prospect, he told his wife that "there's something to stir the blood in such a bold operation as that." Others might fear what lay ahead, he said, but "I wouldn't miss going on this expedition for 6 months pay. I hope I may see Milledgeville. I have wanted to see it ever since I was an urchin stumbling thro' my Geography in Newark." Sheridan's eastern soldiers had devastated the Shenandoah Valley, and now Sherman's western soldiers threatened to do the same to the fertile farmland of Georgia. Moreover, Lincoln's growing confidence in his chances on the second Tuesday in November probably had a great deal to do with his change of heart concerning the march. In Richmond an official confirmed that suspicion when he wrote three days before the election, "I infer that the government is convinced President Lincoln will be re-elected, else some desperate effort would have been made in his behalf by his generals." Lincoln had already given approval to Sherman's plan, but a show of support at the ballot box would eliminate the need to worry about the political consequences of the general's action.[8]

Lincoln received the victory he hoped for on Tuesday, November 8. The election was close in several key states, but Lincoln won 55 percent of the popular vote and enjoyed a margin of 212 to 21 in the electoral college. The Republican Party also gained seats in Congress. Sherman well understood the importance of this election and the significance attached to the soldiers' vote. Not all the Northern states allowed soldiers to vote in the field or by proxy, so Sherman tried to grant furloughs to men from those states that did not. Just days before the election, the secretary of war directed Thomas to furlough all the soldiers in the hospitals and those men unfit for field duty from Indiana, Illinois, Michigan, Wisconsin, Ohio, Connecticut, and Massachusetts. These prospective voters would be furnished transportation to and from their homes. Not surprisingly, this list contained three states (Illinois, Indiana, and Massachusetts) where men could not vote in the field, and large numbers of men in the western armies were from the two midwestern states. Lincoln won only 54 percent in Indiana and Illinois, or a majority of slightly more than 50,000 out of more than 628,000 votes cast. Lincoln personally calculated that the soldier vote in the states where the men had to go home to cast a ballot could not be "less than 90,000." Indeed, Lincoln received an estimated 75 percent of the soldiers' vote, for the army, particularly soldiers in the West, firmly backed the president's war policy.[9]

This election was significant, for it was the first time in American history that soldiers in the field had exercised the franchise. In past wars a man lost his right to vote when he joined the army and marched off to war; that privilege extended only as far as the boundaries of his home district. Still, the soldier vote was not universal, for some people feared allowing men under military control to have a say in civil matters. Therefore, those states that did not allow soldiers to vote unless they went home had been important to Lincoln, particularly in the October elections. Sherman had tried to accommodate his president in the first election, but he was unable to be as generous with his men in November. Not all who wanted to vote had the opportunity. One soldier complained from his campsite, "Yesterday was election day; many soldiers voted here, but we Illinoisans are disfranchised." Yet a German-born Iowa soldier proudly declared from his bivouac near Atlanta: "We participated in the election and I cast my first vote for Abraham Lincoln as President of the U.S."[10]

President Davis tried to downplay the significance of the Northern election for he had always refused to conduct military operations for purely political reasons. He had hoped Hood would fight Sherman in October, but the October campaign had neither lured Sherman into a position where he could be destroyed nor forced him to withdraw troops from Atlanta for lack of supplies. Davis had agreed that the best way to secure peace was to demonstrate Confederate military strength, and he still hoped that offensive action could end the war. With Lincoln pledged to the war, Davis needed to encourage Southerners, and he insisted that the Confederacy was still "as erect and defiant as ever." The North could not change Southerners' goals, he told the Confederate Congress on November 7, nor could Northern might crush the "indomitable valor" of Southern troops or the "unquenchable spirit" of the Southern people. No Northern military success could destroy the South. A correspondent for the London *Daily News* reported, "I am astonished the more I see and hear of the extent and depth of determination" of the secessionists "to fight to the last."[11]

That assessment was not entirely true. Hood's soldiers had mixed feelings about the future; some clearly wanted to fight to the end while others favored a negotiated peace. In the Confederate camps there was a detached but marked interest in the outcome of the Northern election. Accurate information was almost impossible to obtain. Just a few days after the vote, James M. Lanning in the Tenth Alabama noted, "It is rumored that Lincoln is reelected." Four days later, his curiosity was sparked when he heard that McClellan had won. He had already decided there was little difference in the two men as far as the Rebel army was concerned, for he did not believe that a McClellan victory would necessarily assure a negotiated settlement. Still, what the soldiers wanted most was for the war to end before spring, one way or another. But more immediately, Lanning added, he knew the soldiers hoped Hood would go into winter quarters soon.[12]

There was no talk of winter quarters among Sherman's men. Confident that Northerners had approved Lincoln's war policy, Sherman set his columns in motion a week after the election. Before leaving Atlanta, Federal soldiers put to the torch everything that the Confederates might later find useful. Although Sherman did not plan to destroy the entire city, Maj. George Nichols, an aide-de-camp to the general, recalled watching as flames spread through the business district. "The heaven is one expanse of lurid fire; the air is filled with flying, burning cinders; buildings covering two hundred acres are in ruins or in flames," he wrote. It was, he judged, a "grand and awful spectacle" to see the beautiful city now in flames.[13]

Sherman realized there would be criticism of this seemingly callous act, but if Georgians "raise a howl against my barbarity and cruelty," he had told Halleck in September, "I will answer that war is war, and not popularity-seeking." Many Northern soldiers had already come to this conclusion. Henry Hitchcock, a member of Sherman's staff, told his wife, "General Sherman is perfectly right,—the only possible way to end this unhappy and dreadful conflict . . . is to make it *terrible beyond endurance*." He agreed with Sherman that if Southerners wanted peace, they would have to surrender. But Confederates spurned talk of surrender, and as the Federal troops marched out of Atlanta with bands playing, men cheering, and flags held high, they headed into the heart of the Confederacy, where they would make Southerners regret their arrogant defiance. "A brigade of Massachusetts soldiers are the only troops now left in the town," Major Nichols recorded, "they will be the last to leave it. To-night I heard the really fine band of the

Thirty-third Massachusetts playing 'John Brown's soul goes marching on,' by the light of the burning buildings. I have never heard that noble anthem when it was so grand, so solemn, so inspiring."[14]

As Sherman left Atlanta, he knew exactly what he wanted to achieve. His goal was to break the South's will to fight, not to ravage the land or its people unnecessarily. Indeed, for all his threats, Sherman did not allow his soldiers to destroy everything in their path. Although there had been problems with discipline in the weeks preceding the march, the only incident of note came at Cassville. The village had provided a haven for Confederate cavalry that preyed on Federal wagon trains, and the colonel of the Fifth Ohio Cavalry received instructions to burn it to the ground on November 5. The colonel had orders to give the inhabitants time to remove their possessions before setting the houses aflame. Still, a Confederate congressman later complained that "the Yankees gave Mrs. Headden fifteen minutes to move out her things, and as fast as she carried out any thing they wanted they took it and any thing they did not want, they broke it to pieces."[15]

To Georgians, of course, Sherman bore the responsibility for these crimes. The Union commander personified the Confederates' fear and hatred. Even his own soldiers admitted that he looked the part. He was tall and lean, his reddish-brown hair outlining a craggy, hard face lined with many deep wrinkles. His dark eyes often looked cold and unfeeling, warning Southerners that they would find little sympathy from him. Moreover, Sherman was not the Southern ideal of a gentleman-soldier. He was usually disheveled and always seemed to have a cigar in his mouth. Despite this rough veneer, however, he was "Uncle Billy" to his men. One Yankee said it was not unusual for him to walk along the road with his hands in his pockets and talk "good earnest common-sense with the person nearest him, regardless of rank." Another remembered seeing him ride by: "You would think that he was somb oald plow jogger [with] his head bent a little to one side [and] with an oald stub of a sigar in his mouth," although an Illinois soldier remarked: "It is always about half-gone, but I never saw it lighted. He is the most peculiar-looking man I ever saw." Nonetheless, after the surrender of Atlanta bolstered his reputation, an officer pronounced, "Every man under Sherman has the greatest confidence in him, and make up their minds that where he strikes it is sure death to all rebs within his range."[16]

To carry his war to civilians, Sherman split his army into two wings. The right, which included the XV and XVII Corps under the command of Maj. Gen. Oliver O. Howard, would march in the general direction of Macon. The thirty-four-year-old Howard, a native of Maine, had been an abolitionist even back in his days at West Point, where he had graduated in 1854, fourth in his class. At the outbreak of the war, he was a mathematics instructor at the military academy. The left, including the XIV and XX Corps under Henry W. Slocum, would head toward Augusta before turning in the direction of the capital at Milledgeville. Slocum, also a West Pointer, was a New Yorker who had resigned from the regular army in 1854 to open a law office in Syracuse. As a volunteer, he had risen rapidly, becoming the second youngest major general at the time of his appointment in the Army of the Potomac. After Chancellorsville, Slocum had a falling-out with Joseph Hooker and refused to accompany him to Tennessee in 1863. Slocum agreed to join Sherman in Georgia only after Hooker left. Hooker, angered when Sherman selected his junior Howard to take command of the Army of the Tennessee following McPherson's death, had resigned in the summer.[17]

As the two wings tramped out of Atlanta, panic spread through the state. "We have all been very much frightened here for fear that Shermans army would pass through," young Carrie Timberlake wrote her cousin Tom, who was with Hood's army. Carrie lived near Macon, and her concern was genuine. If Sherman headed for the Rebel prison at Andersonville, the army would march right by her home. Hundreds of refugees streamed past her house, and she told her cousin the roads were "thronged with hogs, sheep, and cattle of all kinds," and the women, children, and slaves carried everything imaginable.[18]

Even before Sherman commenced his march, Georgians were suffering from the effects of his presence. As Union columns marched out of Atlanta, a Newton County widow noted in her diary the ever-present shortages and resulting high prices. "Paid seven dollars a pound for coffee," she complained on November 16, five dollars for an ounce of indigo, twenty dollars for twenty-five sheets of paper, five dollars for some flax thread she valued at ten cents, six dollars for pins, and forty dollars for some machine-made thread. On her shopping expedition, she heard that Sherman was headed her way but decided that it could not be so, and it was certainly only a foraging party. The next day, after learning the rumor was true, she wrote: "What shall I do? Where [shall I] go?"[19]

Unknown to the Rebels, Sherman had issued stern orders to his men regarding their action while in hostile territory. He prohibited soldiers from entering dwellings, although they could take food from the locals. Only the corps commanders had the authority to order the destruction of mills, houses, cotton gins, and other property, and then only if guerrillas or bushwhackers molested the troops or if the inhabitants burned bridges, ob-

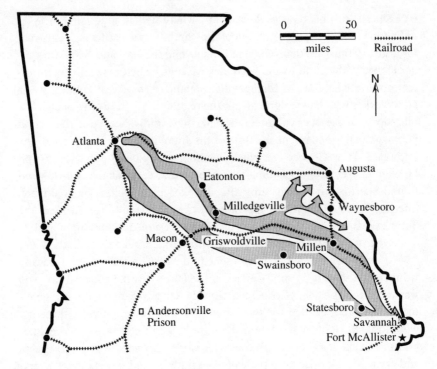

0   50

miles   ┄┄┄┄ Railroad

N

Atlanta

Eatonton

Augusta

Milledgeville

Waynesboro

Macon   Griswoldville   Millen

Swainsboro

□ Andersonville
Prison

Statesboro

Savannah

Fort McAllister ★

3. The March to the Sea

structed roads, or indicated animosity. Army commanders could then "order and enforce a devastation more or less relentless according to the measure of such hostility." Nontheless, it was impossible to police everyone and orders were often ignored. A Wisconsin soldier had told his fiancée that outside Resaca in May 1864 after twenty-three Rebels had surrendered, the Union soldiers killed all of them. "When there is no officer with us, we take no prisoners," he admitted. There is no reason to believe that this disregard for regulations changed on the March to the Sea.[20]

Fear spread as Sherman moved deeper into Georgia. Governor Brown's boast to Beauregard in October that he could raise thirty thousand men to fight alongside the Confederate cavalry had proved empty. Sherman, unaware of the number he faced, would have been pleased to know it was only a fraction of his total: the Confederates could muster only ten thousand men. If Beauregard had not insisted that Hood permit Wheeler's cavalry to remain in the state, Georgia would have been virtually abandoned to its own resources. On Friday, November 18, Brown pleaded for help from Richmond. "I hope you will send us troops as re-enforcements," Brown telegraphed Davis, for we "have not sufficient force." No troops came, but Beauregard offered encouragement in the form of a message to the people in an effort to inspire them to fight the invader. President Davis implored Howell Cobb to use every able-bodied Georgian during the emergency and put blacks to work to obstruct the roads.[21]

Words did little to improve the state's plight. Governor Brown sent Davis a twenty-five-page letter in which he demanded the return of the thousands of Georgians serving in the Army of Northern Virginia. Brown had a point, for more than thirty Georgia regiments and assorted other units manned the trenches at Petersburg. Many of these soldiers agreed. As Sherman had marched toward Atlanta, a young private in Lee's army had told his cousin that "most of the Georgians are wanting to come and protect their own state." Still, Davis refused to weaken the defenses around the Confederate capital, and the Georgians remained in Virginia. These soldiers were also ignorant of Sherman's progress in their home state, for on November 29, two weeks into the march, a Georgian wrote home, "It is the expectation of most every body that Sherman will be captured."[22]

To stop Sherman, Beauregard needed more help than the Confederacy could provide. Hood, two hundred miles to the west, could do nothing. Beauregard asked Hood to send more cavalry, but the Texan replied that he could not spare any "without seriously embarrassing" his own operations and retorted that Wheeler's force was sufficient. Beauregard tried reasoning with Hood, pointing out that Wheeler was greatly outnumbered. He finally asked Hood to send reinforcements to the southeast or begin his own march north. To Samuel Cooper in Richmond Beauregard wrote, "It is left optional with him to divide and re-enforce Cobb, or take the offensive immediately to relieve him." Beauregard told Tennessee's governor Isham Harris the same thing. He also telegraphed Davis that he had ordered Hood north with the ultimate goal of reinforcing Lee in Virginia. Moreover, Beauregard assured Howell Cobb that a "victory in Tennessee will relieve Georgia."[23]

Whether Hood's reasoning was grounded in patriotism, wisdom, or just plain hardheadness did not matter. Certainly he was too far west to send reinforcements to Georgia, for it would take several days for men to return to the southeast, even under the best circumstances. Moreover, the Confederate command was still unclear about Hood's intentions. As late as November 22 President Davis wanted to know if Hood had ordered reinforcements to the southeast. "If it is not too late," he telegraphed. "I wish that Forrest with his cavalry should be sent to impede the march of Sherman's army, and prevent it from foraging on the country." While the Confederates telegraphed a flurry of messages from Virginia to Georgia to Alabama, Sherman remained fixed on his own objective. If Hood wanted "go to the Ohio River," Sherman declared, "I will give him rations. Let him go north. My business is down South."[24]

Sherman hoped to find favorable weather to the south, but as soon as the columns left Atlanta, rain started to fall, sometimes steady, sometimes just a drizzle, turning the thoroughfares to muddy trails. "Such roads I've never seen," complained one soldier, "and still it rains." As the red clay became thick, syrupy mud, another recalled that "nearly every man on foot, both officers and men, fell down, some of them dozens of times." Henry Hitchcock recorded in his diary: "Horrible weather and bad roads—very bad. Our luck for the last forty-eight hours in these respects has changed." Delays and more delays prompted him to add, "At last we get off, foundered through heavy clay mud, under rain sometimes heavy, sometimes drizzling, threading our way through and by wagons laboring along, up hill and down, or stuck fast." The ruts in the road, he marveled, were "fully 18 to 24 inches deep through stiff heavy red clay, some half liquefied, some like wax, or thickened molasses." After watching teamsters struggle to move the wagons and soldiers wading through the slop, he concluded, "No wonder that weather is such an element in warfare." The rain drenched the men to the skin, and when the temperature dropped, it turned to tiny snowflakes on their clothing.[25]

Despite the weather, Sherman made steady progress through the fertile heart of Georgia. He had given his troops permission to "forage liberally," but because they had orders not to enter houses, the civilian population generally remained untouched. Before the march ended, Sherman's foragers would be known as "bummers." There are varying definitions of the word *bummer*, but the easterners in Sherman's army tended to use the term to refer to self-appointed or unauthorized foragers; most of Sherman's men considered a bummer anyone who foraged regularly, with or without permission. One artilleryman described a bummer as "a man dressed in a nondescript suit part blue, part homespin grey or Butternut, with a white hat and tremendous rents in his Breeches, and perhaps barefooted, with his Belt & cartridge box on (for we always go well armed) his trusty carbine by his side, and a revolver stuck in his belt." Another depicted bummers as "a rough looking set of soldiers" who "care for nothing." Although Sherman knew that illegal foraging occurred, he did little to prevent it. In fact, he commented to Henry Hitchcock that he had tried to curb stragglers from pillaging for three years, but "they are harder to conquer than the enemy."[26]

Sherman wanted to frighten Southerners, and he knew that any unauthorized foraging certainly accomplished that without his having to assume direct responsibility for it. He later explained to General Halleck that some of his men were a "little loose in foraging, they 'did some things they ought not to have done,' yet, on the whole, they have supplied the wants of the army with as little violence as could be expected, and as little loss as I calculated." In some instances individual soldiers helped those in need. When members of the Twenty-first Michigan found two tiny girls, dirty and starving, they took them in after failing to locate their parents. For the remainder of the trip, soldiers took turns carrying them, and after the war one of the Michigan officers adopted the two. Such tales of benevolence on the part of Northern soldiers were not unknown.[27]

In fact, Georgians often complained that it was the Rebels, not the Yankees, who gave them the most trouble. When Sherman's bummers arrived, many civilians already knew what to expect, for they were used to visits from troops commandeering food and animals—Wheeler's cavalry had a reputation for doing just that. The *Savannah Daily Morning News* concluded that Wheeler had "demonstrated to every man in the Confederacy, except the President and Gen. Bragg, that he is not capable of commanding 10,000 cavalrymen." A resident told President Davis, "Unless something is done, and that speedily, too, there will be thousands of the best citizens of this State, and heretofore, as loyal as any men in the Confederacy, that will

not care one cent which army is victorious in Georgia." Another Georgian
told a Federal officer that "the Confederates were a great deal worse than our
men, that they pillaged and plundered everybody, and the inhabitants
dreaded their coming."[28]

Yet it was the weather, not pillaging, that was Sherman's main concern
his first days out. The cold rain intensified the problems of moving wagon
trains, artillery, thousands of horses and mules, and large herds of cattle.
When wagons overturned, men had to shovel mud off into the ditch and
roughen the underlying roadbed with picks to provide traction. Soldiers
abandoned overloaded wagons that bogged down and shot animals that fell
from exhaustion. Everything became so wet that it was even difficult to burn
rail fences for warmth. The howling wind made each step a battle with the
elements. Sherman, traveling with the left wing, learned from civilians that
this was the coldest November that many could remember. As he neared
Milledgeville, Sherman took refuge in the house of an overseer not too far
from the state capital. He soon learned that he was enjoying a warm fire on a
plantation belonging to Howell Cobb. Before he left, Sherman instructed
his men to destroy everything except the slave cabins.[29]

The left wing marched east in the direction of Augusta before turning
south toward Milledgeville. Some thirty thousand wet and muddy men
marched into the town on the afternoon of November 22. Sullen residents
watched through frosted windows of gracious homes and listened to the
bands playing "The Battle Hymn of the Republic" as the endless procession
of Union soldiers passed in front of the governor's mansion and state capitol
building. Most of the troops did not stay in the town but crossed the toll
bridge over the Oconee River, which they burned, and camped to the east.

Sherman occupied a capital bereft of politicians, for the legislators had
fled to safer havens. When the general rode into the town, he headed for the
governor's mansion and made the handsome columned structure his headquarters. Brown had left, barely reaching Macon before Federal cavalry obstructed his route. Twenty-year-old Anna Maria Green told her diary that
before the lawmakers ran, "The scene at the State House was truly ridicu-
lous, the members were badly scared, such a body of representatives made
my cheeks glow with shame. . . . They could [not] stand for the defense of
their own capital." Although the town's residents were generally unharmed,
unruly soldiers entered the capitol and conducted a mock session of the leg-
islature in which they revoked Georgia's ordinance of secession. They destroyed the arsenal and depot and plundered the statehouse and state library. A handful of residents retaliated, and a woman who spat on a soldier

had her home burned. When an overseer, Patrick Kane, tried to defend his employer's property, he was shot; Kane was the only fatality of the invasion of Milledgeville. Nonetheless, Major Connolly wrote in his diary. "Here I am, finally, at Milledgeville. My boyish desire is gratified." Another proclaimed, "'First act of drama well played, General!' 'Yes, sir, the first act is played.'"[30]

As the left wing entered the state capital, the right wing drove toward Macon. The city was an industrial center, but it was also on the itinerary if Sherman decided to head for Andersonville. Richard Taylor, hurrying to join the state's defenders, arrived in the city in the "bitterest" weather he remembered for that far south. Other notables congregating in Macon were Howell Cobb, Governor Brown, Robert Toombs, and Gustavus W. Smith, the latter three fleeing Milledgeville some thirty-five miles away. But Hardee, who was in Savannah directing operations, concluded that Sherman's true objective was not Macon but Augusta, the site of one of the Confederacy's most valuable munitions factories. Confederate concern for Augusta was logical, for the powder works provided goods to Lee's army in Virginia. Davis had even dispatched Braxton Bragg there to prepare a defense. Naturally Hardee believed that no competent military commander would pass up an opportunity to destroy such an important site. Therefore, he ordered all the units he could collect from around Macon—a mixture of troops from the Georgia State Line and Gustavus Smith's Georgia Militia (accompanied by some artillery) under Pleasant J. Phillips—to head for Augusta to reinforce the meager defenses there.[31]

This decision resulted in disaster for the Confederates. The Rebels' path intersected with that of Sherman's cavalry at Griswoldville on November 22, and the small factory town east of Macon became the site of the only real battle between Atlanta and the coast. At the sound of skirmishing between the Union horsemen and Rebel troops, Brig. Gen. Charles C. Walcutt rushed his infantry toward the clamor, deploying his men behind a barricade of fence rails. Phillips had instructions to avoid an engagement, but he was not a military man, and it was later said he had enjoyed too much whiskey. Unwisely he ordered a frontal assault. As the Rebels advanced across an open field, Walcutt's experienced soldiers, armed with efficient Spencer repeating rifles, took aim, fired, and watched men writhe and fall as the bullets hit their mark. Capt. Charles Wills of the 103d Illinois reported, "It was awful the way we slaughtered those men." After the battle, Northern soldiers were distressed to discover that their opponents were not regular Confederate soldiers but mainly old men and boys, some not even fifteen years old. A Union soldier who walked across the batt'efield the next day recalled: "Some one was groaning. We moved a few bodies, and there was a boy with a broken arm and leg—just a boy of 14 years old; and beside him, cold in death, lay his Father, two brothers, and an Uncle." Another Union veteran concluded, "I hope we will never have to shoot at such men again." A Georgia militiaman wrote home that after the battle the doctors were busy cutting off arms and legs. "They was wounded in all possible manner that you can imagine," he noted. "It was the distressingest time I ever saw in my life."[32]

Griswoldville was not much of a battle, and the loss on the Union side was relatively light: 13 Union soldiers died and 79 were wounded. The Rebels, however, counted 51 killed and another 472 wounded. Yet as Georgia families mourned their dead and tended their maimed, Northerners celebrated. Thursday, November 24, was Lincoln's day of Thanksgiving.

When Sherman's columns skirted Macon it became clear that he had decided not to bother with Andersonville, the notorious Confederate prison camp southwest of the city. The compound, officially named Camp Sumter, was near Americus in Sumter County, and the first prisoners had arrived in February 1864. By July 1, the stockade held more than twenty-six thousand prisoners in an area designed for ten thousand; the next month the population had risen to thirty-three thousand. Conditions quickly deteriorated as overcrowding increased. Latrines built along the lone creek inside the walls filled with human waste and eventually overflowed, creating a swamp of disease-producing sewage in the middle of the compound. Men dug holes for wells, but it was almost impossible to avoid sickness, and during the hot summer, at least one hundred men died each day. After Atlanta fell, Richmond authorities recognized the vulnerability of the location, particularly if Sherman moved on Mobile. Just days after Atlanta fell, Hood asked Davis to empty the compound so that he would be free to maneuver without having to stay between Sherman and the prison. Many Union prisoners were transferred to Millen, a small town on the railroad between Augusta and Savannah. Therefore, by the time Sherman began his march, Andersonville was almost deserted.

Although Andersonville was not on Sherman's agenda, Millen was, and the prison near the town was directly in his path. Designated Camp Lawton, the compound was named for Alexander Robert Lawton, who served as the quartermaster general, and as Sherman approached, it still held ten thousand prisoners. An order came to move the men, and in the early hours of November 20, guards herded them into open railroad flatcars destined for Savannah. The prisoners, weak and debilitated, suffered intensely from the cold wind and rain.

Sherman's decision to ignore Andersonville was justifiable because he certainly knew it was empty; his decision to bypass Augusta was not as easily excused. Indeed, after the war, the general would have to explain why he avoided the city and the valuable ammunition works there. He claimed that it was not necessary to take Augusta, for he had planned to destroy the railroad to Virginia when he marched through South Carolina, effectively cutting off the supply of munitions from Georgia. Of course, in November 1864 Sherman would have no way of being sure that would happen, for even after reaching Savannah he would have to argue his case with Grant again before receiving permission to make the trek through South Carolina.

There are various theories to explain his decision. A favorite story among the locals is that Sherman avoided the city because of his infatuation with a young Southern beauty he had known during his years at West Point. According to the tale, Sherman had met Cecelia Stovall when her brother was a cadet at the academy. During his Georgia campaigns, the general had spared her plantation home in Cass County (although she had already fled) and had sent her a note by a slave that read: "My Dear Madam: You once said that you pitied the man who ever became my foe. My answer was that I would shield and protect you. That I have done. Forgive all else; I am but a soldier. W. T. Sherman." It is possible that Cecelia, who had married Charles Shelman, was with her brother's family in Augusta when Sherman's columns passed, and it certainly makes for an engaging tale. But Union soldiers had a more practical explanation. They feared that because of the importance of the powder works, the Confederacy had probably sent adequate reinforcements to defend the facilities. There were even stories that Longstreet or Johnston might be there. "Sherman don't know what is at Augusta," worried one, "neither do we know. A rebel army of 50,000 men may be on us before daylight tomorrow." Yet the possible presence of a Confederate army at Augusta does not seem to have concerned Sherman. He was more worried about supplies, for he knew that once he left the fertile region of Georgia he would need to link with the Federal navy on the Atlantic coast to receive provisions.[33]

As Sherman plunged deeper into Georgia, the land changed. Fertile fields became pine woods with trees thirty to sixty feet tall. Pine needles carpeted the ground as the sun fought unsuccessfully to penetrate the thick forests. Correspondingly, as foodstuffs became harder to find, the soldiers increased their looting and unauthorized foraging. And provisions were not all they took. A Georgian recalled that "4 or 5 yankees came, professing they would behave as gentlemen. These gentlemen, however stole my gold watch, and silver spoons, besides whiskey, tobacco, and a hat or two apiece." Later that day, "4 more came, and got a few hats, and one fiddle, and some whiskey." After sundown two more appeared "and got some whiskey, a few hats, etc." Few civilians tried to prevent the foraging parties from taking everything, for the Federals punished armed resistance by burning houses, barns, and fences. Nonetheless, Confederate cavalry and Rebel guerrillas often retaliated. At least sixty-four Union soldiers were executed. Some had their throats slit, and their bodies, left for the army to find, carried signs such as "Death to all foragers" or "Hear Hangs Hams."[34]

Although Union soldiers did not maim or murder civilians, it is impossible to calculate the number of unreported assaults on civilians. A white woman shamed by being raped by a Yankee might never divulge the incident outside of the family, regardless of how brutal or degrading the experience had been. One incident occurred in the small community of Midway, just outside of the state capital. Twenty-seven-year-old Kate Latimer Nichols, the wife of Capt. James H. Nichols of the Governor's Horse Guards, part of Phillips's Legion in Virginia, was ill when two Union soldiers forced their way at gunpoint into her bedroom. A local resident confided in her diary: "The worst of their acts was committed to poor Mrs. Nichols—violence done, and atrocity committed that ought to make her husband an enemy unto death. Poor woman I fear she has been driven crazy." The Savannah paper reported on December 6 that "the incarnate devils ravished some of the nicest ladies in Milledgeville. One of their unfortunate victims was, we learn, consigned to the Asylum on Monday."[35]

Black women suffered too, although soldiers often contrasted them, "particularly good looking ones, decked in satins and silks," with backwoods white women. A letter written from Clinton (between Milledgeville and Macon) on November 26 claimed that "female servants were taken and villified without mercy, by their officers; and in some instances when they were reared as tenderly as whites." One former slaver recalled that "dere wuz a heap of talk 'bout de scandlous way dem Yankee sojers been treatin' Negro 'omans and gals." On one plantation, black men put the women in a house and staked a guard.[36]

Free black women did not fare any better than their white counterparts, for the Union soldiers often confiscated property belonging to them just as quickly as that of the white inhabitants. Mary Ross Bellamy, a free woman of color who lived near Milledgeville, complained that soldiers emptied her barns and fields and took her horse and hogs, even though she had initially rejoiced at their arrival.[37]

Federal commanders were not unaware of the violence against women. One court-martial convicted sixteen-year-old John Bass, an Illinois private, for attempted rape even though the evidence in this particular incident was flimsy, and the woman admitted during the trial that Bass had never threatened, much less touched, her. She claimed he had pulled a revolver, although she did concede that she had provoked the incident by calling him a "Nigger Stealer." The court found the young man guilty; his head was shaved and he was dishonorably discharged. Bass's commander complained, but to no avail, for General Howard replied that "he must make an example of some one and just as well a 48th [Illinois] man as anyone else."[38]

Depredations were not confined to Sherman's soldiers, for runaway slaves, deserters from both armies, and Confederate cavalrymen plagued the countryside. While citizens might expect brutal treatment from the first two, it was often the Rebel cavalry that proved most trying. Still, whatever Georgians might have thought about Wheeler's cavalry, it was the only regular army command standing between their homes and the enemy. Indeed, the Rebel cavalry was the only serious obstruction in Kilpatrick's drive toward the prison compound near Millen.

The twenty-eight-year-old Kilpatrick was not popular, even in his own army, for he could be obnoxious, boastful, and a notorious womanizer. Wheeler was the same age, and the two had known each other during earlier days at West Point. On the morning of November 27, Wheeler attacked Kilpatrick's camp, taking prisoners, flags, and hundreds of horses. Kilpatrick, reportedly enjoying female company in a house nearby, was "very nearly captured." Regrouping his command, Kilpatrick battled his old classmate throughout the day in a fighting withdrawal. When he reached the little town of Waynesboro, having burned everything else in his path, he set it aflame, but Wheeler's men managed to drive him out and extinguished the blaze. The fighting continued throughout the night and into the next day, with some eighteen hundred Rebels chasing about thirty-seven hundred Union horsemen. Kilpatrick finally retreated, bareheaded, to the safety of the infantry camps. "Confound the cavalry," wrote a Federal officer when he learned of the fiasco. "They're good for nothing but to run down horses and steal chickens. I'd rather have one good regiment of infantry than the whole of Kilpatrick's cavalry."[39]

While horsemen continued to battle, the infantry moved without opposition. After the army left Milledgeville, the weather had cleared and the temperature began to rise just as Sherman hoped. As the roads dried, the wagons rumbled steadily along. The rolling hills faded as the landscape leveled. James Connolly observed, "We are now in the country where the 'Spanish Moss' begins to show itself." He, like others new to the Deep South, had never seen the gray-green streamers hanging from tree limbs. Moreover, the warm, pleasant days offered the men a welcome respite from the cold of the previous week, and with the weather cooperating, Sherman could turn his attention to making connections with friendly forces along the coast. As his columns neared the ocean, Federal authorities on the South Carolina side of the Savannah River tried to provide assistance. On the last day of November, Union troops under Brig. Gen. John P. Hatch advanced on the Charleston & Savannah Railroad, the supply line for the Confederate defenders in the Georgia seaport. Among the units accompanying Hatch on his expedition were several regiments of African American soldiers.[40]

The Confederates quickly responded. Col. Charles J. Colcock, who commanded the area from his comfortable headquarters in the antebellum resort of Grahamville, had barely over four hundred available men, and many of those were along the railroad where they manned artillery up and down the track. In any case, he was absent when the crisis unfolded, and his second in command, Maj. John Jenkins, called for reinforcements from Charleston and Savannah. One of those to respond was Gustavus Smith. After the fight near Macon, General Smith had hurried to Savannah and, when learning that the railroad was in danger, promptly agreed, in an unusual move, to take the Georgia militia across the state line. Smith's troops would prove critical in the battle that followed.

The clash came at Honey Hill, not far from Grahamville. For the Confederates, it was Griswoldville in reverse. The slaughter was immense for so small a battle, but this time it was the Union soldiers whose bodies covered the ground after several futile assaults through a swampy expanse covered with trees and brush. "We fought in a forest dense and marshy," recalled Sgt. James M. Trotter of the Fifty-fifth Massachusetts (Colored), "and it was almost impossible on this account to maneuver more than half our troops." Capt. William D. Crane of the Fifty-fifth, who tried to encourage his men by yelling that the opponents were only Georgia militiamen, was quickly killed by a canister ball. After the carnage ended, a Southerner claimed that outside the Rebel earthworks he saw "some sixty or seventy bodies in a space of about an acre, many of which were horribly mutilated by shells, some with half their heads shot off, and others completely disemboweled." Rows of black troops "lay five deep as dead as a mackeral." Smith later reported his victory: "The flight of the enemy during the night and the number of their dead left upon the field is evidence of the nature of the attacks as well as the defense."[41]

The battle took a heavy toll on the Federals. When the fighting ended, 750 men had become casualties. Although 138 were from the Twenty-fifth Ohio, the remainder were black. Those participating in the battle were the Fifty-fourth and Fifty-fifth Massachusetts (Colored) and the Twenty-sixth, Thirty-second, Thirty-fourth, Thirty-fifth, and 102d U.S. Colored Troops. This was the first battle for the men of the Thirty-second and 102d USCT; the former lost 64 men, the latter 23.[42]

The black soldiers had certainly indicated their willingness to fight, but that had not been enough. The Confederates had successfully defended the rail line, and the militiamen headed back for Savannah, pleased with the victory and proud they had redeemed their loss at Griswoldville. For these Georgians, Wednesday, November 30, was a day of celebration. Far to the north, soldiers in Hood's Army of Tennessee would recall the thirtieth, the date of the battle of Franklin, with anguish.[43]

Jefferson Davis knew about the fighting in South Carolina, but he had no idea what was going on either with Sherman in Georgia or with Hood in Tennessee. In fact, the previous two weeks had been among the worst he had endured during the war simply because of the uncertainty. As soon as he heard that Sherman had struck out from Atlanta, he had telegraphed Robert E. Lee, "Please give me your views as to the action proper under the circumstances of Sherman's movement upon Macon." He then decided that a written reply would not suffice, and so he sent another message inquiring if the general could come to Richmond as soon as possible. One of the topics he wanted to discuss was troops. Beauregard, he told Lee, needed help from beyond his department. This was no surprise, for several times in the past the Creole had suggested that troops from the Virginia theater should be sent as reinforcements to the West. Almost every time (with the exception of Longstreet's trip to Georgia in the late summer of 1863) Lee had convinced Davis that such a move was impractical. There is evidence to suggest that Davis agreed with Beauregard this time but was unable to persuade Lee to release any men. Not long after conferring with Lee, Davis told Hardee at Savannah "Beyond the force sent some time since to Augusta, General Lee has not thus far found himself able to detach troops from his command. Should a change of circumstances permit further aid to be sent, no time will be lost."[44]

The Confederacy could do nothing to alleviate the suffering of the people in Sherman's path. Although it is difficult to assess the damage accurately, a woman at Covington determined as the Union army disappeared, "This ended the passing of Shermans army by my place leaving me poorer by thirty thousand dollars than I was yesterday morning. And a much stronger rebel." After seeing the damage inflicted on her neighbors and living in fear of a return visit, she realized the impact of Sherman's march and added two days later, "Oh the horrors the horrors of war." Another Georgian complained to her cousin that the government had done nothing to prevent the march. "I never could understand the policy of Hood's going off to Tennessee and leaving the Yankees in our midst to make their way undisputed to our seaport cities," she declared. "We feel the deepest anxiety, and know not what to expect."[45]

Leaders in Richmond did not know what to expect either. On Wednesday, November 30, Sherman's march was two weeks old and still there was no news of Confederate fortunes in Tennessee. Davis had told Beauregard that day: "Until Hood reaches the country proper of the enemy, he can scarcely change the plans for Sherman's or Grant's campaigns. They would, I think, regard the occupation of Tennessee and Kentucky as of minor importance." That same day, an official in Richmond recorded in his diary, "It is reported that Gen. Hood is still marching North, and is near Nashville." Although Davis had no idea of Hood's exact position, he had assured a crowd in South Carolina on his visit just weeks before that Confederate soldiers would "plant our banners on the banks of the Ohio." What Davis did not know as November ended was that Hood was trying his best to fulfill that promise. An Ohio infantryman told his brother: "Sherman and Hood here both playing 'smash' Hood has come one way and Sherman gone the other. Neither one having any line for supplies of rations or ammunition. But Hood cannot take any important place here and Sherman can go just where he pleases."[46]

CHAPTER FIVE

Hood's Advance into Tennessee

During the last days of November, travel became easier for Sherman's troops as the temperature rose and the terrain leveled out, but for Hood's Confederates, thinly clad and poorly fed, the last week of the month proved grueling. As the Rebel army set off for Tennessee, the ragged columns that followed the tattered battle flags seemed a far cry from the army of earlier days. The weather frowned on the Rebels too, for the conditions rapidly deteriorated. Hood's decision to march north tested the loyalty and endurance of every soldier, for the winter storm that plagued Sherman's progress out of Atlanta made the trek into Tennessee miserable and exhausting. A Texan remembered how he tucked his head into the blustering wind and, fighting the elements, pressed on as the "snow came down thick." One column covered twelve miles the first day out, but steady snow flurries and intermittent sleet made progress arduous. At night, the intense cold disrupted sleep as men struggled to stay warm.[1]

So as Sherman moved south, leaving the winter weather behind and moving into fertile Georgia farmland, the Confederates headed north, where they were greeted with freezing temperatures and a landscape that had already suffered from more than two years of war. Unlike central and southern Georgia, where most civilians had never seen a blue-clad invader, middle Tennessee was one of the Confederacy's most fought-over regions. Little actual damage could be attributed to invading armies, but as the breadbasket for the Union's western armies and a gateway to the Deep South, it was the site of smaller actions and a target for scores of guerrillas. The fighting might only now be touching anxious Georgians, but Tennesseans already knew what a destructive war was like. Sherman and Grant may have initiated a policy of exhaustion in the spring of 1864, one that Sherman was now implementing his March to the Sea, but many civilians in Tennessee would argue that soldiers had been given a free hand to wage unlimited war long before Sherman struck out for the coast.

Although modern historians offer differing interpretations of how "total" the Civil War was, many Tennesseans certainly recognized unrestricted war. Sherman, with sixty thousand soldiers, would march into history, but in reality his passage through southeastern Georgia was so rapid that the devastation was not absolute. His armies occupied many towns after he left Atlanta but destroyed none completely, and even two of Georgia's state capitals, Milledgeville and Louisville, suffered only minor damage. Only Millen, the site of a Rebel prison, became a target for angry Union soldiers. Georgians would remember the terror that accompanied Sherman's campaign far more than the actual physical destruction—that devastation came later, in South Carolina.[2]

Middle Tennessee, by contrast, had been a crossroad for Rebels and Yankees since 1862. Farmers could only watch as soldiers took horses, pigs, corn, and other goods the armies needed. "This is a dreary, desolate, barren and deserted looking country," a Federal officer noted in 1862. "It is really sad to see this beautiful country here so ruined," wrote a Union soldier the following year. "There are no fences left at all. There is no corn and hay for the cattle and horses, but there are no horses left anyhow and the planters have no food for themselves." A Confederate south of Nashville wrote, "The Federal soldiers have taken every horse mare and mule that I have." They had even "broken into my smoke house repetedly and have taken all my hams. They have taken a goodeal of my corn and all of my hay and near all my fodder. My health is very bad. I will certenly go crazy." There were around ten thousand permanent Union garrison troops in Nashville, but detachments stationed along the railroads and turnpikes constantly needed supplies. "When we have eaten a place empty," wrote an Indiana cavalryman in 1863, "we go a few miles farther and take everything there we can find." Occupation forces also controlled civilian activities, including travel and correspondence.[3]

Long before Georgians fled from Sherman's armies during the Atlanta campaign, Tennesseans suffered from problems of refugees, slaves, and a flood of Northerners who followed the Union columns. The Federal army attracted escaped slaves, and by 1864 the unofficial policy was to "keep all we get, and get all we can." An Illinois officer told his wife that Union soldiers also took all the horses and slaves they could find. "Now what do you think of your husband," he wrote, "degenerating from a conservative

young Democrat to a horse stealer and 'nigger thief,' and practicing his ne-
farious occupation almost within gun shot of the sacred 'Hermitage' and
tomb of Andrew Jackson?"[4]

The war had a dual effect on the region's farmland. Non-slaveholding
farmers had joined the army and their fields often lay fallow, while plantation owners suffered because many of their slaves had fled to the Federal
army. Without workers in the fields, both farms and plantations barely produced enough for their immediate needs and could not provide goods for
those in the towns. Even firewood became scarce. By 1862, angry residents
claimed there was hardly a day when they did not lose food, stock, fencing,
or equipment to soldiers from one side or the other. A farmer and preacher
near Franklin had observed, "The yankies hear for something to day . . .
every day 2 or 3 times in the day never pay anything." Indeed, the man of
God recalled that one soldier, after aiming a gun at him, had "called me a
damn old sun of a bich and said he would blow my brains out." Although the
trooper only took the man's corn, such actions had a devastating effect on
both the people and the land. In Georgia, Sherman led his bummers
through the heart of the state, the location of the most fertile land and afflu-
ent plantations. In Tennessee, Hood would march into an impoverished region, devastated and demoralized by the unending war.[5]

Yet for many of Hood's Rebels this was a special crusade. Tennessee was,
after all, home. "How every pulse did beat and leap, and how every heart
did throb with emotions of joy, which seemed nearly akin to heaven," wrote
Tennessean Sam Watkins, "when we received the glad intelligence of our
onward march toward the land of promise, and of our loved ones." As the
soldiers trundled their wagons across the river, a Trans-Mississippi Confederate had a different view. "The crossing of the river did not awaken enthusiasm," he declared. "Most of the army felt they were placing what seemed
to them a formidable barrier between themselves and their homes." He did
admit that the Tennessee soldiers were an "exception." They were jolly, for
they were going home, "many of them for the first time in years."[6]

On the morning of November 21, after a three-week lull along the banks
of the Tennessee River, the march began, a march fateful in the life of John
Bell Hood and in the history of the Confederate Army of Tennessee. Hood
had numerous explanations for the long delay, but precious days had been
lost. Part of the holdup was the result of Hood's poor planning; part was
simply bad luck. The Texan had transferred his headquarters from Tuscumbia to the Florence side of the river on November 13, but the next day
the heavens opened and it rained for almost a week. While Sherman wel-

comed the downpour, Hood watched the river rise, further hampering troop movement. In addition, Davis had proclaimed November 16 a day of prayer, and the men were encouraged to attend church services. Although that was just another frustrating delay for Hood, some men were encouraged by hearing the preachers ask for divine guidance and protection. A soldier wrote his mother in Savannah, "We expect to have a hard time and to have some fighting to do, but we intend with Gods help to ruin Thomas' Army."[7]

Even the true believer must have recognized that if God was listening to the Rebel entreaties, he had a strange way of showing it, for the rain continued for several days after the prayers ended. Accordingly, Hood grew impatient to strike out. Food grew scarce when the roads connecting the camps with the railroad became so muddy that supply wagons bogged down in the mire. The one bright spot in November was the arrival of Forrest's cavalry in mid-month, although any optimism resulting from his appearance was muted by his badly depleted numbers and worn-out horses. Forrest had furloughed part of his command for the purpose of replenishing tired mounts, and many of the men had not returned before his unexpected march to join Hood. For the religious, the trials of getting the campaign under way must have seemed a sign from above, and to the superstitious, a forewarning.

Beauregard simply saw the delays as a lack of appropriate groundwork on Hood's part. Critics would blame Hood harshly for his excessive delays, but he could not control the weather. He could, however, make adequate preparation for the march, and frustration gave way to exasperation when Beauregard discovered that Hood planned to move without sufficient provisions. On Friday, November 18, Beauregard demanded, "Where are your supplies?"[8]

With or without enough supplies, Hood was about to embark on the most critical campaign of his career. A simple notation attached to a report briefly announced: "Crossed Tennessee, November 21, 30,600 men." For so modest a statement, the event held great fascination for the participants. Just moving the men, wagons, and supplies across the river was an ordeal. "I stopped on a high bluff bank to see the army crossing," wrote a Rebel. "Each Brigade had its band playing ahead of it, all marching by fours. The pontoon bridge is flat on the water and one and a half miles long, and at the distance I am, it looks like the men were walking on the water. It is a pretty and at the same time a strange sight, a sight that is not seen more than once in a life time." Another soldier described the structure as a "very imperfect and unsafe affair" because it was constructed of boats, rafts, and barges.

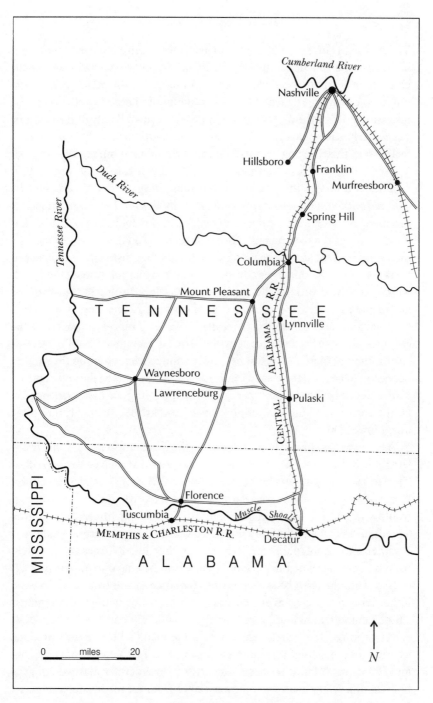

4. Tennessee Theater of Operations

The powerful current caused it to bulge into a crescent shape, and the center often disappeared below the water. Even though Hood had ordered the bands to play, a man recalled that the "gay notes of music merely echoed and bounded down the rugged cliffs. Not a shout nor cheer nor yell, except the necessary cries of the drivers of the cattle and teams." Many of the soldiers, particularly those not from Tennessee, were apprehensive. "The general feeling was this," claimed an Arkansan. "'We are marching to certain ruin. We will fall back in less than a month, or Hood will have us all captured!'"[9]

The land across the river appeared uninviting. The ravaged country, studded with vacant houses, promised little fodder for the horses or food for the men. Making a new camp every night in the cold required almost as much effort as the day's march. After a fitful sleep on the frigid ground, the men were roused, and in the predawn darkness they dismantled and packed their goods for the this day's advance. Under normal conditions, the march would have held little challenge for these hardened soldiers, but this was one of the most demanding they ever experienced. The storms alternated between rain and severe frost, recalled a Federal officer stationed in the region, and covered "the roads with a frozen crust over deep mire, just strong enough to make the utmost obstruction, without getting the solidity necessary to bear up the wagons and teams." Moreover, the flat river bottom of the Tennessee gave way to rugged hills, putting an increased burden on the animals pulling the supply wagons and artillery through the frosty quagmire.

As the wagons slowly rumbled forward, the weather was not the only problem. The barren, mountainous country also provided a haven for guerrillas. "These robbers and cutthroats were on neither side," related a soldier. "They could have done us no harm, had we preserved order. But our men would stray off the road foraging. Not until twelve or fifteen poor fellows were found dead and horribly mutilated did the danger become realized." Another soldier noted that the country was "filled with Tories and diserters from both armies who buswack our men when they have an opportunity."[10]

Slaves might have been responsible for some of the trouble, for as the Rebel army advanced, many slaves and contrabands fled to safer regions. Those behind Union lines were fearful of what might happen if the Confederates captured the Federal garrisons, while many still on the plantations worried that they might be impressed, or worse. Just a couple of weeks before Hood crossed into Tennessee, a party of Texas cavalry masquerading as Federal officers kidnaped six former slaves from a contraband settlement south of Huntsville. Two of the frightened prisoners escaped while being taken across the river, but another two of the "meddlesome blacks" were killed, one shot and one hanged. George Griscom, with the Ninth Texas Cavalry, recorded in his diary on October 30: "Catch a negro spy & hang him."[11]

Thus the presence of Hood's infantry, preceded by Forrest's cavalry, heightened the tension in an already edgy countryside. The three corps marched along parallel routes. Lee led the way, following a backwoods road that ran roughly halfway between the towns of Waynesboro and Lawrenceburg. With him were some 8,600 soldiers under division commanders Carter L. Stevenson, Henry D. Clayton, and Edward Johnson. Cheatham moved out next and took the longest route to the west through Waynesboro. Cheatham, with around 10,600 men, had Pat Cleburne, William B. Bate, and John C. Brown leading his divisions. The last to cross the river was Stewart, whose 8,800 infantrymen were divided among the divisions of Samuel French, William W. Loring, and Edward C. Walthall. Stewart followed the shorter route to Lawrenceburg but had to turn west when the army reunited on the Waynesboro-Mt. Pleasant Road. Forrest's horsemen, in divisions under James R. Chalmers, Abraham Buford, and William H. Jackson, provided the screen. Forrest reported that his command engaged the enemy several times and was constantly skirmishing "but drove him in every encounter."[12]

Hood steered clear of Pulaski, a Federal garrison on the railroad south of Columbia. Although it was a pleasant locale before the war, a Union officer described Pulaski in 1864 as a "nice town but like all Seceshdom gone to Seed." According to an article in a Nashville newspaper, the conditions around Pulaski were dreadful. It was almost impossible to "form any conception of the great scarcity of every thing necessary to sustain life that exists there." Many residents had fled to Nashville, and a local Unionist who spent the war in the state capital recalled that "day after day I saw the wives and daughters of the once wealthy and well-to-do planters of my own acquaintance getting out of [railroad] box cars, clad in tatters, carrying bundles of bedding, and staring about themselves vacantly as not knowing where to look for food or shelter."[13]

Pulaski was more than just a Union depot. The town provided temporary shelter for escaped slaves who came into the lines and quickly became a contraband center. Concerned Northerners soon arrived to help the newly freed families learn how to survive on their own. They taught the blacks to cultivate the land, build cabins and barracks, and work at various trades. Missionaries established schools, and the government provided medical care. By 1864, one historian noted, the experiment was applauded as "a well-managed enterprise generating profound social repercussions throughout its environs by safeguarding the black family and severing the last bonds of slavery." With the presence of Unionists, Federal soldiers, and black refugees, it was easy to see why guerrillas plagued the region. In 1862 Rebel guerrillas had lynched two Unionists and left the bodies hanging as a warning to others. "These people are proud, arrogant rebels," wrote the garrison commander in 1863. "I propose, so far as I can, to let these people know that we are at war." He apparently had little success, for guerrillas continued to be a problem. After frightening a Unionist out of the county, guerrillas auctioned his property to Rebel neighbors. In 1864 a local woman had an encounter with guerrillas who rode up to her home. They inquired if her husband was in the Union army and then told her that they were going to burn her "damned old 'shebang.' " She fled the house with her children in tow before they put the torch to the beds, although the leader shouted that "he ought to burn the house with the whole family in it."[14]

Guerrilla warfare quickly generates its own grim rules. As General Cox headed toward Columbia he surveyed the aftermath of vicious irregular fighting. At Lynnville, a small town between Pulaski and Columbia, he saw piles of ashes and charred wood, all that remained of most of the homes. Troopers of the Tenth Tennessee Cavalry (Union), claiming that Rebel guerrillas in the neighborhood had fired on the regiment, had burned the structures to the ground. It is not surprising that, as hatred intensified on both sides, after the war Pulaski became the birthplace of the Ku Klux Klan.[15]

The Pulaski garrison was under the overall command of George Thomas. From the beginning Thomas operated with the handicap of having to pull together a makeshift army out of scattered commands. Sherman had sent him north with two divisions, partly to consolidate troops in the region and partly to protect Union communications from raiding Confederate cavalry. Additionally, when an invasion by Hood became a possibility, Sherman sent the IV Corps from the Department of the Cumberland to join Thomas and a few days later ordered the XXIII Corps from the Department of the Ohio into Tennessee. John Schofield arrived the second week of November and assumed command at Pulaski. A week later, Maj. Gen. James Wilson took charge of the cavalry.

The twenty-seven-year-old Wilson was one of the youngest stars in the Union army. He was a friend of Grant's and had risen from regular army lieutenant to brigadier general of volunteers by December 1863; nine months later he had become a brevet major general. Wilson had gone east with Grant, where he commanded a division under Philip Sheridan (while men such as George Custer commanded only a brigade). His success had been mixed, and not everybody was as enamored of Wilson as Grant. Custer, for one, called him an "upstart and imbecile" who lacked the brains and experience to lead cavalry in the field. But after Sherman complained about the inability of his cavalry to handle the Rebels, Grant had sent Wilson west.[16]

Sherman had not requested Wilson. He initially asked for Joseph Mower but found that Mower was off chasing Sterling Price in Missouri and not available. Still, he needed someone experienced to organize his horsemen for Kilpatrick, he believed, was good only "for small scouts." Sherman told Grant he wanted a "man of sense and courage" to manage his cavalry, but he would take anyone who satisfied the commanding general. Grant sent him Wilson with assurances that he would "add 50 percent" to the effectiveness of his cavalry. When Sherman embarked on his march to the coast, he took Kilpatrick along but ordered Wilson to report to Thomas. In late November, Wilson would have a chance to prove Grant had not misplaced his faith.[17]

Even before Wilson had an opportunity to assess the situation properly, Federal scouting parties had a pretty good idea of what Hood was doing. Although Brig. Gen. Edward Hatch, who commanded two cavalry brigades tracking Hood's progress, had thought that the wet weather would keep the Rebels from attempting any movement through the sea of mud, he soon realized his mistake. On November 21, as a piercing north wind howled and snow blinded both horses and riders, Hatch telegraphed Thomas a fairly accurate assessment of the strength and location of Hood's columns. He estimated that Hood was moving toward Columbia rather than Pulaski with from thirty thousand to thirty-five thousand men, around sixty pieces of artillery, and some ten thousand cavalry. "There is no doubt of their advance," he concluded.[18]

Although Thomas was skeptical about a Rebel drive across the snowy, windswept landscape, he could not ignore the possibility. Just in case the report was true, Thomas ordered Schofield to occupy Columbia before Hood could reach the town but informed Henry Halleck in Washington that he did not have enough men to attack and would have to operate on the defensive until reinforcements arrived. Stanley's corps, he pointed out, numbered only twelve thousand men and Schofield's corps a mere ten thousand. Wilson, he added, could field just three thousand troopers. Thomas counted on reinforcements from A. J. Smith from Missouri, but Smith had not received his marching orders until November 21 and was still two hundred miles from St. Louis. Moreover, the bad weather that hampered movement in Tennessee had also made the roads almost impassable across the Mississippi River.[19]

Federal troops were not any more anxious than the Confederates to brave the elements, for the intermittent snow, driven by a cutting wind, promised intense suffering. It was not cold enough to freeze the roads, and an Ohio soldier told his sister, "We wade in mud fight in mud cook in mud sleep in mud or on brush or rails and eat mud as we do not keep anything without mud on it." After the Federal troops abandoned their huts at Pulaski and took to the road, General Cox chose to walk for several miles in an effort to keep warm. The race for Columbia was on.[20]

Columbia was another of the prosperous towns that had suffered from three years of war. In 1860, its population was fifty-four hundred; the only place in middle Tennessee with more people was Nashville. Both Union and Rebel cavalry frequently visited Columbia, and the region was infested by guerrillas. Nimrod Porter, whose farm was near the town, recorded in his journal that the guerrillas' favorite method of coercion was to approach a "house in the dead of the night gitting the doore open & punishing the inmates by partially hanging & choking them until they tell where there moneys & valuables are." Even most of the churches had ceased to operate. "Owing to the disturbances in the country," wrote the clerk at Zion Church in April 1864, "we have had no communion since October 1862; & Session have had no meeting since that time." In May an Episcopal rector watched as soldiers invaded his sanctuary and stole everything they could carry off, even trying to remove the cornerstone in search of hidden valuables.[21]

As Schofield hurried troops to Columbia, the Confederates continued their steady march toward the same objective. When the Rebels left Alabama and entered Tennessee, they found that the land was testimony to the ravages of war, for the Rebel columns passed darkened houses with yards overgrown with weeds. The carpet of snow that blanketed the fallow fields and covered the roadways made movement treacherous. An officer recalled that the "roads were in such terrible condition that the men marched in the woods and fields to escape the mud." One of Stewart's commanders complained that it proved "almost impossible for the artillery to move at all, the teams being very poor and greatly exhausted from constant and excessive service. Until we struck the old Nashville road heavy details (sometimes one, and often two regiments) were required to move with the artillery to assist in getting it up the hills." A soldier in the Thirty-seventh Mississippi added that the horses were "so poor and jaded that entire regiments were detailed to help the artillery along, the combined strength of horses and men often being required to get the pieces up the hills." Urging along the heavy supply wagons with their wheels churning in the mud was arduous, even though men laid fascines of brush, branches, and wooden boards.[22]

But on they marched, and as the miles passed, conditions improved. Even when the weather began to moderate, a Rebel still complained that his "hand's & feed were near frozen off." Despite the cold, women and children turned out to watch the army pass, and an Alabama soldier noted that the people were all loyal Confederates who "received our arrival with joy. White handkerchiefs are waved by the ladies in every house we pass that is inhabited." At one home a lady stood next to a barrel of molasses and filled cups and canteens while offering words of encouragement. One soldier recalled that he trudged along with a tin cup of molasses in one hand and a stick slung across his shoulder with a pair of shoes taken from the black prisoners at Dalton dangling off the end; his feet were too sore to wear the captured boots. But the unexpected reception along the route made many tired and weary infantrymen forget their suffering. The soldier added that thousands of men still wore moccasins in spite of Hood's attempts to replenish the footwear in Alabama, but "we didn't care—*just then!*" After an absence of over a year, the army had reentered Tennessee.[23]

Parts of middle Tennessee were a vast improvement over northern Alabama and southern Tennessee for the landscape changed from the uninviting expanse of undergrowth and timber that had greeted them on the northern side of the Tennessee River to a region where many people enjoyed wealth and prosperity. "Land rich, very rich," wrote a soldier in Cleburne's division on November 26. "Water very good and plenty of it, and the finest timber we have ever seen." He marveled at the tall trees and enclosed fields of bluegrass. "To day we pass the Polk place in Maury Co. The prettiest place I have ever seen in my life." Even travel improved when the division reached the gravel turnpike, which was hard and solid. That night the Rebels camped four miles from Columbia.[24]

Maury County was the home of former president James K. Polk, and when he died, his land was divided among several relatives. The family had four separate residences, including Ashwood Hall, an impressive mansion built in 1836 and the home of Lucius J. Polk, brother of Leonidas Polk, the Confederate general who had been killed during the Atlanta campaign. Hood made his headquarters at Ashwood, and the other stately homes in the region opened their doors to other Confederate officers. Bishop Charles T. Quintard, who stayed at Hamilton Place, another of the Polk residences, gave a prayer of Thanksgiving in honor of the army's safe return to Tennessee. "I did not move out of the house," he added, "but just rested and tried to realize that I was once more in Tennessee."[25]

The Polk plantation church, St. John's, was located nearby. Ivy climbed the red brick walls of the twenty-two-year-old gothic structure that stood beneath imposing magnolia trees, an inspiring breath of spring amid the signs of approaching winter. Behind the chapel was a small, well-kept cemetery. When General Cleburne rode by he was struck by the beauty as well as the similarity to his native Ireland and remarked to his staff that it would be "almost worth dying for, to be buried in such a beautiful spot."[26]

Although scores of Rebels saw the region for the first time, Columbia was familiar to some Confederates. The town, located on the south bank of the Duck River, was roughly fifty miles from the state capital. Nathan Bedford Forrest had been born just east of Columbia in 1821 (and named Bedford for the county of his birth). In 1863, the town's Masonic Hall had been the site of a violent confrontation between Forrest and one of his men. Despite being wounded in the fight, Forrest inflicted a fatal knife wound on his would-be assassin. Twenty-five-year-old Sam Watkins, whose wartime reminiscences would later become a popular book, had also been born nearby. Watkins, a member of the Maury Grays, recalled that when his company left Columbia in 1861 there were 120 men. As they approached their home, only 12 of the original members remained.

But when Hood arrived at Columbia, he found Schofield's army drawn up in a strong position, ready to oppose any Rebel assault. The Confederates deployed in a line opposite Schofield's, and, with the Duck River to his back, Schofield feared that the Rebels would outflank him. He quickly decided to withdraw across the river. When he abandoned the town, delighted Confederates rushed to visit friends and relatives they had not seen in many months. On the morning of November 28, as the sun rose over the abandoned Federal works, the Confederates congratulated themselves on a job well done; Schofield had fled.

Hood had a plan to bag his old West Point classmate. He intended to leave behind the wagons, most of the artillery, and the majority of Lee's corps and, unencumbered by the slow-moving wagons and heavy caissons, swing around Schofield with the remaining two corps. Lee would remain in Columbia and deceive Schofield into believing that the Confederates were still on his front while Hood crossed the Duck River east of town and stealthily slid to Schofield's rear. "The situation," Hood later declared, "presented an occasion for one of those interesting and beautiful moves on the chess-board of war . . . which I had often desired an opportunity" to execute.[27]

Hood still lamented what he thought had been a lost chance to flank the Federal line at Gettysburg and had visualized himself emulating T. J. "Stonewall" Jackson's successful march around the enemy at Chancellorsville. Now he had a chance for the military operation he had always dreamed of, and as the rain let up on the twenty-eighth, Hood made plans to use his pontoon bridges to cross the river. Unfortunately, the wagons carrying the pontoons were far behind because of a lack of draft animals. Steers taken from the huge herds that furnished beef for the soldiers made obstinate substitutes. Hood had cause to hurry, for on the twenty-fourth Beauregard had telegraphed that Sherman was moving rapidly toward the coast, "doubtless to re-enforce Grant." The news spread quickly through the ranks. "Sherman is advancing in the direction of Savannah and Charleston," an Alabamian told his wife. The Confederacy needed immediate action, and Beauregard warned Hood, "It is essential you should take offensive and crush enemy's force in Middle Tennessee [as] soon as practicable, to relieve Lee." Hood confidently answered on the twenty-eighth: "The enemy evacuated Columbia last night and are retreating toward Nashville. Our army is moving forward."[28]

The next few hours would be a major test of the skill of both Hood's men and commanders. To cut off Schofield, Hood planned to occupy Spring Hill, a small village situated on the turnpike connecting Columbia with Franklin. Schofield would then be caught between Lee at Columbia and Hood at Spring Hill. To reach Schofield's rear, Hood turned east, crossing the Duck River on the Davis Ford Road, a rutted and little used country route that proved nothing more than a soggy path. The going was slow because Hood seemed unable to make heads or tails of his outdated map. Fearing an attack while en route, he moved cautiously rather than aggressively. Moreover, the men were tired, for the week of plowing through rain and snow had taken its toll. "We had marched through fields in the heavy mud," recalled a Rebel, "and the men, weary and worn out, were just dragging themselves along." The head of the column reached the crossing at Rutherford Creek, about two and one-half miles southeast of Spring Hill, in mid-afternoon. After expending about an hour of the sun's precious late autumn rays in preparation, Hood began to advance on the Yankee defenders around 4:00 P.M., as the gathering gloom heralded the coming dusk.[29]

Spring Hill, about eight miles north of Columbia and fourteen miles south of Franklin, had been a comfortable rural community before the war. The village had become the focus of national attention in May 1863, when a local doctor murdered Earl Van Dorn, a flamboyant Confederate general, in Martin Cheairs's elegant Greek revival home. The assassin, George Peters, fled to the safety of the Union lines and later claimed that Van Dorn had seduced his wife, Jessie Helen McKissack Peters, who, twenty-six years younger than her husband, was described as "a very handsome woman." The McKissacks' red brick residence, located on Spring Hill's main thoroughfare, was a frequent society gathering place and a regular stop for Confederate officers in the area. As the Confederate army neared the town, many soldiers hoped they might catch a glance of the infamous lady.[30]

Cavalry skirmishes had erupted around Spring Hill hours before the infantry arrived, but Forrest did not find the Federal troopers, only about two hundred men, much of a match. Wilson was nowhere near. In fact, Wilson, thinking that the Confederates were aiming for Franklin, had withdrawn all the way back up the turnpike, which placed him far from Forrest and effectively out of the action. When Wilson vanished, only a hodgepodge of cavalry and a small infantry force—men from the 103d Ohio and four companies of the Seventy-third Illinois—remained to hold off Forrest's assault. The infantrymen had a good position from which to fire their Spencer carbines and Colt rifles, and they put up a determined fight for more than two hours. Just as it looked as if the Rebel cavalry might overwhelm them, Federal reinforcements appeared on the pike from Columbia. As happens so often in war, only a matter of minutes separated the Confederate chance of success from failure.[31]

Schofield had a dilemma. He did not want to battle Hood, but he also understood that Thomas expected him to delay the Confederates until Smith arrived from Missouri. He knew Thomas did not want him to abandon Columbia, but if he remained in the town much longer, he would be trapped. After wiring Thomas for instructions, he ordered a withdrawal. He needed to ford the Harpeth River at Franklin before Hood cut him off if he wanted to reach Nashville safely. With the recent heavy rains and flooded waterways, there were few other places that Schofield could cross his artillery and cumbersome caravan of some eight hundred wagons. One of his greatest fears, of course, was that he would either have to destroy the valuable supplies and ammunition or see the lot fall into enemy hands. In an effort to save the train, he hurried Stanley along the Columbia-to-Franklin Turnpike with the wagons. Stanley, accompanied by Brig. Gen. George Wagner's division (the brigades of Cols. John Q. Lane, Luther P. Bradley, and Emerson Opdycke), clearly grasped the importance of reaching Spring Hill before Hood blocked the route. With the advantage of a macadamized road, Stanley's infantry had arrived in time to overpower Forrest's weary horsemen. Still, Schofield was not thinking about confronting Hood; his immediate concern was how to escape.

The Confederates would capitalize on Schofield's inexperience and his lack of audacity. After crossing Rutherford Creek, the Confederates hurried up the Rally Hill Pike, a road that entered the town from the southeast. As they neared Spring Hill, Hood instructed Cheatham to join Forrest for an assault on the town. But no sooner had Cheatham departed than Hood changed his mind. He ordered two of Cheatham's divisions to turn toward the turnpike rather than north toward the town. Following Hood's instruction, Cleburne formed his three-thousand-man division en echelon, a stair-step formation, and started an advance across a cornfield in the direction of the Columbia-to-Franklin Turnpike where he could cut off the Federal columns. Mark Lowrey's brigade of Alabama and Mississippi infantry was on the right, nearest the town, and in front. Daniel Govan's all-Arkansas brigade was in the center, slightly behind Lowrey, and Granbury's brigade, primarily Texans, was on the left. Hood told Bate, on Cleburne's left, to move his division to the turnpike, turn south, and sweep toward Columbia, snaring Schofield as he came up the road. Without making his intentions clear to Cheatham, Hood had sent Cheatham in one direction but two of Cheatham's divisions, under Cleburne and Bate, in another.

Each commander had a different goal. Cheatham thought the objective was Spring Hill, while Cleburne and Bate focused on blocking the turnpike. Hood, apparently unaware of the incongruity of his orders, retired to the home of Absalom Thompson, a comfortable 1835 classical revival house south of the action, where he remained until the following morning. His absence from the field was inexcusable, especially in light of the growing confusion. Hood had failed to clarify his objective, and his orders made unit coordination impossible. Worst of all, he had left implementation of the plan in the hands of subordinates unwilling to take the initiative.[32]

The result was predictably frustrating to all participants. As Cleburne moved out, Lowrey's brigade came within range of Federals on the south side of the town. Luther Bradley, a former Chicago salesman and militia officer, had positioned his two thousand men on a high plateau one-half mile east of the turnpike and about three-quarters of a mile south of the town. As soon as the Rebels left the safety of the trees and broke into an open field, Bradley's men opened fire. With his right exposed, Cleburne ordered Govan

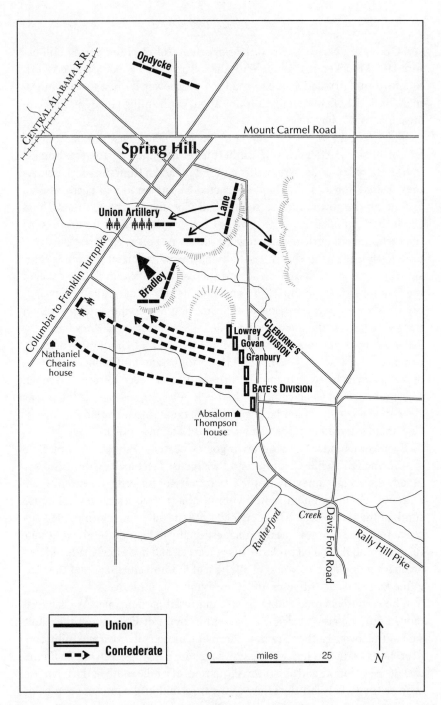

Central Alabama R.R.

Opdycke

Mount Carmel Road

Spring Hill

Union Artillery

Lane

Bradley

Columbia to Franklin Turnpike

Nathaniel
Cheairs
house

Lowrey
Govan
Granbury

CLEBURNE'S DIVISION

BATE'S DIVISION

Absalom
Thompson
house

Rutherford   Creek

Davis Ford Road

Rally Hill Pike

Union

Confederate

0   miles   25

N

5. Spring Hill

and Granbury to wheel and move to Lowrey's assistance, but because of the stair-step formation, the Irishman's other two brigades were some distance behind. As the Rebels turned, recalled an Ohio captain, they "pulled down the rims of their old hats over their eyes, bent their heads to the storm of missiles pouring upon them, changed direction to their right on double-quick in a manner that excited our admiration." The line swept forward, through wide gaps between the Forty-second Illinois and the turnpike, and fell on the Federals. "Our line stood firm," insisted the Buckeye, "holding back the enemy in front until the flank movement had progressed so far as to make it a question of legs to escape capture." The veterans under Cleburne overwhelmed the Union troops, and in the fight, Bradley was wounded. He was the highest-ranking officer on either side to be wounded at Spring Hill.[33]

Cleburne, one of the finest division commanders in the Confederacy, pushed his advantage until stopped by a massive volley from Federal artillery directly in his front. Cleburne had just instructed his former law partner, now his aide, Lt. Learned H. Mangum, to find Granbury and tell him to form his men along a fence running parallel with the pike in preparation to advance when his horse, Red Pepper, was hit in the hip and reared out of control. Cleburne, who had never been a skilled horseman, was thrown. "I remained a moment to see if the General was hurt," recalled Mangum, but Cleburne answered, "No; go on, Mangum, and tell Granbury what I told you." Nonetheless, Cleburne's breakthrough ended as the last rays of the sun slipped beyond the shadowy horizon. Mangum later described how Cleburne called off the assault after receiving an order from Cheatham to halt and not move any closer to the pike until instructed. This, believed the aide, was the fatal mistake. Cleburne had struck out west as Hood wanted, but he had been forced to turn north when he came under fire, and his command had changed fronts. Mangum loyally stated, "Cleburne would have been on the pike and had the position of Spring Hill in less than ten minutes; then there would have been no battle of Franklin." Although this might have been true, the Confederate casualties would have undoubtedly been high, for they would have had to storm the Federal guns.[34]

Cheatham, in the meantime, knew nothing of the change of plan. He still thought that the town, not the turnpike from Columbia to Franklin, was the main objective. He had waited at the Rutherford Creek crossing for Bate to come up so he could direct him to Cleburne's left. Cheatham planned to cover Cleburne's right with Brown's division. Stewart's corps, not yet on the field, would operate as support. Confusion was inevitable. Cheatham was new to his position and had never worked with Stewart and Lee at this level of command. All three men were battle-hardened division commanders, but none had more than a few months' experience heading a corps. Hood, an outstanding leader with a smaller command, had still not demonstrated he had the skill to lead an army to victory. More critically, he was not at the front when the conflicting orders stymied the assault.

Everything began to fall apart. Cheatham had planned for Brown to lead the attack on the town, followed by Cleburne, then Bate. But when Brown finally moved forward he discovered that the Federals had outflanked him on the right and he halted. Cheatham, not hearing any firing from the direction of Spring Hill, anxiously asked an aide, "Why don't we hear Brown's guns?" To complicate matters, Stewart never arrived. He had taken the wrong road and became lost in the dark. Confusion quickly turned to bewilderment; none of the commanders knew what to do next.

When it became clear that the Confederate advance had stalled, Stewart halted, told his men to bivouac, and went in search of Hood. It was 9:00 P.M. in a very long day, and nearly all the soldiers had collapsed from exhaustion. A few boiled coffee and devoured hardtack, but many had marched fifteen miles or more since dawn and almost a hundred arduous miles since leaving Florence the previous week; they fell asleep even before they built their fires or prepared something to eat. "The weather was now getting quite cold," recalled a Texan, "and the men, still wet from wading the deep creeks during the day, sought what sleep they could get on the damp, frosty ground." Even Bate, who had his men in position to cut off the turnpike, pulled back and camped for the night. Neither of the two corps commanders, Cheatham nor Stewart, was willing to take any chances without first consulting the commanding general.[35]

By relinquishing the advantage, the Rebels ensured that the night would become fateful in the history of the Army of Tennessee. In those critical minutes around sunset, when the army had its best chance to overwhelm the Spring Hill defenders, Hood was not in a position to make the tactical decisions required of a commander. When the Confederates halted, they still had a three-to-one advantage: around nineteen thousand infantry facing Stanley's single division of some six thousand men. Hood, who had earned his reputation with the Army of Northern Virginia, probably expected more from both commanders and men. Upon learning that the attack had not unfolded, he was annoyed. Hood later claimed he rode out to where Cheatham was still trying to sort things out and demanded, "General, why in the name of God have you not attacked the enemy, and taken possession of that pike?"

Even if this was true, by this time the lengthening shadows would have made an advance difficult. Cheatham later wrote, "I was never more astonished than when General Hood informed me that he had concluded to postpone the attack till daylight." In truth, Hood seems to have taken the failure to occupy the town with equanimity, for he still believed he could trap Schofield at Columbia the next day.[36]

Unfortunately for Hood, Schofield was no longer at Columbia. He had arrived at Spring Hill around 7:00 P.M. and established his headquarters in the imposing residence of William McKissack on Main Street. Not that he felt very confident. Two-thirds of his army was still in Columbia, and an observer recalled that he spent the evening pacing the floor and wringing his hands. The eight miles of turnpike that separated Spring Hill from Columbia were a deathtrap if the Rebels caught his army. Destroying the wagon train was an option; so was surrender. When Mrs. McKissack heard that her home might be used "unpleasantly" during the night, she feared it would be destroyed, as had some of the homes in Columbia. Her concern was calmed when told, "No, madam, we will not burn the house, but here we will have to surrender this army to the Rebels."[37]

While Schofield fretted, the Rebel commanders settled in for the evening at Hood's headquarters. According to some accounts, there was much eating and drinking, and Hood, tired from the long march and undoubtedly in pain from his stump of a leg, probably took some laudanum to help him sleep. He was awakened several times during the night and given information about the Federal movement, but at no time did he get up to check the situation personally. Laudanum, a tincture of opium, usually works in progressive stages. At first, it blots out pain and anxiety, but it can also act as a mental stimulant. As it begins to take effect, the drug carries a person off into a trancelike slumber. This latter stage seems to have been Hood's condition on that fateful night. When a lone private disturbed him around midnight with news of movement on the turnpike, Hood told his chief of staff, Maj. A. P. Mason, to instruct Cheatham to investigate, then fell back asleep. Cheatham did nothing, and Mason did not even remember sending him a note the next morning.

As Hood slept, his commanders took advantage of local hospitality, and some soldiers later speculated that liquor had a prominent role in the events of the night. One Confederate concluded that "John Barleycorn played his part in the drama," and a Tennessee cavalryman concurred when he wrote, "Whiskey—whiskey that accursed thing—had a great deal to do with it." True, some officers had spent the evening drinking and frolicking at the home of the alluring Jessie Peters, located just a little over a mile and a half from Hood's headquarters and just half a mile from Forrest's headquarters at the Caldwell house. One Federal officer claimed that "there were queer doings in the rebel lines among some of the leading officers. . . . There was music and dancing and feasting, and other gods than Mars were worshipped." There was even talk that Cheatham, a hard-drinking bachelor, had spent the night with Jessie. In 1903, one of Forrest's cavalrymen wrote that he had seen Cheatham "full Drunk." He did not, however, mention a woman. The horseman also claimed that Cleburne (who abhorred liquor) and Granbury "drank quite Freely."[38]

As Rebel brass held carnival, the enemy escaped. Long columns of Federal infantry, with all their wagons and artillery, pulled out of Columbia and passed right by the Confederate position. Understanding the importance of a stealthy passage, an Indiana captain warned his men to move by the Rebel camps along the east side of the turnpike as quickly as possible and to ensure that there would be no noise. As the silent line inched forward, Federal soldiers stumbled through the darkness. Men could not even move a few feet before being brought to a "sudden halt." One fellow would bump into the dark figure in front, recalled an officer, "immediately followed by the man in your rear bumping up against yourself."[39]

Besides the confusion in the Federal lines, the mental stress was enormous. The suspense was almost unbearable as the Union troops waited to leave Columbia. All the men were impatient to start before the Rebels discovered their passage. This tension, combined with the lack of sleep over the previous three days, strained nerves to the breaking point. Rebel horsemen had an opportunity to thwart the advance, but lacking adequate men and ammunition, they did not try. Luther Bradley, who was resting from the wound he had received earlier in the day, concluded: "It was the most critical time I have ever seen. If only the enemy had shown his usual boldness, I think he would have beaten us disastrously." Another Federal officer was less generous. While the Confederates were "sacrificing at their shrines," he chided, "the whole of Schofield's . . . force moved silently and fearfully by. . . . But in the morning there was much swearing. . . . Cheatham and Forrest and the others who had given themselves up to the charms of society the night before were more chagrined at the disappearance of the enemy than at their own lapse from duty."[40]

Meanwhile, the people in the countryside tried to survive the unexpected arrival of thousands of soldiers. In contrast to Sherman's handiwork in Georgia, neither army brought wanton destruction. But unavoidable devastation did occur, and innocent civilians suffered. During Cleburne's attack, Arkansan Daniel Govan and his adjutant general spotted a house in flames. A frightened young couple clutching two small children stood in the yard, "terror-stricken," unable to decide which way to flee as shells from the Federal artillery burst all around. Govan rode to the edge of the enclosure and told the father to pass the children over the fence, and each horseman took one while the parents followed, "shrinking and dropping at every shell." Besides rescuing the family, volunteers from Govan's brigade entered the burning structure as shells exploded all around and saved some of the family's household goods.[41]

On the morning of November 30, as the sun peeked up over the trees to the east, Hood discovered that Schofield was no longer at Columbia. He was furious. He directed most of his anger toward Cheatham, but there was certainly enough to go around. Hood refused to accept that he was the one ultimately responsible for the army's failure to pin the Federals at Columbia. Cheatham deserves his share of the blame, but so does Brown as well as Edward Johnson, whose division of Lee's corps had squandered a chance to occupy the pike. Forrest also fell short of expectations. In any case, even if Hood had succeeded in holding Schofield at Columbia, or in even blocking the Columbia-to-Franklin Turnpike, there were alternate routes that Schofield could have used to reach Nashville. Stewart later concluded that the disaster at Spring Hill was the result of "a Divinity that shapes our ends," and a Confederate wrote after the war "that a hand stronger than armies had decreed our overthrow."[42]

Naturally, not everyone laid the disaster to providence. Initially Lee blamed Cheatham, but after the war he changed his mind and told a friend that the responsibility for failing to attack did not fall on Cheatham but on another officer no one suspected. Lee claimed that Brown, who commanded Cheatham's old division, "either lacked nerve on that day or was drunk (no doubt the latter)." Whatever the truth, Bishop Quintard commented, "My own opinion has always been that General Cheatham was in no way at fault in his conduct at Spring Hill."[43]

No one really knew who was at fault, but Rebel soldiers wanted to believe that they had a real chance to catch Schofield, and a Georgian told his mother that if it had worked, "Hood would have bagged the whole of Thomas's force." An Alabama soldier observed that the Rebels "gave the Yanks a race for Franklin and got ahead of them at Spring Hill but for some reason unknown to me the army was halted and the enemy" passed by safely. This, he judged a month later, was "the greatest blunder of the Campaign." Another Confederate decided that the "effect of the Spring Hill mishap was bad on our men. Whether reasonable or not, the thing was looked upon as a terrible blunder, and the army was divided as to who was to blame. Some said Cheatham, some said Hood. The thing cast a shadow, and chilled the new found feelings of confidence." He was less sympathetic to Hood. "Following this most dismal episode at Spring Hill," he added, "Hood seemed to lapse into his old self again. The sudden flash of skill and prudence that he had been evincing, proved short lived. After Spring Hill he became the same old thing again, blind to but one idea of fighting, deaf to all suggestions, and singularly incapable of hand[l]ing troops." Union general Jacob Cox concurred. He later wrote that Hood alone was responsible for "a commander who is personally with the head of column in such a movement and upon the field, has the means of enforcing his orders by direct commands to the divisions."[44]

As news of Schofield's escape spread through the camps, the Confederates learned the full extent of the damage, and gloom settled over the army. Not only was Schofield gone, but rumors that the Republicans had won the White House had been confirmed. "Sure enough Lincoln is elected," an Alabama soldier told his wife, "so we may expect four years more of war." There would be no negotiated peace now, and if the Confederacy won independence, it would be because the army secured it on the battlefield. For Hood and his men there was no turning back.[45]

CHAPTER SIX

Hood at Franklin

As Schofield's soldiers slipped past Hood's encampment in Tennessee, Sherman's army in Georgia spent a night of peaceful repose. Although Sherman was still a long way from the ocean and the supplies that he would soon need, the army's confidence mirrored the improving weather. The afternoon of November 29 was superb, recalled military secretary Henry Hitchcock, and the evening gave way to a pleasant, star-filled night. Hitchcock left his tent to stroll around the camp and fix the setting in his mind. It was, he decided, a scene of tranquil serenity and camaraderie of the kind that a man fondly cherished long after the horrors of war had faded from his memory. The thousands of soldiers resting amid the tall pine trees had no way to know that their comrades in Tennessee were in trouble, and before he retired to his tent Sherman looked with satisfaction at the campfires sparkling among the trees. Sometime after midnight the red-haired commander stirred and, with a blue cloak pulled over his worn dressing gown, sat by the fading embers of his fire. He often awoke in the early morning hours. Certainly in the quiet time before dawn he must have thought about the fate of the soldiers he had sent to Tennessee.[1]

Fatigued Union soldiers in Tennessee would look back on the night too, but it would be the hours of suspense that were indelibly etched in their wartime recollections. And unlike Sherman, Schofield did not have to wonder where Hood was; he knew the Rebel commander and his army were still at Spring Hill. Indeed, as dawn broke Hood was at the Nathaniel Cheairs house on the Columbia Pike south of the town having breakfast with his corps commanders. A staff officer described him as "wrathy as a rattlesnake . . . striking at everything." Hood knew he had relinquished the initiative. Even worse, it seemed his old classmate from West Point had outfoxed him.

Until the morning of November 30, the Federals had scrambled to respond to his advance into Tennessee. Now those roles were reversed: Hood's next move would depend on Schofield.[2]

As Hood saw it, he had no choice. Too proud, too sure of his destiny, he had ventured too far to turn back now. With every day that passed, the problems facing him would grow more acute. He had only two realistic choices. Hood rejected retreat. To retrace his steps was repugnant to him; it would confirm publicly that the entire campaign was a failure. The second alternative was bolder and therefore more to his liking—he would push forward and press his duel with the men in blue. He had not broken camp in Alabama only to winter in a place further north, and because food and fodder in the ravaged countryside were inadequate, he could not stand where he was for long. The Texan now obsessively committed himself to a pursuit that might bring on the decisive, overwhelming battle he fantasized might end the war in the West. Unfortunately, he failed to consider a most important concept in war: he needed a blend of grand strategy and tactical purpose. At this point he considered only righting the wrong of the night before, and he thought only of where his counterblow should fall. He had hoped to bag Schofield; now he was determined to fight.

As the Confederates dogged Schofield's columns, they saw encouraging signs of an army in panic. Debris cluttered the turnpike, and wagons, hastily abandoned by the enemy, smoldered in the ditches. This, concluded one soldier, was heartening evidence of "the wreck of a flying army." Even Schofield, as he rode north, tried to ignore the remains of his supply wagons and the dead animals, for horses and mules too tired to pull their load were shot in their harness. He knew that Hood was not far behind, and he had no time to worry about either broken-down wagons or men who could not keep up. Many new recruits had overloaded their knapsacks, and the rear guard had to hurry them along by cutting the straps on backpacks.[3]

Schofield's hasty retreat certainly seemed to suggest that the Federals did not want to fight the Army of Tennessee, and Hood began to feel confident that he could salvage something from the debacle at Spring Hill. Still, he could not avoid the reality that his best chance had probably eluded him the night before. Riding at the head of the columns, Hood told Samuel French that the army had "missed the great opportunity of the war." French agreed and added that he heard that the Yankees even "lit their pipes at our camp fires." French later explained that his comment was a "*little* figurative" but that some fellows who overheard the exchange spread rumors that enemy soldiers had boldly walked into the Rebel camps.[4]

While the notion of Federals straying off the turnpike made a good story, it was probably an exaggeration that soon became a frequently repeated myth. Schofield's soldiers were simply too tired and too intent on escape to risk detection so foolishly. Most of the men marched quietly and rapidly north, and around dawn they streamed into Franklin. As soon as Schofield arrived in the town, he began preparations for the wagons to cross the Harpeth River, the only obstacle between him and the safety of Thomas's fortifications at Nashville. He knew he had been lucky to evade Hood at Spring Hill, and a historian of the Army of the Cumberland concluded: "Rarely has an army escaped so easily from a peril so threatening." Yet on the morning of November 30 that was not yet apparent to the commanding general, and Schofield understood the danger he still faced.[5]

As Union soldiers reached the crest of hills overlooking the fertile Harpeth River valley, they saw the town of Franklin below. In earlier times, this land had belonged to nomadic Indians, and along the river not far from the town were ancient burial mounds, the largest measuring more than two hundred feet long, one hundred feet wide, and sixteen feet high. White settlers had claimed the area by 1800, and the village of Franklin had flourished as the seat of Williamson County. The town sat along a main road running southwest from Nashville, and during the war its residents had suffered during the endless months of civil strife. After the Confederates abandoned the state capital in the winter of 1862, many civilians fled when martial law replaced the peacetime government, and Union authorities confiscated newspapers and other property. By June 1862, the local government had ceased to function in Williamson County, and the people struggled to survive. Bridges were out, slaves surreptitiously sabotaged their owners' property, and the churches had trouble maintaining regular services. Although the region was predominantly pro-Confederate in sympathies, spies operated for both sides and more than one unfortunate informant had died at the end of a rope.[6]

When an invasion by Hood's army seemed imminent, military governor Andrew Johnson ordered civilians to enroll in the state militia. Williamson County's sixty-year-old magistrate Isaac Ivy answered that his district had few able-bodied men left. His county, insisted Ivy, was large and "thinly settled," and the forested hills and mountains made it a haven for robbers and guerrillas. The situation for civilians was so wretched that he told Johnson he would have little luck convincing men to join the militia.[7]

Even though the county could not furnish more troops, it would become an important location in the war, for it was here that Schofield stopped on

his flight to Nashville. When the soldiers topped Winstead Hills, an elevation along the Columbia Turnpike about two and one-half miles south of the
town, they could look down on the village below. The town lay in a sharp
curve in the river. Off to the immediate right was the railroad line that connected Nashville with Decatur, Alabama. Further east, hugging the Harpeth River for about a mile below the town, lay the Lewisburg Pike. To the
west, the Carter's Creek Pike completed a trio of roads that converged in the
town's center. The roads resembled an inverted V with the Columbia Pike
dissecting the middle. Across the river near the railroad, at the eastern point
of the river's curve, was Fort Granger, an abandoned Union earthwork built
earlier in the war.

Schofield hoped to cross the river as rapidly as possible, but he had destroyed his pontoon bridges at Columbia and needed replacements from
Nashville. Those, he discovered to his dismay, had not arrived. In an unusual burst of energy, Schofield personally directed the repair of bridges and
improvement of the fords over the Harpeth. He had avoided being trapped
with his back to the Duck River just days before, and now he faced a similar
situation, but this time he could not cross and put the river between his
army and the enemy.

Schofield wanted to escape without a battle, but he knew he had to prepare for a defensive stand. From his headquarters in the Benjamin Franklin
Carter home on the Columbia Pike, he ordered Jacob Cox to position soldiers on both sides of the high ground around the house to protect the army
as it crossed the river north of town. Carter, whose 1830 house had been
commandeered by exhausted officers now sleeping on his floor, watched as
Union soldiers deployed in his yard and across the pike by his cotton gin.
His heart filled with trepidation as he saw the deadly preparations, for in the
advancing Confederate army was his twenty-four-year-old son Tod.

The Federal position was strong, stretching for more than a mile and a
half long. The line ran in an arc, anchored at both ends on the Harpeth. Its
focal point was the Carter house and gin. The terrain in front of the fortifications was flat, but between the Carter gin and the river to the east was a row
of leafless Osage orange that had been clipped into a thick hedge. On the
west side of the pike was a grove of locust trees whose bare limbs could be
sharpened into crude abatis. The soldiers thinned the Osage orange to create a thorny palisade and used the pruned limbs to build an obstruction in
front of the line. Cox also placed batteries to protect the gap where the Columbia Pike cut through the fortifications. The opening could not be closed,
for the wagons and artillery still coming up the road had to pass through.

Wagner's division, serving as the army's rear guard, halted about three miles south of the town. When Confederates appeared on the crest of the surrounding hills, the division withdrew to within a half mile of the main line, while one of Wagner's brigades under Col. Emerson Opdycke moved into reserve behind the Carter house.

Although the Federals continued to construct a strongly fortified line, no one really believed that the Confederates would attack such a formidable position. The availability of the rifled musket had vastly increased the strength of defenders, for one man behind field entrenchments was equal to several outside of them. Unfortunately for attackers, tactical thinking had not changed much in the official manuals even though the common soldier understood the basics—a frontal assault was costly. Hood understood that, but he still believed that élan could overcome the advantage of entrenched defenders, and he had earned a reputation for his offensive tactics at such battles as Gaines's Mill, Second Manassas, and Sharpsburg. In his postwar writings Hood even claimed that Johnston's use of the tactical defensive and entrenchments had ruined the Army of Tennessee. To be sure, few commanders demonstrated that they really comprehended that traditional ideas about the offensive, élan, the bayonet, and formations were becoming obsolete. The rifle made the tactical defensive dominant over the offensive. Moreover, as the Rebels approached Franklin on November 30, even Lee's Army of Northern Virginia was safely behind strong field entrenchments— with the exception of the one last offensive effort at Fort Stedman in late March 1865, it would never attack again.[8]

In Tennessee, Schofield never believed he would be lucky enough to have Hood hit him head-on, and while the soldiers entrenched, he supervised work at the river crossings. Escape was his primary concern. The ford, though poor, could be negotiated with care, and construction crews rapidly covered the railroad bridge with planking to create a sound footing. Although the Columbia Pike bridge had been destroyed, its foundation was sound, and workers quickly made repairs that would allow wagons and artillery to pass. Weary from the long night's march, both animals and men took short naps as they waited in line to ford the river. South of Franklin, in the trenches, exhausted soldiers fell asleep as soon as they completed their breastworks.

The townspeople, grown accustomed to troops moving through their streets, tried to carry on life as usual. Students arrived at the Franklin Female Institute on this Wednesday, just as they did on every weekday. Classes did not begin, however, and a bell called the students to the chapel, where they were instructed to gather their books and go home, for after some hurried discussion, the school's administration feared there might be trouble. The students thought that possibility exciting. The thrill of watching Union couriers "dashing hither and thither" and officers gathering in squads delighted all who peered from the school's windows. The students knew, as did the rest of the town's residents, that this Wednesday would be unlike any before. "I had been sitting on the back porch playing at backgammon," recalled Carrie Snyder. "A few shots from the infantry had been heard; then, as it became quiet . . . I began to fear there would be no fight." Betraying the innocence of civilians who have never experienced war, she added, "I wanted to see a battle, or hear one." Hardin Figuers, a teenager, remembered, when he discovered there might be a fight, "No mortal can tell with what a thrill of excitement I heard this announcement."[9]

Both civilians and soldiers waited expectantly as the shadows lengthened on the mild autumn afternoon. "The day had proved to be a bright and warm one," wrote Jacob Cox, "a good sample of Indian summer weather coming after the first sharp frost and snows of opening winter." By midafternoon, after all the wagons had crossed the Harpeth, Schofield concluded that Hood's only option was to attempt the same strategy the Rebels had tried at Spring Hill. But this time, if Hood tried to flank the Union position, he would not be caught off guard. Feeling more confident that he could escape unscathed, Schofield moved his headquarters to the north side of the river at Fort Granger.[10]

The fatigued Rebel soldiers dogging Schofield's trail also hoped Hood would not attack. Over the previous forty-eight hours they had felt cautious excitement and anticipation, as well as one of intense mental and physical stress. It had been three months since the two sides had fought a major battle. Hood had played cat and mouse with Sherman in north Georgia during October, but the armies, so familiar with each other during the Atlanta campaign, had not fought a true battle since before the city's surrender. Most Confederates did not want to remember those last disastrous encounters outside Atlanta, and their trepidation increased when the gray-clad columns topped Winstead Hill. Standing at the summit of the elevation, Hood halted his mount and swept his telescope up and down the Federal position. In the foreground lay the Union siege line, and from the heights the hastily constructed defenses presented a formidable sight. They looked impressive: a ditch, backed by an earth rampart studded with sharpened stakes, the chevaux de frise. As Hood viewed the fading sunlight reflected off rifles and artillery, Confederate soldiers watched with anticipation, for the fate of thousands depended on his decision.

"We will make the fight!" he turned to Stewart and announced. Cheatham promptly complained that he did not like the odds and stated what was obvious to all: "The Federals have an excellent position, and are well fortified." Forrest, who also opposed Hood's plan, offered an alternative; he requested an experienced infantry division to work with his cavalry and boasted that he could flank the Federals out of their works in two hours. Forrest claimed he knew every hogpath in the county and could show Hood a route that would at least give the Rebels a chance. He knew, like everyone present except Hood, that small and exhausted armies did not normally attempt to storm fortified lines. Moreover, a frontal assault was always a bloody affair and rarely produced decisive results, for unless Hood planned to cut off Schofield's line of retreat, the Federals would certainly escape. Even Lee had failed in the frontal assault at Gettysburg, and Hood was certainly no Robert E. Lee.[11]

But Hood was inflexible. To remain inert in the face of the enemy was impossible, to retreat equally impossible; the only solution seemed to be assault. He was still angry with both soldiers and commanders, all of whom he believed had failed him at Spring Hill just hours before. Now, with one bold stroke, he would decide everything. Cleburne, knowing that Hood placed part of the blame for the previous day's debacle on him, dismounted his horse at the top of Winstead Hill, looked at the Federal line through his field glasses, and commented quietly that it appeared "very formidable." Seating himself on a stump, he took out a pocketbook and scribbled down a few observations. He opposed the attack, but as his aide later recalled, Cleburne "was too blunt and frank" to influence Hood. When Daniel Govan commented that "there will not be many of us that will get back to Arkansas," Cleburne replied, "Well, Govan, if we are to die, let us die like men." In contrast, Hood claimed in his postwar account that Cleburne, after forming his lines, had stated that he was ready to attack and had more hope in the final success of the cause than he had felt at any time since the first gun was fired. But this seems unlikely. The Irishman recognized, as did every veteran there, that in an attack like this the odds overwhelmingly favored the defenders. When he stated that he would take the works or fall in the effort, Cleburne was doing what he had always done, following orders with the personal bravery and professionalism that had made him a fine division commander.[12]

Hood, they all realized, had already made up his mind, and there would be no dissuading him. This time, he would make sure there were no slip-ups. If Schofield escaped again, Hood would face a far larger task at the Tennessee state capital. He told his officers that he preferred to fight where Schofield had "only eighteen hours to fortify, than to strike them at Nashville where they have been strengthening themselves for three years." Riding along the Confederate lines, Hood tried to rally the troops by exclaiming that the Yankees were weak and if the Rebels broke the enemy lines, no one would "exist who will dare to oppose your march to Ohio."[13]

Had the assault worked, Hood would have been a hero, which was clearly apparent to the tall moody Texan. But he was in an unreasonable frame of mind and failed to acknowledge what everyone else on the summit of Winstead Hill sadly understood: the chances for success were very slim. Unlike the men who counseled him, Hood was reckless. It was the pattern of his life, from childhood through his West Point days to this moment when he stood on the range of hills overlooking the peaceful little Tennessee hamlet. During his years at the military academy, Hood lived precariously close to expulsion, graduating with 196 demerits, 4 short of dismissal. He tempted fate, even though demerits often indicated nothing more than being late falling into the ranks (1 demerit); underclothes not properly piled on shelves with folded edges out (2 demerits), or being caught smoking (6 demerits). He was a natural for life on the Texas frontier, where he had tracked Indians, Mexicans, and outlaws in the years before the Civil War. In those days, Hood enjoyed horse races in his idle hours. He was a gambler and, like all who fall prey to the passion, believed he could win. An old story told how he had once wagered a thousand dollars on one card in a faro game and scored. Gamblers like Hood could not, did not, admit defeat.

So eighteen Confederate brigades descended into the valley and deployed in line of battle. There was a chance, Hood thought; a concentrated assault on the line might pierce it before sufficient reinforcements could be brought up from other sectors. Success, of course, depended on the discipline and skill of his soldiers, for once inside the break, the men must exploit the chaos that ensued. In preparation, Forrest divided his cavalry, directing half to each flank, while Stewart's corps of infantry moved to the east of the railroad, with Cheatham to his left across the tracks. Stewart's men formed between the railroad track and the Harpeth with Loring on the right, Walthall in the center, and French on the left. In Cheatham's corps, Bate occupied the extreme left; Brown was to his right; and Cleburne moved into position to the right of Brown, between the Columbia Pike and the railroad line. Forrest had W. H. Jackson's cavalry east of the river and Buford to the west between the Harpeth and Stewart; Chalmers's horsemen were near the Carter's Creek Pike in the extreme west.

Through the morning and afternoon, both sides diligently prepared for battle. A Tennessean in Walthall's division described the Federal activity he could see from his position between the river and the railroad tracks. He watched enemy couriers galloping along the lines carrying orders from one position to another while "sappers and miners, or fatigue parties," worked hard completing the fortifications. From his vantage point, he saw spades and picks flash, then disappear, as dirt flew to the top of the parapets. The Yankees were, he decided, "as active and industrious as gopher rats and prairie dogs when they are trying to burrow into the earth." From the time his company arrived in position before noon until nearly four in the afternoon, the men had orders not to break ranks. Their fatigue intensified as hunger increased.[14]

Anticipation rose and tension mounted as a curious melancholy settled over Rebels in the valley. They knew what an assault would mean, and even as Cheatham issued the order to move forward, he declared that it was a mistake. Cleburne agreed but told his men that they would give it a try. Like other officers, Cleburne seemed depressed because he understood the desperate nature of the assault. "Silently the ranks were formed," related an Arkansan, "and as they descended to the plain, their places atop the hills were filled by crowds of men, women, and children from the surrounding country who waited with bated breath and quivering hearts the impending shock." In the distance, the Rebels could see women "on the housetops in the town . . . fluttering their handkerchiefs as though signalling them to come on."[15]

Thousands of Rebel foot soldiers, massed in blocks of dirty gray, purposefully fixed their bayonets and advanced across the field toward the Union line. This was the supreme trial for the Rebel soldiers. A Tennessean remembered the "profound silence" like "one of those sickening lulls that precede a tremendous thunderstorm." The surrealistic atmosphere was broken as music filled the air. A South Carolina colonel recalled that "bands were playing, general and staff officers and gallant couriers were riding in front of and between the lines, 100 battle-flags were waving." The bands struck up "Dixie" and "The Bonnie Blue Flag," but as the men came to within a few hundred yards of the Federal works, the instruments fell silent. More than sixteen thousand men moved forward. Their courage was not in question, and they advanced with the same discipline seen in Pickett's Charge at Gettysburg.[16]

It began to dawn on Schofield that, as incredible as it might seem, the Rebel army was about to storm his position. The astonishing display also astounded the men in the trenches. "For the moment we were spell-bound with admiration, although they were our hated foes," wrote a soldier within the Union lines. Another Federal admitted, "It was worth a year of one's lifetime to witness the marshaling and advance of the rebel line of battle." Indeed, "few battlefields of the war were so free from obstruction to the view," recorded General Cox, for along a mile-and-a-half front, an "imposing array" of Rebels advanced at quickstep. Confederate brigadier general George W. Gordon later wrote that after the Rebels moved to within four hundred paces of the Federals' advanced position, the columns halted and deployed into two lines in preparation for a charge. The Federals who would absorb the first shock were the brigades from Wagner's division under Col. John Q. Lane and Col. Joseph Conrad (who had replaced Bradley after Spring Hill). Deployed on a small rise about a half mile from the main line, they would act as skirmishers, then withdraw when the Confederates attacked.[17]

The Rebel army made an unforgettable sight. Slowly, steadily, the infantrymen advanced, holding their fire until the last minute. They moved forward with a calm determination that was anchored in months and years of experience. Musket barrels reflected the fading afternoon light, flags that gave each unit its individuality whipped in the breeze. Hood intended to use the old tactic of delivering a hard blow on the Federal line, hoping to break through, spread confusion, and thus roll up the opposing army, aided by the resulting panic. When the order to charge rang out, chilling Rebel yells replaced the bands' patriotic songs. Under the bright autumn sky, Hood watched the breathtaking spectacle explode. From his vantage point, he had an unbroken view of the level plain his men must cross. Seated on a blanket, he could see the entire battlefield, an opportunity of solemn proportions that few military leaders experience. In these few moments, before bloodshed ushered in the reality and sheer horror of war, the Army of Tennessee looked proud and defiant.

"With a wild shout," recalled General Gordon, the Confederate line "dashed forward." After the Federals opened a volley on the approaching Rebels, the bluecoats in the advance position on the pike broke and fled in panic. "Go into the works with them," came the cry. The Confederates sustained few casualties until they neared the main line, when, recalled General Gordon, "Hell . . . exploded in our faces." A Northern newspaper correspondent reported from Nashville: "At precisely four o'clock in the after-

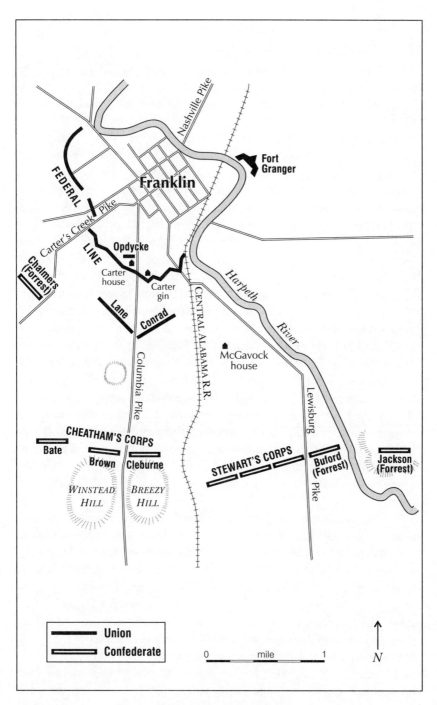

6. Battle of Franklin

noon the entire rebel force made a charge, and succeeded in making a temporary break in our centre, commanded by Wagner. With characteristic impetuosity the soldiers . . . dashed into the breastworks and, cooperating with the attacking party on their left, attempted to envelope and destroy our right."[18]

The charge, although not unexpected, caught several Federal officers unprepared. While waiting for the soldiers to complete the defensive line, some officers had stopped at the house of John McEwen, where an Indiana colonel asked one of McEwen's daughters to sing for him. McEwen told the man that his daughter would perform a new piece, "Just before the Battle, Mother," but as the young woman prepared to sing "Hark, I hear the bugles sounding, 'Tis the signal for the fight," a shell exploded nearby. McEwen looked at his startled guests and exclaimed, "Colonel, if I am any judge, it is just about that time now!" Sprinting out of the house, the unidentified colonel was wounded and out of the battle before he ever reached his regiment.[19]

Although most of the Confederate artillery had not arrived, a few fieldpieces followed the advance and occasionally dropped a shell into the Federal line. (Hood later claimed that the artillery had been instructed to take no part in the battle because of the fear of injuring women and children.) It is true that most of the artillery was far behind, hurrying to reach the field before the battle ended, but Hood's later assertion that there was no artillery shelling the Federal line is incorrect. Moreover, once the artillery did arrive, Hood raised no objection to the cannoneers firing into the Federal works the following morning. In fact, cannoneers in one Texas battery aimed over the heads of the Confederates in the direction of the cotton gin, for that building gave Union soldiers an effective site from which to direct their destuctive barrage.[20]

As shot and shell rained over the little town, civilians no longer clamored to see a battle. Nothing had prepared the residents of this quiet Tennessee community for the horrifying events in store for them that day. Most families headed for the safety of basements. "We had not been in the cellar very long before a bombshell, a twelve-pounder, of conical shape, struck the main sill of the house just over our heads and within a few feet of us," recalled Hardin Figuers. Alice Nichols described how "Grandpa had already put rolls of rope in the windows" hoping "to keep the bullets out." As shells fell like rain, dust and gravel splattered the women and children huddled in dark corners. During Sherman's siege of Atlanta, Georgians had built bombproofs, or underground holes, where they hid, but Atlantans had weeks to prepare. Franklin residents had only hours. "We thought, down there in that cellar," remembered Carrie Snyder, "that a shell would come through those walls, explode inside of the house and blow us all into 'Kingdom come,' the next minute."[21]

Outside, the peaceful town had become a bloody battlefield. Cannons roared and flashed, infantrymen struggled to keep formations and follow commands to load and fire, while around their knees writhed the bodies of shattered comrades. Whistling cannonballs chopped bloody holes in the Rebel ranks. The fire was so intense and deadly that the attackers were simply shot to pieces; some fell before they ever reached the Union line. Men shouted and screamed, horses stumbled and fell. As the carnage spread, blood colored the ground and, over it all, in the autumn sky, drifting clouds of thick, blinding, choking smoke.

Rebels from Cheatham's corps under Cleburne and Brown had struck the Union's exposed brigades when Wagner did not fall back to the main line as instructed. In the distance, Federal soldiers could only watch the bloodshed, holding their fire for fear of hitting their own men. But as the Rebels advanced, it became clear that they had no choice but to open on the intermingled mass of blue and gray. Confederate George Gordon, just to the left of the Columbia Pike in Brown's division, vividly recalled that the "booming of cannon, the bursting of bombs, the rattle of musketry, the shrieking of shells, the whizzing of bullets, the shouting of hosts, and the falling of men in their struggle for victory, all made a scene of surpassing terror and awful grandeur." Another soldier observed that many Rebels reached Wagner's line before the Yankees could withdraw and there was vicious hand-to-hand fighting. The barrier that Union soldiers had rapidly constructed that morning proved as much a hindrance for the retreating Federals as it would to the advancing Rebels. This, noted Colonel Lane, "caused some delay which enabled the enemy to get within fifty feet of us." The scene evolving below Hood was one of intense confusion, but the smoke had become so thick that it was difficult to distinguish an object just twenty feet away, and the sun, low in the sky when the battle opened, slowly retreated below the horizon. Thus, as smoke and darkness obscured the field, Hood was spared from witnessing the appalling panorama in the valley below.[22]

Just over a year earlier, at the battle of Chickamauga, the Confederates had won a victory when a gap appeared in the Union lines. Now, at Franklin, it seemed that might happen again. The Federals had not obstructed the Columbia Pike because the supply wagons and artillery needed to use the road, but as Wagner's soldiers fled through the opening in the breastworks, Hood's veterans quickly followed. As the breach widened, Cleburne and

Brown, sensing victory, urged their men on, and a desperate struggle exploded in the area around the Carter house that soon spread toward the cotton gin. At Chickamauga, George Thomas had saved the day for the Federals. At Franklin, it would be Emerson Opdycke. His brigade, waiting in reserve some two hundred yards behind the breakthrough, waited to advance if the line snapped.[23]

The bearded thirty-four-year-old Opdycke was an unlikely hero. He was not a military man, although his father had served in the War of 1812 and his grandfather in the Revolutionary War. A native of Ohio, he had twice traveled to California to pan for gold. Returning to Ohio none the richer, he had settled down and became an ardent abolitionist. Rising through the ranks, he became colonel of the 125th Ohio in January 1863. His regiment was one of those to hold fast with Thomas on Horseshoe Ridge during the battle of Chickamauga, and he distinguished himself again at Chattanooga and during the Atlanta campaign. He was not a striking figure. Opdycke's curly hair receded at his temples, and his beard was scraggly and thin, but now at Franklin he had the opportunity to be a hero if he could stop the advancing Rebel line. Neither Opdycke nor Col. Samuel White, commanding the second defensive line, waited for orders to charge; they were in motion before the instructions reached them. White was wounded in the face but refused to leave his men until dark had fallen. Opdycke, for his part, fought personally "in the thickest of the deadly tussle on the turnpike."[24]

It was into this maelstrom that Cheatham sent his men. Division commanders Cleburne and Brown would follow orders; they always had. When Cleburne's aide, L. H. Mangum, asked the Irishman what he wanted him to do, the general cryptically replied, "It is too late," and spurred his mount in the direction of Govan's brigade. "When I last saw General Cleburne," Mangum recounted, "he was going up to the enemy's works mounted on a brown mare, which was soon killed; and while he was in the act of mounting another horse this animal too was shot dead, by many bullets. Then Cleburne rushed on foot to the works. He must have been killed between where his last horse was killed and the works, about where his body was found the next morning." General Gordon, whose brigade touched Granbury's on Cleburne's left, added: "Amid this scene General Cleburne came charging down our line to the left, and diagonally toward the enemy's works, his horse running at full speed, and if I had not personally checked my pace as I ran on foot, he would have plunged over and trampled me to the earth. On he dashed, but for an instant longer, when rider and horse both fell, pierced with many bullets, within a few paces of the enemy's works." Although accounts vary about exactly when and how Cleburne died—on foot or on horseback—there is no dispute that Hood had lost his finest division commander that day.[25]

Mangum, who had left Cleburne to join the Texas brigade of Hiram Granbury about halfway between the first and second lines of defense, watched the Texan fall when a bullet struck him in the cheek. Before Granbury fell, he yelled, "Forward, men; never let it be said that Texans lagged in the fight." Born and educated in Mississippi, the curly-haired, thirty-three-year-old Granbury had moved to Texas in the 1850s, where he settled in Waco, became a lawyer, and eventually chief justice of the county court. Recruiting the Waco Guards, which became Company A, Seventh Texas Infantry regiment, he had been captured at Fort Donelson in 1862. After being exchanged, Granbury led his regiment at Vicksburg, Chickamauga, and Chattanooga, winning a promotion to brigadier general in February 1864. He headed a brigade of Texans during the Atlanta campaign and at Franklin led them toward the Federal breastworks. [26]

The veterans under Cleburne and Brown hit the Federal line with a curious rashness seldom displayed in battle. A member of Cheatham's staff explained that the two divisions were the "Siamese twins" of the Army of Tennessee and very competitive. This time the men fought side by side and in full view of each other. For years each had claimed recognition as the "crack division" in the army, and as the soldiers raced across the open expanse toward the Federal position, the demeanor of officers and men seemed to say, "Here is the field upon which that right shall be decided." Brown's men, west of the pike, pushed as far as the Carter house, while Cleburne's men made it to the Carter gin. Both divisions paid a high price for their attempt to take the Union works and earn the title of best division in the army. As the Federal counterattack drove Stewart's corps back, Cleburne's men were caught in a deadly crossfire when Yankees to their right opened on them with repeating and breech-loading rifles. "I never saw men put in such a terrible position as Cleburne's division was in for a few minutes," judged an Illinois soldier. "The wonder is that any of them escaped death or capture." Cheatham had no way to know that thousands of his men lay dead and dying, for he was several hundred yards behind the battlefield. From atop a hill, he had an excellent view of the plain below as the assault unfolded, but after the firing began he could distinguish little through the smoke. As the battle continued into the darkening shadows of the November evening, only the flash of guns and exploding shells illuminated the darkened sky.[27]

Cheatham suffered irreparable losses. Before it was over, Cleburne was dead, Brown badly wounded, and five of seven brigade commanders gone. Brown had been hit while riding along the line and fell forward on his horse's neck, seriously wounded. He was quickly carried from the field. In front of the Carter house, where the soldiers of Brown's division were devastated by enfilading fire, Brown's four brigade commanders, States Rights Gist, John C. Carter, Otho Strahl, and George Gordon, were in the fight of their lives. Gist a South Carolinian, was killed early in the assault, waving his hat from atop his horse. Brigadier General Strahl, who found himself trapped in the ditch, loaded guns like any other private and passed them up to those who were firing above. "The battle lasted until not an efficient man was left between us and the Columbia pike, about fifty yards to our right," wrote a Confederate, "and hardly enough [men] behind us to hand up the guns." The likelihood of surrender came closer each minute. A soldier in the Twenty-fourth Tennessee claimed, "I myself lay so close to a Federal battery that every time it fired I could feel the heat." In spite of the perilous position, Strahl defiantly told his men to "keep firing" just before he was struck in the neck by a ball. The general crawled about twenty feet, over the dead and wounded, before his staff officers reached him. As they headed for the rear, Strahl was hit again and then a third time. Before he died, the general turned over command to Lt. Col. Fountain E. P. Stafford of the Thirty-first Tennessee. Early the next morning, Stafford's body was found in the ditch, half standing among piles of corpses, "as if still ready to give command to the dead!" John C. Carter, also wounded, died ten days later, and George Gordon, the only one of Brown's brigade commanders not fatally wounded, was captured. Thus four of Brown's brigade commanders were gone.[28]

Still, the Confederates came. Each attack broke and sagged away into unnerving quiet, only to be succeeded by the next surging wave. While each assault was frightening, the calm that followed was worse. "First, there was a sound in the distance, as of a great multitude in motion, coupled with a fearful yell, which culminated in a rush and roar, as the living human wave struck upon the beach, and broke and rolled back again," Henry Field poetically recounted. "Then for a few minutes there was a lull, as the enemy were gathering their forces to renew the onset—a comparative silence, broken only by the groans of the wounded and the dying." A soldier later told Field "that the charge itself was not so dreadful as these moments of expectation." Each time the Rebels rushed forward, shouting "the same terrific yell," their confidence ebbed, "for they came, not with erect, martial air, but with heads bent low, as when facing a tempest, and caps drawn over their eyes, as if to shut from their sight the fate that awaited them."[29]

Rebels scaled the enemy works in several places, and the ditch filled with dead and dying. The wounded who toppled into the trench were buried under the dirt that tumbled down as other men mounted the works. The firing was so intense that the ground, torn with bullets, resembled a field that a harrow had crossed. As the Rebels charged again and again, it was impossible not to stumble over bodies. "No man," lamented a soldier, "could have been so particular as not to have bloodied his shoes," for the wounded could not be removed; all the litter bearers were shot down. The terrific fire that came from behind the fortifications killed hundreds of men as they lay immobile on the field. Because they could not be rescued, scores bled to death or died of exposure as the night air turned cold.[30]

While the battle raged, Hood waited for word of the outcome. When a courier from Cheatham arrived to report that the Rebels had carried part of the Federal line but could not hold it unless reinforced, Hood asked about Cheatham's losses. Half of his men were either killed or wounded came the reply. "O my God!" Hood was heard to exclaim, "this awful, awful day!" Nonetheless, he quickly recovered, turned to one of his staff, and instructed the officer to tell Stephen Lee to hurry his corps forward.[31]

The men of Stewart's corps, between Cleburne and the river, were also trapped as the afternoon gave way to dusk. Stewart's men had to navigate between the Harpeth and the railroad track, but as they advanced, the line contracted. As the Rebels neared the enemy line, Federal batteries, particularly those at Fort Granger across the river, poured down a deadly fire. Fighting through the Osage orange abatis, the Confederates reached the Federal defenses only to discover the enemy armed with deadly repeating rifles. General Walthall later reported that many fell back, but those who pushed forward were either captured, killed, or wounded in the effort to climb the embankment. A Tennessean observed that the enemy fired "by turning their backs to the breast works, taking their guns by the breach and raising them above their heads over the head-logs, so as to point the muzzle downward, firing them at us this way, and having nothing exposed except their arms and hands."[32]

Stewart lost a valued brigade commander when Brig. Gen. John Adams died a couple of hundred yards to the left of the cotton gin. Adams, the son of an Irish immigrant, was a Tennessean who had resigned from the Old Army in May 1861 to offer his services to the Confederacy. He received no

glowing commendations as he rose through the ranks, but Gen. Joseph
Johnston had called him "valuable" during the Vicksburg campaign, and
his brigade had led the advance in Hood's October march through north
Georgia. Early in the fighting at Franklin, Adams was wounded in the right
arm but declined to leave the field. When he attempted to leap his mount
over the fortifications, both horse and rider were pierced with bullets; neither survived. Old Charley was a veteran war horse and did not balk, for his
hooves lay on the palisade. The animal was almost as well known as his master, and "the powerful creature was very striking in death."[33]

As the fighting finally ended in the early morning hours, it was time to
count the casualties. Bodies lay everywhere. Men cried for help, calling for
friends and relatives who were dead or dying and would never come.
Twisted forms rested in every position, and many of those who were not
dead wished they were. One Confederate officer, whose horse shied at the
strong smell of blood, had to dismount and proceed on foot. A soldier with
Walthall remarked that "for seventy-five yards on either side of the works
we could have walked upon the dead without ever stepping on the ground."
Another Rebel agreed. "You could see squads of these veterans who had
fought together, and slept together, kneeling down around the body of some
dying comrade, and their grief was so great that they wept like women," he
later wrote. A young Franklin woman reflected: "Horrors! what sights met
our girlish eyes." Many of the maimed died, never knowing which side won.
One Rebel, whose lower jaw had been shot away, defiantly scratched on an
envelope before he expired: "John B. Hood will be in New York before
three weeks." On the Federal side, Schofield tried to evacuate his wounded
to Nashville, but the seriously mangled had to be left behind, where, as prisoners, they filled the local Presbyterian church.[34]

Schofield had to leave behind many of his soldiers, but he herded captured Confederates along the road to Nashville. Guards often forced the exhausted prisoners, many with blood trickling from their bare feet, to run in
order to stay out of the range of Hood's gunners. One Confederate thought
the guards were more concerned for the prisoners' safety than the prisoners
themselves. When they finally arrived in the city, more than one hundred
Rebel officers and a thousand enlisted men endured being put on public display for several hours. Nearly five thousand—including, it was rumored,
the newly elected vice president, Andrew Johnson—came out to view the
ragged group.[35]

Back in Franklin, the residents struggled with the battle's aftermath. Every building housed casualties. Wounded men covered the floors of private

homes as well as the female institute, the female college, the courthouse, and local churches. One resident counted forty-four hospitals, only three of which held wounded Federal soldiers. From morning until night local women rolled bandages to dress the wounds. A Georgian wrote three days after the battle, "The people are the kindest in the world *especially the ladies.*" In spite of the care, men continued to die, and burying the dead became a heavy burden. Union corpses, strewn on the battlefield, were not interred for several days. One of the Confederates buried in a common grave was Thomas Stokes, the brother Mary Gay had visited at Dalton before the Atlanta campaign began. Another who fell was Benjamin Franklin Carter's son Tod.[36]

Conditions were made worse for the people of Franklin when the temperature soon dropped again, and for more than two weeks the weather alternated between ice, sleet, and snow. Food became scarce, not only for the wounded but also for the town's residents. Furthermore, the uncertainty of the future weighed heavy on the minds of all, for they knew that Hood had not finished in Tennessee.

Back in Washington, Lincoln learned about the battle from a dispatch Thomas sent to Henry Halleck. Instead of being pleased by Schofield's escape, Lincoln and Grant fretted about the flight to Nashville. Both preferred to have Thomas's soldiers on the offensive and were not happy when Schofield joined Thomas behind the fortifications in the Tennessee capital. Thomas, it seemed, was too willing to wait for Hood to attack. Secretary of War Stanton warned Grant: "This looks like the McClellan and Rosecrans strategy to do nothing and let the Rebels raid the country. The President wishes you to consider the matter." Lincoln could not have been happy with press coverage either. Depending on an editor's political stand, the fight at Franklin was either a great victory or a terrible defeat. "Great panic prevails among the people in the country around Nashville," reported the *New York Herald*, "and they are fleeing to that city in crowds for safety. They say Hood is gathering up all the horses, hogs, mules, cattle, &c., he can find, and sending them South."[37]

The press, of course, exaggerated. In reality, the Rebel army was in no condition to cause panic anywhere. Hood had lost eleven generals, five killed, five wounded, and one captured. In addition, fifty-five regimental commanders were among the casualties, and the roll call indicated that only about twenty-five thousand soldiers were still fit for duty. The Confederates celebrated the Union retreat, but the Army of Tennessee had suffered a grave loss. Although Hood congratulated his men the day after the battle, praising the soldiers for their success, it was impossible to ignore the army's casualty list. Moreover, Hood knew he had to pursue Schofield; he had already rejected retreat. Beyond that he had no clear plan of action.

Over the next week or so, as news slowly filtered back to Richmond about the battle at Franklin, the president felt the stress of coping with the twin campaigns in the western theater. "Alas for President Davis's government! It is now in a painful strait," wrote a government official. "If reinforcements be sent from here, both Savannah and Richmond may fall." The political atmosphere in the capital became volatile. "Gen. Bragg will be crucified by the enemies of the President, for staying at Augusta while Sherman made his triumphant march through Georgia; and the President's party will make Beauregard the scape-goat, for staying at Charleston—for sending Hood North—which," he added, "I am inclined to think he did not do, but the government itself." Davis's enemies attacked him bitterly and attributed all the current problems to his incompetence. Of course, as the situation worsened, the president's opponents denounced him loudly for removing Johnston back in the summer. All Confederates were worried about how events in the West would affect the rest of the nation. If Savannah fell, for example, Confederate money, already critically devalued, would experience another serious depreciation.[38]

Beauregard, who was in Macon on the thirtieth, could operate only with the information he received from Hood; he had no idea of the actual situation. He did know that A. J. Smith had finally joined Thomas and had heard rumors (untrue) that Frederick Steele was en route to Nashville from Little Rock, so he asked Jefferson Davis if he could order Gen. Edmund Kirby Smith and his Trans-Mississippi soldiers to the army in Tennessee. Davis agreed but warned Beauregard that since Smith had "failed heretofore to respond to like necessities" he should not depend on his compliance. The president had tried throughout the summer to move troops across the Mississippi River but had abandoned that idea by August. One Texan had commented, "It is reported, and I believe it is true; that this Army is ordered over the Mississippi, and I am sorry to say that a great many will desert before they will go." This flat refusal on the part of the men, coupled with food shortages, infrequent furloughs, no pay, and talk that the cavalry might be dismounted, only increased discontent in Smith's department. By autumn, Smith finally had to dismount many of his cavalrymen when food and forage gave out for both horses and men. He could not help the armies on the east side of the river.[39]

Clearly the Army of Tennessee needed help, but with Sherman steadily advancing toward the coast, Hood's situation did not require the immediate attention that the southeast did. The Confederates were spread too thin for the dual crises that faced them in Georgia and Tennessee. Yet after weeks of refusing to take advice from Beauregard, Hood finally realized he needed help. Perhaps he wanted someone to share the responsibility should the campaign fail. One week after Franklin, Hood wired Beauregard a single sentence, "Whenever you can I will be pleased if you could visit this army." But it was too late. Beauregard, after a short visit to Montgomery, had promised Howell Cobb he would return to the southeast coast. So as the last month of 1864 opened, Beauregard headed for Charleston, arriving on December 7, knowing the Confederates would have to fight both Thomas in Tennessee and Sherman in Georgia with the troops on hand. Neither Smith on the west side of the river nor Lee in Virginia could see the way clear to furnish reinforcements. Those troops in the western theater were on their own.[40]

CHAPTER SEVEN

Sherman at Savannah

While officials in Washington pondered the news from Tennessee, a Richmond resident gloomily recorded in his diary: "The Northern Papers say our army under Hood in Tennessee has met with a great disaster. We are still incredulous—although it may be true." The repulse at Franklin had done immense damage to the Rebels, but that did not satisfy Lincoln and Grant. As soon as news of Schofield's victory arrived in Washington, Grant telegraphed Thomas and encouraged the Virginian to put forth every effort to finish off the Rebel army. Grant's anxiety, of course, was increased because of Washington's concern over Sherman's continued silence. Schofield might have damaged Hood on November 30, but fourteen days had passed since there had been any word from Georgia.[1]

Unlike Thomas, Sherman had encountered no serious resistance, but neither Lincoln nor Grant knew that. The infantry plodded along roads of red Georgia clay while the cavalry continued to drive ahead, skirmishing with scattered Confederate troopers. As the landscape changed, the soil became sandier, the terrain flatter, and cypress swamps, dotted with silt and algae, appeared along the roadbeds. Houses were fewer and farther apart, and the encounters between horsemen became more desperate as Joe Wheeler realized that time was running out to frustrate the infantry's advance.

Facing Wheeler was the flamboyant Judson Kilpatrick. Sherman had specifically requested the New Jersey native from the Virginia theater in spite of lingering doubts that he was the right man for the job. An 1861 graduate of West Point, he was young for a brigadier, only twenty-eight, and his reputation for "notorious immoralities" had preceded him west. Nicknamed "Kill-Cavalry," he seemed confident of his own abilities, and a Federal major sarcastically told his wife that Kilpatrick was the "most vain, conceited, egotistical little popinjay I ever saw" with only one redeeming quality: he did not often drink to excess. He was, however, "a very ungraceful rider," pronounced the foot soldier, "looking more like a monkey than a man on horseback."[2]

Although the cavalry skirmished daily, it was not until the fighting near Waynesboro that the Federal superiority in strength became evident. "This has been a regular field day, and we have had 'lots of fun' chasing Wheeler and his cavalry," wrote a gleeful Federal officer of the fighting near Buckhead Church on December 4. "Kilpatrick is full of fun and frolic and he was in excellent spirits all day, for Wheeler and he were classmates at West Point, and he was elated at the idea of whipping his classmate." Being part of a cavalry fight was "just about as much fun as a fox hunt," he added, if not for the fact that men were being "hurt all the time." Kilpatrick, in fact, was proud of his victory over Wheeler, whom he described to other officers as "a great sloven" during their days at the academy. Moreover, he had already accused Wheeler's men of numerous depredations, including slitting the throats of their enemies. Sherman was aware of the personal differences between Wheeler and Kilpatrick, and these allegations prompted the general to caution Kilpatrick about hasty accusations. Although Sherman warned Kilpatrick to be extremely careful when investigating charges that the Rebels murdered or mutilated Federal soldiers, he also instructed him to communicate to Wheeler that this behavior would not go unpunished. "When our men are found and you are fully convinced the enemy have killed them after surrender in fair battle, or have mutilated their bodies after having been killed in fair battle," Sherman harshly ruled, "you may hang and mutilate man for man without regard to rank."[3]

Sherman left Kilpatrick to deal with the Rebel cavalry while he contemplated the obstacles that lay in his path. Only days before he had heard that Braxton Bragg had ten thousand soldiers in Augusta that might march on the Union columns at any moment. Brimming with confidence, he told General Slocum that if they could draw Bragg toward Savannah, "we can turn on him and send him off at a tangent." Sherman knew the Confederates in Georgia had not concentrated, for on December 2 he had obtained a Savannah paper that reported Rebels occupying Macon, Augusta, and Savannah. Yet many soldiers worried about what steps the Confederates might take to slow their march, for this was the first time the Rebels had allowed them to advance virtually unopposed.[4]

There was little Wheeler could do, however, and Sherman's left wing finally reached into Millen, the site of Camp Lawton, the first week of December. To no one's surprise, the prisoners were gone, and nothing remained except a sign that read, "650 buried here." A Union chaplain inspected the abandoned camp and recalled that it made his "heart ache" to see the "miserable hovels, hardly fit for swine to live in" that had housed the prisoners. One soldier feared reprisals against civilians if the army saw the site. Every soldier who visited the facility, wrote an officer, "came away with a hardness toward the Southern Confederacy he had never felt before." A staff officer recorded in his diary that the enclosure was "a hideous prison-pen," and the Union photographer George Barnard, who inspected the compound, told Henry Hitchcock that it used to bother him when he saw soldiers burn houses, but after visiting Camp Lawton he decided that it was justified retribution. This elicited from Hitchcock the response, "If B. feels so from *seeing* the prison pen, how do those feel who have suffered in it!" To avenge the prisoners who had died, Sherman gave permission to burn the train depot that had served as transfer point for the captives. The fire quickly spread to the town, destroying some buildings.[5]

The conditions at Camp Lawton appalled the men, but the plight of the slaves following the army also touched a nerve in many Northern troops. Sherman's soldiers held a wide range of racial attitudes. A large number approved of Sherman's well-known opposition to the use of black soldiers, while others exhibited abolitionist sentiments and wanted radical change. Neither, however, was prepared for the scores of refugees the army attracted as it traversed the state. One Wisconsin soldier complained that they were "a great hindrance, if not to say nuisance," but another observed that it was enough "to start the tears on a pretty hard looking fase to see wih what joy our troops are greeted with by the poor down trodden slaves." An Indiana soldier thought that although the slaves wanted freedom, they "realy dont seem to know just what freedom means," but a Michigan man believed that they were willing "to endure all the hardships of a long march to secure their liberty."[6]

Still, they proved a burden to army quartermasters, who now had an estimated additional ten thousand mouths to feed. The army had left Atlanta with fewer than two hundred contrabands, but by the time the columns reached the Ogeechee River the number had grown. They rode on mules, often several crowded on one old animal. They came in wagons pulled by oxen and buggies taken from plantations. "Columns could be written descriptive of the harrowing scenes presented by this unfortunate class of fugitives," concluded one observer.[7]

Racial conflict was impossible to prevent. Many soldiers did not want the blacks around the camps; some resented their presence, blaming them for the war and, by extension, their own long absence from home. "The silly prejudice of color is as deeply rooted among northern as among southern men," decided an Ohio captain. "Very many of our soldiers have as yet no idea of treating the oppressed race with justice." In one instance a soldier, tired of marching, shot and killed a refugee. The unfortunate victim's only crime was sleeping by the side of the road at a time when the soldier could not obtain permission to stop and rest.[8]

The most onerous incident involved Brig. Gen. Jefferson C. Davis and the refugees following his wagon train. Even before the march, Davis, who carried a name of no little irony, was a controversial personality. Earlier in the war he had argued with his superior, twenty-year navy veteran Maj. Gen. William Nelson, while serving in Louisville, Kentucky. After several altercations, Davis had challenged Nelson to a duel. When the old veteran refused, Davis confronted Nelson, who insulted him and knocked him down. Davis then borrowed a pistol, walked into the hotel where Nelson was staying, and shot him. Although Nelson died within minutes, Davis was never brought to trial for there were not enough officers available to form a court-martial. Instead, through the intervention of Indiana's governor, Davis received a transfer. In Georgia, Davis was not popular with the men, particularly after he threatened to shoot looters. His justice, they complained, was often random. Nonetheless, he was a favorite of Sherman even though James Connolly was not alone in grumbling, "I do think our Government is hard up when such men are allowed to command."[9]

But Davis did command, leading the XIV Corps, and his actions would cause a stir back in the North. At the end of the first week of December, his soldiers reached Ebenezer Creek, a swift, deep stream about one hundred feet wide, not far from Savannah. Davis, known for his proslavery leanings, intense dislike of black camp followers, and coarse vocabulary, ordered the refugees to stand aside while his men crossed on a pontoon bridge. When Major Connolly rode up and asked if the contrabands would be allowed to follow, he was told that Davis had left orders that only soldiers could use the bridge. Connolly angrily protested the "inhuman, barbarous proceeding," but to no avail.[10]

Other Federals also condemned Davis's action. An Indiana chaplain said that when the slaves saw the bridge being removed, they sent up a collective "cry of agony." Then, when someone shouted "Rebels," men, women, and children panicked. Wildly rushing forward, some plunged into the water and were able to swim across, while others ran up and down the bank, shaking with terror. Pvt. Harrison Pendergast of the Second Minnesota counted hundreds of refugees on the far creek bank, "huddled as close to the edge of the water as they could get, some crying, some praying, and all fearful that the rebels would come before they could get over." Many drowned trying to ford the swollen stream, while others, according to Union soldiers, died at the hands of the Rebel cavalrymen. Sympathetic Northern soldiers tossed logs and tree branches into the water, and some refugees ferried back across on a makeshift raft to rescue as many as they could. The chaplain blasted Davis as "a military tyrant, without one spark of humanity in his makeup." An appalled surgeon in the XVII Corps wrote that if he had the power he would see the general hanged. "I should not wonder," he concluded, "if the valiant murderer of women and children should meet with an accident before long."[11]

Davis justified his deed by pointing out that he needed to disassemble the bridge, but this was not the first time he had taken such a measure. Several days before, Major Connolly had noted, "I heard tonight that General Davis turned back a lot of contrabands at Buckhead Creek, and I don't doubt it, for he is a copperhead." A blue-clad soldier observed, "Let the 'iron pen of history' write the comment on this action of a Union general," while another believed it was "a burning shame and a disgrace" to abandon the slaves, "for they prefer sinking in the water to returning to slavery." A Union private questioned, "Where can you find in all the annals of plantation cruelty anything more completely inhuman and fiendish than this?" Although this act did not directly involve Sherman, he would nonetheless receive criticism when the incident became public knowledge. Remembering his outspoken policy against the use of black troops, abolitionists could only conclude that Davis's action was yet another example of Sherman's proslavery feelings.[12]

The first report of this incident broke in Northern papers shortly after Sherman made contact with the fleet. When the story appeared in the press, Davis initially seemed to be a victim of circumstances. He had, the correspondent wrote, removed the bridge only because of military necessity. It was the Confederates who were responsible for any atrocities. A biased account claimed that Wheeler's cavalry had charged the unfortunate refugees, drove them mercilessly into the water, and watched women and children drown. The reporter, whose information came secondhand, conceded that he might have exaggerated for the sake of a good story. "How far true this may be I know not," he admitted, "but all the negroes who escaped, with whom I have talked, seem to agree in their account of the hellish slaughter." As soon as Major Connolly reached Savannah, he composed a letter that eventually appeared in a New York paper vilifying Davis's deed. Connolly later noted with pleasure that Davis was passed over for promotion to brevet major general.[13]

Davis's actions served to add fuel to a growing controversy, for his treatment of the refugees polarized soldiers who had strong opinions about slavery. While many condemned his decision, there were those who regarded his conduct as practical, even necessary. Protecting his own command was his primary duty, not providing an escort for the escaped slaves. Davis, his supporters argued, had no way to know what problems might arise with the Rebel cavalry, and he pointed out that he did not want to be forced into abandoning a valuable pontoon bridge. Undoubtedly, Davis's checkered reputation magnified any controversy, but the affair also brought to light a more serious concern, the question of what to do with escaped slaves.[14]

This issue troubled both sides. Georgia society was in total upheaval as Sherman moved through the state, for slaves flocked to the Union columns in increasing numbers. Wheeler admitted that he had shelled the XIV Corps "with good effect" during the night of December 8, causing the Yankees to abandon clothing, arms, and other goods they could not quickly gather together. When the Federals broke camp, they abandoned a "great many negroes," who were returned to their owners. One black who feared the consequences if he was captured by the Rebels pragmatically told a Union soldier, "I am too old to go with you's, and I am too young to stay here an' be murdered." There was good reason for the slaves to fear retribution if caught by the Rebels, even though they were only a secondary concern for Wheeler. During the weeks that the Confederates dogged Sherman's heels, Wheeler estimated that he captured nearly two thousand blacks. Whether he returned all of these men, women, and children to their owners is unclear, for once Sherman moved on toward Savannah, Wheeler crossed into South Carolina.[15]

First, Hood had abandoned Georgia by marching his armies west; now Wheeler virtually handed the state to Sherman by taking most of his troopers east. General Hardee, who was making preparations to receive the Federals at Savannah, wanted the Confederate cavalry to protect the northern route into the city. Unfortunately, the decision to transfer the cavalry to South Carolina left no significant Confederate barrier between Sherman and Savannah. Moreover, while there were several Rebel generals in the state, there were few soldiers. The only important general available in the western theater and not ordered to the southeast coast, it seemed, was Joseph E. Johnston. After watching events from the sidelines in Macon, Johnston had recently left the state. So when Beauregard published a proclamation saying he would "rescue" Georgia, John B. Jones, a Richmond war clerk, declared, "Here, then, will be war between the two B.'s—Bragg and Beauregard; and the President will be as busy as a bee." The next day Jones added that Johnston had arrived in Richmond, a martyr to those who opposed Davis's decision to remove him from command outside Atlanta in the summer. "If Sherman's campaign should be a success, Johnston will be a hero," noted Jones, "if the reverse, he will sink to rise no more. A sad condition," he concluded, "for one's greatness to depend upon calamity to his country!"[16]

By early December, Sherman had nearly reached the coast, but back in Washington concern for his safety plagued the administration. Lincoln, addressing Congress on December 6, announced that Sherman's march was the "most remarkable" event of the year but admitted that he had received no recent communication from the general. Grant tried to make light of his concern. "Sherman's army is now somewhat in the condition of a groundmole when he disappears under a lawn," he joked to friends one evening. "You can here and there trace his track, but you are not quite certain where he will come out till you see his head."[17]

In truth, a groundhog could not have burrowed a hole where Sherman's men were, for all that lay between them and the sea was a stretch of land unlike any most Northern soldiers had ever seen. As they neared the coast, rice fields on plantations of absentee owners dotted the landscape, and marshy swamps with skeletal trees protruding out of inky water provided sanctuary for numerous alligators and snakes. Midwestern soldiers who had never seen the coastal plain surveyed the landscape with amazement. The inhabitants sounded different too. "The whites and negroes both do not talk like us," an Alabama Confederate had once noted, "and I have seen some intelligent and aristocratic ladies whom I could scarcely understand."[18]

As he neared the coast, Sherman knew he faced new problems. Captured Rebels warned him he would meet strong opposition at Savannah, and he had even heard rumors that Lee had detached Longstreet to Georgia. Added to these concerns, supplies dwindled daily. On December 10, Henry Hitchcock lamented, "How long will it take us to get over the *last* five of our '300 mile march?'" He believed the food reserves could last only a few days more. If Sherman failed to communicate with the fleet soon, the army would "be pinched." A few days later Hitchcock observed that there were enough rations for the men for ten days, but forage for the horses, mules, and cattle had dropped to a critical point. Even the corn and oats carried in the wagons had disappeared. The chief of artillery for the Army of the Ten-

1. (*Top left*) William T. Sherman
(National Archives)

2. (*Top right*) John Bell Hood (Library of
Congress)

3. (*Left*) George Henry Thomas
(USAMHI)

4. (*Right*) John M. Schofield (USAMHI)

5. Hubbard Pryor as slave from Polk County, Georgia (National Archives)

6. Hubbard Pryor, Forty-fourth United States Colored Troops, was captured at Dalton (National Archives)

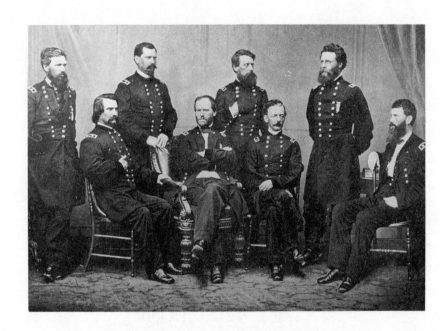

7. Sherman's commanders on the march.
Standing, left to right: Oliver O. Howard,
William B. Hazen, Jefferson C. Davis,
Joseph A. Mower. Seated: John A. Logan,
Sherman, Henry W. Slocum, Francis P.
Blair Jr. (National Archives)

8. (*Opposite top*) The capitol at Nashville
(Library of Congress)

9. (*Opposite bottom*) Union occupied
Nashville (Library of Congress)

10. Nashville from the capitol (Library of Congress)

11. Georgia contrabands (USAMHI)

12. William J. Hardee (National Archives)

13. Fort McAllister, Georgia (Library of Congress)

14. (*Opposite top*) Joseph Wheeler (USAMHI)

15. (*Opposite bottom*) Former slaves on Cockspur Island near Savannah (USAMHI)

16. Sherman's Savannah headquarters (USAMHI)

17. Savannah waterfront (National Archives)

nessee wrote his brother on December 13 that everything was progressing well, except that there had been a shortage of rations for several days. A German in the ranks was more succinct. He complained he was "almost starved and ragged. My shoes have given out and I am as good as barefooted with many others."[19]

Clearly Sherman needed to contact the fleet. He charged Oliver Howard, who commanded the right wing, which was nearest the Atlantic coast, with this responsibility. Howard dispatched a twenty-three-year-old Illinois cavalryman, Capt. William Duncan, and two of his comrades. When nothing was heard from Duncan's party for several days, Howard assumed he had failed. Unknown to Howard or Sherman, the three volunteers had located a Union gunboat, and as a result, Duncan became a hero of sorts. After giving his dispatch to Maj. Gen. John G. Foster at Hilton Head, he continued to Washington, where he personally delivered a second note to Edwin Stanton. On December 15, a New York newspaper proclaimed: "At last the curtain has risen on the grand military drama in Georgia, and we are again in direct communication with the army of General Sherman." Howard had assured the world: "We have met with perfect success thus far. Troops in fine spirits, and near by."[20]

While the Northern press anticipated the capture of Savannah, Confederates clung to a rapidly evaporating belief that the city could be saved. The man in charge of Savannah's defenses was one of the most respected generals on either side, a general who had a distinguished reputation in the Old Army. General Hardee, nearing fifty, had served as commandant of cadets at West Point and was the author of a well-known and widely read textbook on military strategy. He was also a Georgian, and his family's plantation, Rural Felicity, was on the coast south of Savannah. After his dispute with Hood had forced Davis to reassign him in September, Hardee had taken command of the Department of South Carolina, Georgia, and Florida; Savannah emerged as his chief concern when it became clear that Sherman planned to make that seaport his goal.

The city presented a unique situation. To the east, the Federals controlled the entrance to the Savannah River by holding Fort Pulaski on tiny Cockspur Island and the larger barrier, Tybee Island. After Pulaski fell in the spring of 1862, little effort had been expended on taking the city, for closing it as a port was just as effective. Hardee did not expect any immediate threat from that direction. He also felt confident that Confederate gunboats could protect the north side of the city. The terrain in the region also favored the defenders, for Savannah lay between rivers. The inland peninsula was about thirteen miles wide with the Savannah River on the north and the Little Ogeechee River on the south. To the west Hardee ordered the rice fields flooded, some three to six feet deep. A Union soldier noted that it was "awful country to get through, all lakes and swamps" with hardly "dry land enough to camp on." In spite of the flooded fields, the danger lay to the west and, to a lesser degree, the coast to the south, where Fort McAllister had protected the entrance to Ossabaw Sound and the Ogeechee River since early in the war.[21]

Soon after Sherman's columns marched out of Atlanta, Hardee prepared for a siege. The importance of the Confederate victory at Honey Hill on November 30 was not lost on the general, for the Charleston & Savannah Railroad was the only line bringing him supplies and reinforcements. Hardee succeeded in gathering a hodgepodge of some ten thousand defenders, but few of these men were regular Confederate soldiers. As Sherman neared the city, Hardee became concerned about his ability to hold out and wired Beauregard, who had just arrived in Charleston, that he needed to see him immediately. "It is," he emphasized, "all important that I should confer with you."[22]

En route from Alabama to Georgia, Beauregard had given much thought to his part in the present crisis. At Augusta, anticipating the questions that would follow if Savannah fell, he took time to write Jefferson Davis and enumerate his reasons for not countermanding Hood's march into Tennessee. Beauregard explained the obstacles facing Hood in November. To return to Georgia, Beauregard stressed, would have been futile. Because of recent rains, the roads across Alabama were impassable for artillery and supply wagons, and what railroads were actually running were in such poor condition as to cause unavoidable delays. More important, to backtrack to Georgia would have been a "retrograde movement" through a devastated country short of supplies and would have resulted in large numbers of desertions. Beauregard also believed that if Hood had not taken the offensive, Thomas would have, resulting in the fall of Montgomery, Selma, and Mobile. To absolve himself of the current disaster in Georgia, Beauregard pointed out that Governor Brown had earlier declared he had men enough to defend his state. Based on this assessment, Beauregard believed Confederate forces could reach as high as thirty thousand, while he incorrectly estimated Sherman's strength at only thirty-six thousand. None of Beauregard's explanations could change the situation as Sherman's veterans, almost twice the number Beauregard calculated, neared Savannah.[23]

After Beauregard arrived in the seaport, he and Hardee spent most of the day discussing their options. Hardee's immediate concern was the presence of Federal soldiers only six miles from the vital railway bridge across the Savannah River, his only link with the outside world. Beauregard had already told Hardee there would be no chance of reinforcements and that if the Georgian had to make a choice between his army and the city, he should sacrifice the latter. Therefore, he ordered Hardee to construct a pontoon bridge across the river into South Carolina. Beauregard, like Johnston before him, was willing to give up land in Georgia and the city of Savannah in order to preserve the army intact.[24]

Although many of Hardee's troops had never fought in a major battle, his three commanders could claim wartime experience with Lee's Army of Northern Virginia, albeit with varying degrees of distinction. The troops on the left of Hardee's line were under the command of Ambrose R. Wright. "Rans" Wright was a Georgian. He had been born near Augusta, where he settled as an adult. A political general, he had led a brigade under Lee, and although court-martialed for "disobedience towards superior officers" after Gettysburg, had been acquitted after handling his own defense. Following this debacle, Wright decided politics held more attraction than bullets, and in the autumn of 1863 he waged a successful campaign for the Georgia state senate. This duty had required him to divide his time between Georgia and Virginia, and he finally left Lee's army in the fall of 1864. Promoted to major general after he reached Augusta, Wright joined Hardee in Savannah as Sherman marched toward the city. Contemporaries described him as "too self-willed and combative" with "too much dash" and not enough "coolness."[25]

Hardee placed Gustavus W. Smith on the right. The Kentucky-born Smith had a distinguished background but nothing to commend him for any responsibility that might require quick and decisive action. He graduated from West Point eighth in his class of fifty-six, later taught at the academy, but resigned from the army in the mid-1850s. Smith's hour of fame came after Joseph E. Johnston was wounded at the battle of Seven Pines in the spring of 1862, and he had briefly assumed command of the Confederate army on the Virginia peninsula. His tenure was short-lived, however, for an attack of paralysis, a recurring malady that occasionally rendered him unfit for duty, forced Smith to pass the army to Robert E. Lee. This undiagnosed disorder caused some to claim that Smith's immobility was brought on because he knew he could never live up to his own grandiose boasts. No doubt Smith, described as "tall, burly, and unashamedly smug," was convinced that the Confederacy did not appreciate his abilities. He resigned from the army early in 1863 after being passed over for promotion. He served briefly as secretary of war, but his inability to get along with Davis had thrown him into the Beauregard camp, and he served as a volunteer aide-de-camp to the Creole before becoming major general of the Georgia militia in 1864. His performance during the Atlanta campaign and at Griswoldville brought neither recognition nor censure, but he seemed to function well enough when under the command of someone else. As the campaign for Savannah opened, Smith did have the distinction of having just returned from the battle at Honey Hill, where he had led his militiamen in the victory.[26]

Lafayette McLaws, born in nearby Augusta, held the center of Hardee's line. He attended the University of Virginia before graduating from United States Military Academy in 1842. McLaws resigned from the Old Army when the Civil War began and joined the Rebel army. He steadily rose in the ranks from captain to major general, and he fought at Sharpsburg, Fredericksburg, Chancellorsville, and Gettysburg. At Gettysburg, McLaws became frustrated with James Longstreet, who was not only his commander but also an old acquaintance from West Point. In exasperation, McLaws called him "a humbug, a man of small capacity, very obstinate, not at all chivalrous, exceedingly conceited, and totally selfish." To no one's surprise, the two men had a serious falling-out several weeks later, resulting in Longstreet bringing several charges against McLaws after the failed Knoxville campaign. McLaws was married to a cousin of Richard Taylor and had vague connections to President Davis, whose first wife had been Taylor's sister. In any case, Davis sided with McLaws in the altercation. Nonetheless, although Longstreet drew censure from the War Department, McLaws was the one who received a transfer. Clearly Lee needed Longstreet more than the Georgian in Virginia. Yet McLaws was particularly suited for a siege outside Savannah. He had begun his Confederate career in that seaport and had later earned a reputation in the Army of Northern Virginia for his defensive skills. A staff officer recalled the general as "fond of detail," and an artillerist judged that McLaws was "about the best general in the army for that sort of job."[27]

Despite McLaws's meticulous attention to detail, Hardee faced insurmountable odds. He had done everything he could to prepare the city, but as Sherman's columns approached and the Confederates withdrew from the outer perimeter, Hardee had to destroy the Savannah & Charleston Railroad bridge, thus severing his lifeline. He warned Beauregard on December 11: "I have been obliged to extend my line. It is impossible to hold it without immediate reenforcement." Since Beauregard could spare only a few scattered units, Hardee did not receive anywhere near the number needed.

When Federal batteries fired on Confederate ships patrolling the river, Hardee feared that Sherman might challenge him to the north. To eliminate any threat from South Carolina, Hardee had already ordered Wheeler to withdraw from Sherman's rear and move the cavalry to Hardeeville, on the South Carolina side of the river, to protect the crossings. Although the number of Confederate cavalry continued to grow, it was not enough to stop men with Slocum from taking possession of an island in the river, and Hardee knew that if Sherman pressed this advantage by moving more than a regiment onto the island, the Federals could block his line of retreat.[28]

Hardee did have one point in his favor: he understood that Sherman's first objective was not the city itself. Hardee was enough of an old soldier to recognize that Sherman needed to establish communication with the fleet before he mounted any offensive. Hardee guessed that supplies were running low for the thousands of Union men, horses, and mules. As a native of the area, he knew there was little forage in the swampy marshes surrounding the city, and if the soldiers found anything at all to eat, it would probably be only rice. This knowledge comforted Hardee and meant that he would not have to evacuate Savannah immediately, but he realized that he would have to abandon the nearly two hundred defenders at Fort McAllister. As Hardee constricted his defensive perimeter, the fort fell outside that line. The men at McAllister understood the situation, but they were willing to stay, facing certain death or capture. As the Federal columns neared the fort, both sides prepared for battle. The Rebels waited behind their earthworks for the attack, while Sherman's men saw the fort as the last obstacle between them and the Union navy offshore, ships that promised not only supplies but also long-awaited news from home.

McAllister, near the Atlantic Ocean, guarded the mouth of the Ogeechee River. All along the coast, the sharp green of the pine forests contrasted with the brilliant blue of the nearby ocean, and the shore was lined with sandy beaches, dunes, and low mud cliffs. The army would have to march through this flat, marshy country to take the fort, but to the soldiers that challenge presented no worse obstacle than the flooded rice fields. Although concerned about the Rebel defenders, many a Yankee feared the snakes concealed in the swampy underbrush more than enemy bullets.

Storming fortifications was not in Sherman's nature, but neither was a siege. He did not intend a direct assault on Hardee's defensive perimeter unless he had no other option, and he reasoned that opening communications with the fleet might offer other alternatives. With supplies refreshed, he could starve the city into submission. So he wasted no time in making arrangements to take the fort and personally selected the assaulting force: William Hazen's division of the XV Corps. This was Sherman's old division, men he had commanded early in the war from his beloved Army of the Tennessee, and he had every confidence in these westerners. As the Union lines formed for the assault, Sherman watched from atop a shed at a nearby rice mill. There was no question that the Rebels would eventually surrender, for Hazen had more than four thousand men. Although only three thousand of those would actually participate, they outnumbered the defenders fifteen to one. Sherman watched the preparations outside the fort, but his eyes kept scanning the shoreline for any sign of the U.S. Navy. He was confident that the fort would fall, but his signalmen had been searching the water for three days without any sign of the fleet.

Late in the afternoon, just about the time the attack was scheduled to open, a Federal officer spotted a ship flying a U.S. flag. Breathing a sigh of relief, Sherman instructed his signalmen to make contact with the vessel while he turned his attention to the scene unfolding along the riverbank. The general lost patience with Hazen as the daylight hours dimmed and he saw no activity along the Union lines. He reminded his subordinate that he wanted the fort taken before dark. Hazen finally got moving, and when he ordered the charge, men in Federal blue rushed forward. Watching through field glasses, an officer saw the men emerge from the woods, press forward in a solid mass, and with fixed bayonets march up the causeway to the outer work. They did not fire a shot even though they were exposed to a heavy and constant cannonade. Then, with some twenty regimental flags flying in the breeze, they charged the main work. Presently the head of the column sank from view, and for a moment, Sherman feared that the attackers had been repulsed, but then he saw the line reemerge up a hill, reach the parapet, and pour inside. The onlookers in Sherman's party rejoiced, grasping hands and embracing. The general later wrote his wife, Ellen, that watching his old division take the fort was the "handsomest thing" he had seen in the war.[29]

Although greatly outnumbered, the Rebels resisted with dogged determination, and the fighting, although lasting less than twenty minutes, was ferocious. Maj. George W. Anderson, who surrendered the garrison, later commended the gallant conduct of Capt. Nicholas B. Clinch, who refused when told by a Federal captain to surrender. A fight broke out between the two officers that was stopped only when Federal privates came to their commander's assistance. Clinch's "cool bravery" even elicited praise from Sherman. The hospital at Beaufort later reported that Clinch had suffered a bayonet strike and gunshot to his left arm, three saber wounds in the back, four saber wounds in the scalp, and a fractured skull, but he seemed to have a "fair prospect of recovering." On the Federal side, Capt. Stephen F. Grimes of the Forty-eighth Illinois was commended for his conduct in the battle (his sharpshooters silenced two of the ten-inch guns) and for his hand-to-hand fight with Clinch. Major Anderson later insisted that McAllister "never surrendered. It was captured by overwhelming numbers." Still, a Federal soldier cheerfully predicted after the fort fell, "We will have Savannah, sure."[30]

The fall of Fort McAllister removed the first hurdle in a successful conclusion to the campaign. Sherman's frontal assault had succeeded, but unlike Hood, who had failed at Franklin two weeks previously, Sherman had an overwhelming numerical advantage. Also, unlike Hood, Sherman avoided the offensive if he could find another way to achieve his objective. Moreover, he did not want to attack the Savannah defenses. Yet the fall of McAllister was cause for celebration. "We all breathe freer to-night than we have for three months past," wrote Major Connolly. Now that the fort was in Sherman's hands, hungry troops knew the army could contact the fleet. The steady diet of rice, without even meat or crackers and little coffee or sugar, had become monotonous. Moreover, the rice was still in the straw, and the soldiers had to do their own threshing before they could get enough for a meal. Even horses and mules ate rice straw. What the black refugees ate no one could guess, but they camped everywhere except near Davis's headquarters for, noted Major Connolly, "they find no sympathy there."[31]

The surrender of the fort had more than military significance, for it meant that Sherman could reestablish communication with the North, thus bolstering morale more than any battlefield victory could. A letter that Brig. Gen. John W. Geary wrote home probably mirrored thousands the soldiers penned. "Yesterday was a day racy and rare, and under all the circumstances long to be remembered," he told his wife, Mary. "We had been thirty-one days cut off from the world and 'the rest of mankind,' during which period we had not received a single word concerning the affairs of the North, except occasionally through the unreliable and lying *sheets* of the South, but yesterday we had a carnival of letters and newspapers." Even official word of McClellan's loss in November comforted the weary travelers. "The news of the presidential election was all fresh to us," he noted, "although we had learned, through rebel sources, of Mr. Lincoln's election."[32]

This was good news, even though Sherman could not really savor it until he took Savannah. He ordered heavy guns transported from Port Royal in preparation but confided to his wife that he did not plan to assault the city.

He intended to starve the civilians and soldiers into submission. Four days after McAllister fell, he had his brother-in-law Charles Ewing deliver a formal demand for surrender to city officials. Sherman warned Hardee that if he was forced to take Savannah by assault, he would resort to "the harshest measures" and would make little effort to restrain his army. Although this was only saber rattling, a Federal officer heard a rumor that Sherman intended to open the city to the men for two days without any restraints. To emphasize that he meant business, Sherman included a copy of Hood's communication with the Union commander at Dalton in which the Texan had threatened that he would give no quarter if he was compelled to carry the place by assault. A Union officer knew what was going on and wrote: "General Hardee replied that he declined to surrender, and that in the conduct of the war he had always been governed by the usage of civilized nations. They were both 'only talking,' and both knew it."[33]

Sherman's threats were pure rhetoric, but residents of Savannah panicked. Those who had not already fled the city now had little chance of escape unless they left with the Rebel army. Scarcely a month earlier the inhabitants of this peaceful Southern city had been making plans for Christmas; now they faced the possibility of suffering the same fate as the citizens of Atlanta.

Known as Forest City because of its many huge trees, Savannah possessed more Old World charm than most Southern cities, and the beauty of its homes attested to the wealth of many of its residents. Founded in 1733 and planned around squares, the city rested on a high-walled bluff overlooking the Savannah River, and live oak trees draped in pale green moss lined the broad thoroughfares. In the first few decades of its existence, the city had visits by such notable figures as John Wesley, George Whitefield, and the Marquis de Lafayette. Eli Whitney had worked as a tutor at Mulberry Grove, near Savannah, where he had invented the cotton gin.

From a military standpoint, Savannah presented a challenge. Its swamps were its strength, Sherman told Ellen, for they could be crossed only on narrow causeways, all of which were protected by heavy artillery. He even confessed that he had almost been hit while reconnoitering, and a "Negro's head was shot off close by." John Geary wrote his wife, "The enemy have a strong line in our front, well defended with swamp dykes, rice-field marshes." Moreover, the Southerners were "very defiant. We are therefore in the midst of the thunders of a siege." Savannah, he added, was a "great prize, and like all things of great value, very difficult to obtain."[34]

Difficult, but not impossible. The swamps and flooded rice fields could not hold Sherman back long, and even Hardee knew the time had come to evacuate. This must have been a hard decision for the Georgian, for barely three months earlier he had endured bitter criticism for his failure to stop Sherman outside Atlanta. Hood had, in fact, laid the loss of Atlanta at Hardee's door. Remembering Hood's stinging criticism, Hardee wanted to save Savannah. Since communication with Charleston was still open, Hardee would certainly have heard of Hood's disaster at Franklin and knew how badly the Confederacy needed a victory somewhere. But he could not overcome numerical odds and urged soldiers and civilians to pack in anticipation of a withdrawal.

The only route of escape was across the river into South Carolina. Hardee assigned the job of collecting enough rice flats to construct a bridge to Brig. Gen. Pierce M. B. Young. A South Carolinian who had grown up in Georgia, Young had attended the Georgia Military Institute and later West Point, where he would have graduated in the class of 1861 had he not resigned. He fought in the Army of Northern Virginia before being ordered to Georgia to assist Hardee. Yet the task before him was as difficult as any he had encountered in Virginia, for finding enough rice flats and then getting them into position before Sherman cut off the South Carolina escape route was critical. As the pontoon bridge slowly took shape, the residents of Savannah watched with apprehension. It took three separate links to connect the islands with the South Carolina shore, and some thirty rice flats, seventy to eighty feet long, had to be strapped together and then covered with wood taken from nearby wharves. Because of the scarcity of flats, the engineers had to lash them together end to end and not side by side as was typical. Building the bridge took time and required more labor than could be done by the available slaves. Georgia militiamen and sailors whose ships had nowhere to go made up work parties.[35]

Fortunately for Hardee, Sherman was in no hurry to enter the city. He actually had no desire to see Savannah suffer the fate of Atlanta. As a young army officer, he had visited the graceful parks and walked through the gardens, and even though the people he had known in the past were now technically the enemy, he had no appetite for bombarding their homes. He believed he could starve the residents into submission without a substantial loss of life on either side. With this plan in mind, he left for Hilton Head Island to discuss means of isolating the port with Adm. John A. Dahlgren of the navy and General Foster, who commanded the Department of the South. He left strict orders prohibiting any action during his absence. Although Hardee did not know Sherman's plans, it was clear to him that the situation was grave. Skirmishing near the railroad at Pocotaligo on the South Carolina side of the river and the appearance of Union gunboats could only mean that the net was closing tighter. Hardee knew that the Confederate cavalry could not hold the roads open long. He needed to move quickly.

Five days before Christmas, many families abandoned their homes, left behind festive holiday trimmings, and joined the procession slowly crossing the improvised structure that passed for a bridge. Rice straw muffled the sound of hoofbeats as animals pulled both crowded army wagons and elegant carriages across. Frightened horses and mules shied as drivers tried to coax them to walk on the bobbing link to South Carolina, and many animals had to be blindfolded before they could be persuaded to advance. Men and women abandoned their buggies, often crammed with household goods, and gingerly tested the rice flats as the river current tugged at the flimsy creation. Savannah civilians had experienced nothing like this before, for even when Fort Pulaski had capitulated in the spring of 1862, there had been no serious attempt to capture the city. People along the southeast coast, in both Savannah and Charleston, had learned to live with the blockade, and life had gone on much as usual until Sherman appeared. Curious Union soldiers on the South Carolina shore watched the strange scene but made no attempt to stop the procession. Everyone assumed someone else would prevent the exodus, and besides, Sherman had ordered no action during his absence.

Although Hardee abandoned the city, he did not intend to leave anything behind that could be used by the occupying force. As the Confederates moved out of the outlying defenses, they destroyed the guns and ammunition they could not haul. Anxious soldiers spiked old or damaged cannons, while others worked feverishly to save those in good condition. When Rebel gunboats patrolling the river east of Savannah pulled back they left the iron-clad *Georgia*, near Fort Jackson, defenseless, forcing its crew to scuttle the vessel. At the same time, retreating Confederates torched Fort Jackson's barracks, spiked its remaining guns, and demolished the gun carriages. Quietly the Rebels around Savannah withdrew, leaving only skirmishers to man the defensive line.

Melancholy settled over both soldiers and civilians. As the Rebels crossed the makeshift bridge, a Confederate sadly noted, "The constant tread of the troops and the rumblings of the artillery as they poured over those long floating bridges was a sad sight, and by the glare of the large fires at the east of the bridge it seemed like an immense funeral procession stealing out of the city in the dead of night." A soldier told his mother, "I have no words to picture the gloomy bitterness that filled my breast on that dreary march through water, mud and darkness." By this time, it was impossible for the Federals not to realize that something significant was happening, for fires of abandoned Rebel vessels lit the night skies. Yet no one tried to stop the procession and by dawn all was quiet.[36]

Federal soldiers, meanwhile, continued to prepare for an attack on the city's defenses. On Tuesday, December 20, exactly one week after the fall of Fort McAllister and four years to the day since South Carolina seceded, a soldier told his diary, "Another quiet day; but the bustle of preparation for the assault can be seen on all hands, and everybody feels confident of the result." Yet as the first rays of light illuminated the morning sky, the cry, "Savannah is evacuated," reverberated down the line. A jubilant James Connolly recalled that "in less time than it takes to tell it, the heaviest sleepers in the army, as well as the lightest, were out, some dressed, and some *en deshabille*, shouting and hurrahing from the bottom of their lungs. This was indeed a joyful morning. Savannah is ours. Our long campaign is ended." Another Union soldier saw events in more pragmatic terms. "We have," wrote Charles Wills, "just by a hair's breadth missed what would have been a most unpleasant fight." Although no one would be happier than Sherman at the turn of events, he was not on hand for the celebration. Having spent Tuesday at Hilton Head making preparations for his siege, he had been delayed when Admiral Dahlgren's flagship had grounded in a storm. Sherman did not know that Hardee had abandoned the city until a tug arrived to pull his vessel out of the mud bank left by the low tide.[37]

Back in Georgia, Savannah authorities pondered how best to surrender the state's largest city. Mayor Richard Arnold and several aldermen waited patiently for the last Confederate to cross the pontoon bridge and watched in despair as the Rebels on the South Carolina bank cut the structure loose and sent it floating downstream. There was nothing left to do now except locate a Federal officer and ask for terms. The mayor's small party did not go far out the Louisville Road before encountering pickets who escorted them to John Geary. The general, happy to accept the surrender, agreed to protect the citizens and their private property. The first Federal troops, men from Henry Barnum's brigade of Geary's division, reached the heart of the city by six o'clock on December 21, just as the last of the Confederates who had remained behind to destroy the bridges escaped. Only the ironclad *Savannah* attempted to defy the invaders. When the U.S. flag appeared above Fort Jackson, the Rebel sailors harmlessly shelled the old masonry bastion. Federal attempts to sink the vessel failed, but the Confederates abandoned it shortly after dark, leaving it to burn in the middle of the river. Around midnight, when it finally exploded, the blast shook windows at Hilton Head, some twenty miles away. In writing his wife, General Geary left the impression that his men had fought their way into Savannah. "I am now the *Commandante* of the City," he boasted, "in honor of its capture by me, and of the surrender to me."[38]

Sherman rode into Savannah the next day. As he passed the spacious mansions that dotted the city's gracious squares, he knew his decision not to pursue the Army of Tennessee had paid big dividends. He had faced the easier half of the two campaigns, for he had encountered little enemy resistance. Hood had guaranteed Sherman's success by moving into Tennessee. Sherman never really doubted that Thomas could deal with Hood because he knew that when A. J. Smith arrived with reinforcements, the Federals would have a numerical advantage. And Sherman had the utmost confidence in Smith and his veterans. As he enjoyed the graceful elegance of Savannah's tree-lined avenues, Sherman reveled in the knowledge that his strategy was working.

Sherman's march to the coast was over, but he was now faced with political issues. Before, he had successfully evaded Lincoln's attempts to integrate his army. When a black regiment, the 110th U.S. Colored Troops, arrived at his Savannah headquarters, he found ways to undermine the president's design to attach black soldiers to his command. The general disarmed the men and put them to work as laborers, teamsters, and servants. Reports circulated that white troops harassed the new arrivals so viciously that some were killed. One Ohio soldier concluded that the blacks must be "taught to know their place & behave civilly." Clearly, the government could not ignore these acts, and Halleck warned Sherman that if he persisted in his negative attitude toward black soldiers, he would make powerful enemies in Washington. As evidence, Halleck recounted the accusations against Jefferson C. Davis at Ebenezer Creek. Sherman, of course, dismissed the charges as "cock-and-bull" and "humbug," accepting without question the explanation that Davis had given. Davis had, claimed the commanding general, taken up the bridge, not because he wanted to leave the slaves behind "but because he wanted his bridge." From a military standpoint, he reasoned, that was a justifiable argument.[39]

Still, Sherman was accountable for his army's actions, and not long after arriving in Savannah he was visited by Secretary of War Edwin Stanton. Stanton's official purpose was to reestablish Union control of the city and check on the cotton trade, but unofficially he wanted explanations of the rumors concerning Sherman's treatment of African Americans, both military and civilian. Sherman continued to defend Davis's conduct and insisted that he had done nothing to subvert Lincoln's policies concerning the newly freed slaves. Sherman also drafted Special Field Order Number 15, which redistributed land along the southeast coast to blacks. Sherman saw this as a way to prevent refugees from following his army in the future and as a practical alternative to taking blacks into the army. He told Ellen: "I want soldiers made of the best bone and muscle in the land, and won't attempt military feats with doubtful materials. I want [the Negro] treated as free and not hunted and badgered to [be] made a soldier of, when his family is left back on the plantation. I am right and won't change." Sherman thought the experiment along the Sea Islands the perfect solution to the "Negro nonsense."[40]

In spite of these troubling political issues, even Sherman's critics had to give him credit for a successful military campaign through the heart of the Confederacy. It was impossible not to appreciate the logic of dividing his forces and sending Thomas north to deal with the Confederate Army of Tennessee. That is, of course, if Thomas proved successful in his half of the dual campaign.

CHAPTER EIGHT

Hood at Nashville

When Sherman reached the coast, he quickly turned his attention to the situation in Tennessee. As soon as he made connection with the navy, he demanded all the newspapers available and read everything they could tell him about the events of the previous weeks. To his dismay, he found no recent news from Nashville. Sherman knew only too well that if Thomas failed, it would be his failure too. "I hope General Thomas has held Hood," he told Halleck. "My last accounts are of the fight at Franklin."[1]

Sherman appreciated that his success would be spoiled if Hood escaped to do more mischief, and he could not rest easy until he heard from Thomas. He was even willing to order his tired soldiers back on the road if Hood still posed a threat. The general assured Washington that if the Rebels had made any headway he would "not hesitate" to march for Montgomery, which he believed would force Hood to retrace his steps into Alabama. He did not think this would be necessary, for his instincts told him that Hood would have a "bad time" if he undertook a winter campaign in the hills of central Tennessee.[2]

The lack of reliable news was disturbing, for all Sherman could find out was secondhand. He did, however, have several letters from Grant waiting for him, some dating back to the beginning of the month. Through these communications and what he read in the Rebel papers, Sherman had a fairly accurate of Thomas's actions during the past weeks. His concern mounted when he learned that Hood had not only followed Schofield to Nashville but had forced Thomas behind the city's defenses. "I myself am somewhat astonished at the attitude of things in Tennessee," he complained. "I purposely delayed at Kingston until General Thomas assured me that he was 'all ready,' and my last dispatch from him, of the 12th of November, was full of confidence, in which he promised me that he would 'ruin Hood,' if he dared to advance from Florence, urging me to go ahead and give myself no concern about Hood's army in Tennessee."[3]

The general in question, George Henry Thomas, was a career military man, having graduated from West Point in 1840, where he ranked twelfth in the class, six places behind his classmate Cump Sherman. Unlike the two men who now criticized him, Grant and Sherman, Thomas had remained in the army until 1861. His last assignment was with the Second U.S. Cavalry, but by March 1861 he had faced a dilemma. Even though he was on leave at the time, he was a Virginian in a Union army. He requested a transfer to the army's recruiting service but also inquired about a position at the Virginia Military Institute. Fate intervened, for when most of the officers of the Second U.S. Cavalry resigned to join the Confederacy, Gen. Winfield Scott asked Thomas to take command. The Virginian agreed. His wife later wrote: "There was never a word passed between myself or *any one* of our family upon the subject of his remaining loyal to the United States government. We felt that whatever his course, it would be from a conscientious sense of duty, that no one could persuade him to do what he felt was not right." Nonetheless, his sisters did not support his decision and refused to acknowledge him for the rest of his life. From this point forward, their brother no longer existed.[4]

This decision cost Thomas a great deal. The Rebels confiscated his property, and his family, with one exception, disowned him. The South branded him a traitor, and many in the North saw him as suspect. More important to his career in the U.S. Army, he lost any political support he might have from state senators and congressmen. Virginia was out of the Union, and the Northern states generally promoted their own sons, such as Grant and Sherman. Nevertheless, Thomas had earned respect, even admiration, from his colleagues. He rarely blustered or complained but did his job with the able efficiency of a true soldier. He might be slow on occasion, but he was one of the army's strengths.[5]

Relations between the three men—Grant, Sherman, and Thomas—had been strained since 1862. Following the battle at Shiloh, when Grant had temporarily lost command of his army, Thomas briefly took over the Army of the Tennessee. Grant, of course, always suspected that the Virginian had a hand in the embarrassing matter. The Army of the Tennessee was Grant's and eventually Sherman's. Thomas, who later assumed command of the Army of the Cumberland, realized that Grant had cooled toward him. In addition, once Thomas took the Army of the Cumberland, rivalry within the army groups increased the strain in an already tense situation. Although Grant had agreed to the orders announcing Thomas's promotion to replace William S. Rosecrans in October 1863, he had clearly expressed his personal preference when he bypassed Thomas for overall command of the western armies in 1864, selecting Sherman instead. Sherman had fed Grant's suspicions when he complained of the behavior of the Army of the Cumberland in the Atlanta campaign, but he still thought enough of Thomas to assign him to deal with Hood's army in the autumn. Sherman was aware of the discord between Grant and Thomas, and although he did not speak of the problems to Halleck, he freely criticized Thomas's lack of initiative to Grant. "Why he did not turn on Hood at Franklin, after checking and discomfiting him, surpasses my understanding," he said disdainfully. "I know full well that General Thomas is slow in mind and in action, but he is judicious and brave, and the troops feel great confidence in him. I still hope he will out-maneuver and destroy Hood."[6]

Even while Grant and Sherman exchanged worried messages, events at Nashville came to a head. During the first two weeks of December, much had happened in Tennessee. For Hood, the fourteen days after the disaster at Franklin tested the endurance and patriotism of his soldiers to the limit. For Thomas, those same days drove home the realization that if he wanted to maintain command of the army, he needed a victory over the Confederates.

Thomas's failure to capitalize on Hood's misfortunes at Franklin irritated Grant. Just two days after the battle, the general in chief lectured, "It looks to me that instead of falling back to Nashville, we should have taken the offensive against the enemy where he was." Grant nagged Thomas on December 5: "Hood should be attacked where he is. Time strengthens him, in all probability, as much as it does you." When Thomas did nothing, Grant's patience wore thin, and he curtly telegraphed: "Attack Hood at once. . . . There is great danger of delay resulting in a campaign back to the Ohio River."[7]

Crossing the river, of course, had been Hood's original intention, but after Franklin he no longer had a specific plan. He had lost more than six thousand men, but it was December 3 before he wrote the secretary of war and over a week before that report reached Richmond. Hood claimed a technical victory, for Schofield had fled the field, but Davis knew better; he had already seen accounts in the Northern press. In spite of Hood's claim that the Rebels had successfully assaulted the Union line, forcing Schofield to evacuate his position and retreat toward Nashville, Davis suspected the truth. He focused on the casualties. Hood cited the loss of "many gallant officers and brave men." That was an understatement. The names included Cleburne, Adams, Gist, Strahl, and Granbury killed; Carter, mortally wounded; the list went on and on. Although Davis already knew most of this from the newspapers, the confirmation of those accounts was disturbing. For the soldiers in the field, the loss was even more acute. In Granbury's brigade the highest-ranking officer was a captain; other brigades turned for leadership to colonels, lieutenant colonels, or even majors.[8]

Hood led a weakened army, but he had few options once he made the decision to follow Schofield. He could bypass Nashville, cross Kentucky, and strike out for the Ohio River, but the condition of his men made a long march in the winter months not only impractical but virtually impossible. The logistics of such a undertaking would have been complex, and even Hood, who paid little attention to such matters, realized the glaring absence of a supply line. Although the Nashville basin was a rich farming region, Hood's march would not coincide with the fall harvests. More significant, the area had already suffered severely from foragers and guerrillas on both sides. He could also elect to move toward Murfreesboro rather than Nashville. Once there, he might have overpowered the garrison. That would have put him back in the same position the Army of Tennessee occupied two years earlier, but it would also place him between Union troops in Nashville and Chattanooga. He was left only one option, and as a gambler, Hood was willing to take one last chance. He pushed forward. He had hoped to avoid challenging the strong Union fortifications at the state capital, but now he had no choice. He would entrench outside the city—and wait. Hood's initial purpose, it seems, was not to fight a general battle but simply to maintain pressure, to whittle away at the Yankee defenders, to deplete them, wear them down and demoralize them until conditions favored him.

Nashville rested on the banks of the Cumberland River near the center of a bowl-like valley formed by a string of ridges. When city fathers surrendered the city to the Federals early in February 1862, many strongly pro-Confederate residents had fled south. Others, equally pro-Confederate, refused to leave; they preferred instead to remain in their homes and protect their possessions. The city, growing from a population of thirty thousand at the beginning of the war to around one hundred thousand, had become a major depot for the armies in the western theater. Early in 1862, Andrew Johnson had become military governor, and when the mayor and city council rejected the oath of allegiance, Johnson replaced them with Unionists. In the spring of 1862, the townspeople came to know the harshness of martial law as they began the long months of occupation. For the radical Rebels in Nashville, Hood's arrival promised a long-awaited deliverance.

Many Nashvillians, however, had become convinced that the Confederates could not win the war, and they were taken by surprise upon hearing
that Hood was headed in their direction. They had accepted their lot under
Union occupation and even learned how to survive. Boardinghouses, hotels, theaters, eating places, and saloons prospered. When Governor Johnson had required an amnesty oath for all voters in the November election,
citizens quickly denounced it as the "Damnesty Oath" and protested by not
voting but made no effort at organized resistance.

For Union soldiers, Nashville presented a welcome diversion. Like any
city with a transient wartime population, the downtown had become a
haven for prostitutes and gamblers. Even soldiers avoided "Smoky Row," a
dangerous area near the river where violence solicited few comments. Nashville also had the dubious reputation of being the first American city to legal-
ize prostitution. In 1863, both civil and military authorities had recognized
the problem and ordered the offending women north, hoping to exile them
to Louisville or Cincinnati. When neither of these cities would accept the
prostitutes, they were returned to Nashville. The army then tried to control
the profitable trade by requiring medical examinations and licenses. By the
spring of 1864, 352 women had licenses and 92 women suffering from sexu-
ally transmitted diseases had been treated in a new facility established to
deal with the dilemma. By that summer "colored prostitutes" were also li-
censed and examined. Initially, the women had to undergo physicals every
two weeks, but the time was shortened to ten days. Those without a clean
bill of health were shipped off to Hospital Number Eleven, one of over
twenty hospitals operated by the army. This added health protection attracted working women, for the number of prostitutes increased. The surgeon general reported that "many of the better class of prostitutes had been
drawn to Nashville from Northern cities by the comparative protection
from venereal disease which its license system afforded." Dr. William M.
Chambers, a surgeon of volunteers, admitted that, at the direction of the
provost marshal, he visited local "madams" at their place of business; the
fee for a house visit was a dollar.[9]

With such a reputation, it is not surprising that many soldiers wanted to
see the state capital. Even Schofield's men, fresh from the battlefield at
Franklin, recovered quickly when offered a pass into the city. Enterprising
fellows without official passes talked their way out of the camps by deceiving
the guards, many of whom could not read well enough to know they had
been tricked. Once in the heart of the city, soldiers could find almost any-

thing, from exotic food to female companionship. One man remarked that "if ever there was a town that should be burned, that city was Nashville."[10]

Although the Confederates could not enjoy the city's comforts, a glimpse of the imposing state capitol building renewed the confidence of many soldiers, particularly the Tennesseans. "We are in sight of Nashville," proclaimed a soldier on December 6, "and the Yankees are alarmed as to their safety." Another wrote home that the men were "not only cheerful but enthusiastic," while a third told his sister that the army was "in fine spirits." As the army approached Nashville, many soldiers believed that morale rebounded, but after Franklin anything was an improvement.[11]

What Hood planned to do after he invested the city is hard to determine. He does not seem to have had any long-range strategy in mind, for it appears he only intended to react to circumstances. Like Franklin, Nashville sat near a curve in the river with the Federal lines running in a semicircle from Fort Negley in the east back to the safety of the deep waters of the Cumberland in the west. When Hood arrived, he could not besiege the entire position; his line ran only from the Hillsboro Pike on the west to the railroad to Chattanooga on the east. Although his earthworks extended four miles, it covered less than half of Thomas's line. His men were about two miles from the Union trenches on the east, while in the west the distance between the two sides was as close as five hundred yards. Cheatham was on the right near the railroad, Lee in the center, and Stewart on the left, anchored on the Hillsboro Pike. Between this pike and the river to the west were another four miles that Hood could not cover, and between the railroad and the river on the east was yet another mile that Hood left open. Hood spread his troops very thin and husbanded his resources. He had the advantage of high ground, but he refused his artillerists the shells necessary to exploit the position.

Hood understood that his line was weak; he needed more men. He had around twenty-three thousand actually fit to fight, but only slightly over eighteen thousand infantry. Soon after arriving at Nashville, he asked Thomas to exchange prisoners. When Thomas refused, Hood again turned to the Trans-Mississippi as a source of manpower, telling the secretary of war on December 11 that he hoped he could obtain some troops from that side of the river "in time for the spring campaign, if not sooner." Beauregard, already sensing the danger to Hood's army, had requested reinforcements from across the Mississippi. Davis had agreed. Unfortunately, Kirby Smith, recognizing that his soldiers would desert rather than cross the river, continued to decline.[12]

Hood's belief that he could replenish the army with recruits from Tennessee also proved mistaken. Fewer than two hundred had joined the army on its march north. Instead, desertion had become a problem. Angry, Hood instructed his troops to arrest locals who refused to serve, and many Tennesseans fled into the hills, some even taking refuge in Nashville in an effort to avoid conscription into the Confederate army.

Yet Hood longed for a well-oiled machine, an army that could duplicate Lee's greatest victories. But this was not the Army of Northern Virginia, and he was not Lee. Still, he believed that a successful campaign for Nashville would vindicate his right to command. His goal, of course, was impractical, but by this time Hood was not being realistic. Yet it was clear that the army was not functioning with anything near precision. In spite of the boost in spirits prompted by the sight of the capitol building, frustration persisted in the ranks, particularly among the non-Tennesseans. After Franklin, Texan Samuel Foster had angrily told his diary: "He had near 10,000 men murdered around Atlanta trying to prove to the world that he was a greater man than Genl Johns[t]on. . . . And now in order to recover from the merited disgrace of that transaction he brings this Army here into middle Tenn. and by making them false promises and false statements get these men killed."[13]

In spite of the lack of enthusiasm, Hood would not be deterred even though he could only guess at the number of enemy troops hidden behind the fortifications. Initially, the numbers were not that lopsided; each army had fewer than twenty-five thousand. Thomas grumbled that Sherman had taken most of the best units with him, leaving only a skeleton army. That was not exactly true; his troops included Schofield's veterans from the IV Corps and a portion of the XXIII Corps, units that had recently fought at Franklin, and seasoned veterans. Thomas could order noncombatants from the quartermaster and commissary departments to man the trenches if necessary, and he had about four thousand garrison troops available, including various units of railroad guards and reserve battalions, and about forty-three hundred cavalry.

Unfortunately, the horsemen were not ready to meet the enemy; they needed time to rest and reorganize. As an old cavalryman himself from the prewar days, Thomas knew a horse could endure no more than a few hours of fighting at a stretch, and if Forrest was around, he would need every minute. Except for Forrest, Thomas probably felt no great anxiety: an assault on a fortified line of earthworks such as his was a slow and intricate procedure and he knew from experience that it should develop gradually. He told Halleck he thought it best to wait behind his fortifications until Wilson refitted the cavalry. "If Hood attacks me here he will be more seriously damaged than he was yesterday," he asserted on December 1.[14]

Hood had no intention of attacking. The parity in numbers was short-lived, for by the tenth, Thomas had over sixty thousand men, and an assault would only duplicate Franklin. Those precious days lost in early November in camp along the Tennessee River now cost Hood, for the Rebel advance to Nashville coincided with the arrival of A. J. Smith's long-awaited veterans. Hood had sent some of his cavalry to blockade the river, but the horsemen arrived too late to stop the transports carrying Smith's detachment from the Army of the Tennessee. In addition, before Forrest cut the railroad linking Nashville to Chattanooga, another eighty-five hundred garrison troops safely made the trip up the line. As Union numbers increased, an Illinois soldier taunted, "We will defy the whole of Hood's army to get us out of the Rock City."[15]

When it became apparent that Hood might enter Tennessee, the Federals had strengthened the city's defenses. Many of the forts surrounding Nashville had never been completed, so not only did they hurry to finish the existing forts, they planned additional ones. As Hood approached, everyone available, including impressed blacks, worked on a double line of breastworks that would connect the forts. Thomas also needed the cooperation of the navy, for the Cumberland River was a major part of the city's defensive line.

As soon as Schofield arrived on the first, Thomas established his outer perimeter. Schofield's corps manned the left as far as the Nolensville Pike. The distance between the pike and the river was originally held by cavalry, but after Thomas ordered them elsewhere, the soldiers under Maj. Gen. James B. Steedman moved into the trenches. In the center, the general placed Brig. Gen. Thomas J. Wood's corps. Wood, who had the distasteful distinction of being the officer who weakened the Union line to Chickamauga, resulting in a disastrous loss, had taken command of the IV Corps after General Stanley had been wounded at Franklin. On the right, Thomas placed Smith's veterans when they arrived by steamboat.

Wilson's cavalry required Thomas's immediate attention. In an effort to replenish badly needed mounts, he impressed horses from private citizens, giving the owners receipts for up to $160. Yet few serviceable steeds could be found, and detachments scouring Tennessee and Kentucky came back empty-handed. Valuable thoroughbreds, of course, had been shipped out of harm's way early in the war, many ending up along the Texas coast for the duration. What was left had been picked over by Rebel cavalry. In desperation, Union horsemen impressed almost any animal they came across. Carriages and plows sat idle as the animals were taken for military service. Even the performing horses of a traveling circus were confiscated, with the exception of "Mrs. Lake's celebrated trick horse, Czar." Wilson even took the matched bay carriage horses belonging to Andrew Johnson, causing the future vice president to refer to the cavalry commander as a "bumptious puppy." Thomas told Wilson to move his corps to the north bank of the Cumberland River, where he was instructed to work his blacksmiths overtime to shoe the mounts. Well aware that his troopers might face Forrest, Thomas recognized that nothing short of the best preparations would give his cavalry a fighting chance against that stalwart Rebel. Yet Thomas greatly overestimated Forrest's numbers. This concern, however, was not reciprocated in Washington. Edwin Stanton grimly telegraphed Grant at City Point on December 7: "Thomas seems unwilling to attack because it is hazardous, as if all war was anything but hazardous. If he waits for Wilson to get ready, Gabriel will be blowing his last horn."[16]

Besides facing a strong Federal line more than twice their own in length, the Confederates also had to deal with the various isolated garrisons. The closest, Murfreesboro, with around six thousand men some twenty-eight miles away, was Hood's first concern. On December 2 he sent General Bate with two thousand men from Cheatham's corps in that direction and a few days later ordered most of Forrest's cavalry to follow. Fighting broke out there on December 4 and again three days later. Hood apparently hoped that by threatening the garrison, he could tempt Thomas out of his fortifications. Ironically, if the plan worked, Hood would accomplish exactly what Grant wanted by forcing Thomas to attack. Hood confided to a chaplain that "the enemy will have to seek out our armies and fight them."[17]

Thomas was not ready to fight, however, and as this realization dawned on the authorities back east, frustration mounted. Grant not only worried about Hood's army, but he was also concerned about Forrest's cavalry. Moreover, there was the possibility that the Rebels might make a foray into eastern Tennessee. On December 8 Grant, still prodding Thomas to act, asked, "Why not attack at once?" His patience near a breaking point, he blustered: "Now is one of the finest opportunities ever presented of destroying one of the three armies of the enemy. If destroyed, he never can replace it." Grant even appealed to Thomas's ego: "Use the means at your command, and you can do this and cause a rejoicing that will resound from one end of the land to another." The following day, flattery turned to anger when

Grant ranted, "It seemed to me that you have been slow, and I have had no explanation of affairs to convince me otherwise."[18]

Grant was not alone in his anxiety, for President Lincoln, Chief of Staff Halleck, and Secretary of War Stanton all voiced concern. Officials feared they had another dawdling commander and that Thomas's lack of motivation would keep him behind his fortifications indefinitely. Grant even wanted to replace Thomas with Schofield. That would have suited Schofield, who harbored an old grudge against Thomas dating back to West Point. Thomas, he thought, had been too harsh on his youthful indiscretions when he was a student. Now, as a general, Schofield apparently worked to undermine his superior. Some even believed he communicated secretly with Grant, but no records found in the War Department following the war corroborated such rumors. Thomas's supporters, however, claimed that Schofield had tampered with any evidence while serving briefly as secretary of war during the turbulent days of the Johnson administration.[19]

Thomas's predicament also gave rise to criticism of the entire western war effort. Joseph Hooker, commanding at Cincinnati, saw this as the perfect opportunity to carp and whine to political friends about his lack of an active command and his many enemies; he accused Sherman and Grant of conspiring to keep him in the background. Lashing out at those he considered his adversaries, Hooker used the crisis in Tennessee to frame his case. "Had Sherman marched against Hood, there was no earthly reason why he should escape," he pointed out on December 8. "Now Hood is investing Nashville, occupying a position he held two years ago, after two years of campaigning to drive him into the interior." He vented his anger by recalling old stories. "Sherman is crazy," he reminded a senator, referring to newspaper charges against Sherman early in the war, and "he has no more judgment than a child." To the powerful Radical Republican critic of Lincoln Benjamin F. Wade, he wrote: "No matter what the newspapers may say to the contrary, no officer high in command has been more unfortunate than Sherman, and this moment he is engaged in a raid which will tend to prolong the war, when he had it in his power to have utterly destroyed Hood's army. At the time he cut loose from Atlanta, Hood was on the north side of the Tennessee River, but instead of marching for him, he chose to march from him. Blows, not marches, are to kill the rebellion." Although Hooker had old scores to settle, he was not alone in questioning the decision to allow Sherman to head south while Hood turned north. That kind of criticism accounted for some of the tension in Washington over Thomas's delay.

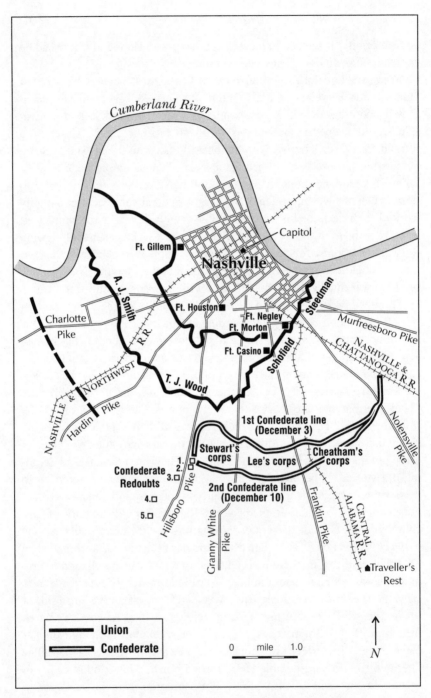

Cumberland River

Ft. Gillem

Nashville

Capitol

A. J. Smith

NORTHWEST R.R.

Charlotte Pike

Ft. Houston

Ft. Negley

Steedman

Murfreesboro Pike

NASHVILLE & CHATTANOOGA R.R.

Ft. Morton

Ft. Casino

Schofield

NASHVILLE & Hardin Pike

T. J. Wood

1st Confederate line
(December 3)

Nolensville Pike

Stewart's
corps

Lee's corps

Cheatham's
corps

1.
2.
3.

Confederate
Redoubts

4.
5.

Hillsboro Pike

2nd Confederate line
(December 10)

Franklin Pike

CENTRAL ALABAMA R.R.

Granny White Pike

Traveller's
Rest

Union

Confederate

0   mile   1.0

N

7. Nashville, the first day

Thomas wanted to wait for the opportune moment to attack, but the situation in the nation's capital denied him that leeway.[20]

Yet he did get a respite of sorts. A winter storm gave Thomas a brief reprieve when a strong cold front passed through the region. Waking up to frozen ground on Friday, December 9, troops in both armies suffered as the rain turn to sleet, then snow, leaving a three-inch cloak over ice-covered fields and tents. After the war, veterans would remember December 11 as "Cold Sunday" for the temperature fell below zero. Men froze to death while on picket duty and in their fortifications. Although Thomas tried to move, the cavalry horses could not navigate the roads, their iron horseshoes slipping as their hooves broke through the snow to hit the ice beneath. Learning of the conditions, even Grant had to admit that an attack might be difficult, if not impossible. In a moment of anger he had nearly replaced Thomas with Maj. Gen. John A. Logan, an old friend who had been on leave. Knowing that Sherman might not be sympathetic to finding him a command, Logan had instead turned to Grant at City Point. Even Logan was amazed when Grant decided to send him to Nashville and to assume command if Thomas had not advanced. On second thought, however, Grant decided instead to go to Nashville himself.

The political intrigue at the top did not alleviate the suffering of the common soldier. While Hood and Thomas rested in comfortable lodgings, the soldiers struggled to keep warm. Many Confederates had no shoes, overcoats, or blankets. Philip Stephenson recalled that men cut down trees, leaving them as logs ten to twelve feet long. "In this way the length of the fire was sufficient to allow eight or more men to lie side by side, feet to the fire, and each get some benefit." Unfortunately for Stephenson, all his messmates had been wounded at Franklin and he had no one with whom to share a bed for warmth. Added to his misery, all he possessed for a cover was a small saddle blanket just four feet square. "There were three or four others in the company in the same fix, but we did not flock together," he added. "I sat up all night. It was hard even to get near the fire, for the row of sleepers monopolized it. . . . At times drowsiness would start me to nodding, but the cold would soon awake me, for it was intense, and the night was long." Toward dawn he was so exhausted that he pushed his way into a tiny space near the fire, but "some of the men got cold, woke up, saw me lying there and grumbled. So I got up again. It was well I did. The back of my jacket had caught fire! A hole was burnt in it as big as my two hands."[21]

The frigid weather required the men to take extreme measures. Without tents or warm clothing, many of them burrowed into the ground. When the snow came, Samuel Foster recorded: "Very cold—No fire wood—No trees nearer than a mile. . . . I have dug out a fire place in the side of the ditch, and burn cedar rails." A Tennessee soldier admitted, "We burned Mrs. Aaron V. Brown's cedar rails that cost Governor Brown 10 cents each." Even those attended by slaves were no better off. A Rebel gunner related that his servant brought him a change of underwear, "for which I had to scrape off the snow on a log at Richmond Creek, strip and bathe in its icy waters to make a change." Although the soldiers suffered intensely from the cold, their comrades who had been captured at Franklin did not have it any better. Texan Charles Leuschner wrote in his diary from his prison cell at Camp Douglas, south of Chicago, that men were losing fingers to frostbite, and "some had to have there feet taken off up to there knees." It was, he added, "one of the hardest winters they had for some time. I have poured water out of a cup and before it would touch the groun it was ice."[22]

Thomas's men suffered too, although certainly not as intensely. On December 11, a Union soldier wrote to friends at home that "both armies are doing their best to keep warm. For three days we have had bitterly cold, winter weather" with "rain, hail, sleet and snow." As a result, "the beautiful woods and groves that surrounded Nashville on all sides, and made it one of the most lovely towns I ever saw, are all going remorselessly down before the axes of the soldiers." He understood that the Rebels also needed firewood, and "away it goes by the thousands of cord daily. If the Rebs coop us up here another fortnight, there won't be a tree left within five miles of Nashville."[23]

The weather damaged Confederate morale, a problem compounded as the immense psychological vacuum left by Franklin took hold. But as the shock of the disaster lessened, many deluded themselves into believing Hood had won a victory of sorts. It was futile, however, to deny the army's loss, for too many friends and relatives had been captured, killed, or wounded. Samuel Foster angrily scribbled in his diary: "General Hood has betrayed us (The Army of Tenn). This is not the kind of fighting he promised us at Tuscumbia and Florence Ala. when we started into Tenn." Another remembered: "Men looked at each other, at each other's rags and thinned ranks, into each other's haggard faces. Men began to miss and mourn their fallen comrades, and men felt in themselves and saw in each other the benumbing effects of that dreadful shock. . . . No noise, no jokes no laughter were there." Besides the obvious emotional response, there was a practical side to the losses. Most of Hood's units had commanders who were new and inexperienced. This often translated into a lack of confidence and certainly affected the esprit de corps.[24]

Logistics was another problem familiar to Hood. He needed the railroad coming from Alabama repaired so he could receive supplies, but by the sixth it was operating only as far as Franklin. Of course, Beauregard, from whom he requested necessary repairs, was occupied with Sherman in Georgia. Beauregard must have been appalled to learn that Hood had only two working locomotives and three cars even though Hood assured him he would have more available in a few days. Beauregard knew that an army could not be sustained on such meager resources. Again seeming out of touch with reality, Hood told Maj. Gen. D. H. Maury, who commanded the Department of Mississippi and East Louisiana and the man in charge of any repairs on the Memphis & Charleston line, that his long-range plans included a winter in Tennessee. He did not explain the reasoning behind this apparent change of plan but simply announced that the "permanent occupation of this country absolutely requires that this road be repaired."[25]

The shortage of shoes was of particular concern. This was not a new problem, but it was accentuated when the weather turned cold. Tempers grew short among those men whose footgear had worn out, and a Rebel estimated that there were as many as thirty-five hundred barefoot soldiers. Texan Samuel Foster considered himself one of the lucky ones, for he obtained some moccasins from the brigade shoe shop. He commented that, made of "green cow hide with the hair side in they are about as pleasant to the foot and about as comfortable as any I ever had."[26]

In spite of clear problems with supplies, Hood remained optimistic. Comfortably situated at Traveller's Rest, the home of Judge John Overton, a wealthy planter and once political campaign manager for Andrew Jackson, Hood enjoyed the hospitality. The rambling structure, located on the Franklin Pike some six miles from Nashville, had been built in the last year of the eighteenth century. Indeed, since his invasion of Tennessee, Hood had rested in some of the state's finest mansions and thus avoided the harsh conditions in the camps. An officer whose tent was in a grove near the house remarked: "We had an abundance of good food, beef, mutton, pork, flour, and potatoes. At the door of our tent stood a barrel of Robinson County whiskey." To add to the festive spirit, there was no shortage of "pretty ladies" who wanted to entertain the famous general with piano and harp. Halsey Wigfall told his sister, "There are several young ladies from Nashville here who are very pretty and agreeable and the most intense Southerners." The wedding of Maj. William Clare, a member of Hood's staff, and Mary Hadley on December 12 was an elegant diversion, and the ceremony, held at Brentwood's Methodist Meeting House, was followed by an elaborate dinner. As he listened to the couple exchange vows, Hood must have thought of Buck and anticipated with pleasure his own wedding day. Just ten days before, Mary Chesnut recorded in her diary: "Buck is happy. J. B. has written, and she says, fancy 'my raptures'—two letters, and he is coming in January to be *married*."27

But before Hood could leave the army to marry Buck, he needed a victory in Tennessee. To strengthen his position and protect his exposed left along the Hillsboro Pike, he ordered the construction of five small forts, or redoubts, each made of logs and earth and capable of holding about one hundred men and their artillery. He hoped these forts would prevent an envelopment of his short line. By using interior lines, Hood rationalized, he could easily shift troops after he drew Thomas out of his fortifications. But when the thermometer fell and the men burned all the trees within walking distance of the camps, Hood had to pull Lee and Stewart back so their units could find firewood. The Rebels settled into new earthworks, anchored on the first redoubt just east of the Hillsboro Pike, on the tenth. As he shifted troops to his right for the Federal move he anticipated toward Murfreesboro, Hood watched Thomas's reaction, and over the next few days, as the temperature first moderated then rose, Hood became convinced that everything would work as he hoped.

As the snow finally began to melt, Thomas prepared to move. He had little choice: he either had to go forward or expect a dressing-down from Grant. He must have heard the rumors that Grant intended to remove him from command. The increasingly agitated tone of the telegrams from his superiors left no doubt that he had delayed longer than anyone back east thought reasonable. Thomas had run out of excuses. Refitting the horsemen had been important, for his main concern was that his cavalry could not compete with Forrest's. As he made his plans to attack, Thomas did not know that most of Forrest's troopers were miles away at Murfreesboro, where Hood had sent them to capture the garrison. Hood, however, could not know that by strengthening his hand at Murfreesboro and weakening his position in the west he had made a major error.

Certainly Hood's most egregious miscalculation was his failure to take advantage of Forrest's talents. Not only did he not employ Forrest usefully, he actually took him out of the action when he ordered him to Murfreesboro. Hood's belief that taking Murfreesboro would draw Thomas out had prompted him to send Forrest off with two divisions, those of Jackson and Buford, leaving fewer than three hundred horsemen to patrol the open ground between the Rebels and the river in the west. Moreover, Hood continually amended his instructions to his cavalry commander, making it impossible for Forrest to operate independently, thus drastically reducing his effectiveness.

While Hood and Thomas jockeyed for position, the common soldiers waited in the trenches. Except for the hardships imposed by the weather and the building of fortifications, there was little activity on either side during the first two weeks of December, and enterprising or curious Confederates often ventured beyond the lines. Robert C. Carden, who had turned twenty-one years old on the fourth of July, described fraternizing with the enemy in the area between the lines. He claimed that when he decided to see the home of former Governor Aaron Brown after the Confederates had retreated beyond it, he found "a big Missouri Yankee" guard. "I had my gun with me and his gun was standing against the stairs," he recalled. But the Missourian did not go for his weapon, instead pointing out that it was a rule of war "not to molest a guard under such circumstances. I told him I understood the rule and I staid there quite a while talking to the ladies and the soldier too." Carden chatted with Mrs. Brown and one of her daughters before taking his leave, but he "had not gone twenty steps" before he spotted "a lot of Yankees around a fire, presumably cooking." When they did not see him, Carden retreated silently, "and if ever a Johnnie Reb moved, I did." In his indignation, he added: "That Missouri Yankee might have told me it was not safe to go very far out that way. Mrs. Brown being a good southern woman might have given me the wink and nodded her head back south and I think I would have taken the hint, but she did not."[28]

Such incongruous incidents amid the inhumanities of war did not mask the seriousness of the situation. On December 14, while Thomas was making final preparations for his advance, Grant's frustration at his subordinate's repeated excuses reached a fever pitch. Leaving City Point, the general in chief headed for Washington to meet with Lincoln, Stanton, and Halleck. If Thomas did not move the army, Grant would do the job himself. It is unclear exactly what Grant knew about Thomas's current situation, and accounts vary. What is known is that Grant never made the trip to Nashville, for he learned of Thomas's advance before such drastic action became necessary.[29]

Grant had reached Washington on December 15, the same day Thomas finally moved out of his fortifications. The Virginian had a simple plan: he would open with a diversion on the Confederate right, while the main assault would come on Hood's left. Thomas hoped to use a turning movement to roll up the Confederate flank by taking the redoubts along the Hillsboro

Pike. He ordered troops down the Hardin Pike with instructions to face east
and attack after the feint shifted Hood's attention elsewhere. Thomas relied
on the crusty A. J. Smith to lead the assault on Hood's western position.

"Smith's guerrillas" were a new addition to Thomas's command. Having
come from the Trans-Mississippi, where they had most recently been chasing Sterling Price across Missouri, they had a distinct western air. "We have
been to Vicksburg, Red River, Missouri, and about everywhere down
South and out West," boasted one of Smith's men, "and now we are going to
Hell, if old A. J. orders us!" Andrew Jackson Smith, aged nearly fifty, carried the name of the renowned Indian fighter and, like Jackson, was quick to
action and easy to rile. (He had wanted to arrest the incompetent political
general Nathaniel P. Banks after he heard the army planned to retreat following the battle of Pleasant Hill in April 1864 but was dissuaded when told
that to do so would be mutiny.) As a dragoon in the Old Army he also had
experience fighting Indians on the frontier. A native of Pennsylvania and
and 1838 graduate of West Point, he was described by one officer at Nashville as "a grizzled old veteran but a soldier all through."[30]

Smith had earned a well-deserved reputation in the Civil War by hard
fighting. He took part in the Vicksburg campaign in 1863 and the Red River
campaign in the spring of 1864, but his fame rested on a victorious battle at
Tupelo in July 1864, where he had routed Forrest. A Northern account
bragged that he "had defeated Forrest as he had never been defeated before." Although Smith never repeated this feat, his reputation as a fighter
could not be denied. He was one of the most competent army commanders
in the Union army, a no-nonsense soldier. A Louisiana Rebel had claimed
that when Federal soldiers set fire to Alexandria earlier in 1864, Smith had
ridden through the streets exclaiming "Hurrah, boys, this looks like war!"
His arrival at Nashville, with the detachment from the Army of the Tennessee, could not have been more welcome. Thomas knew he now had the advantage. Smith's long-awaited arrival at Nashville on November 30 was an
event of celebration. "Thomas (undemonstrative as he was) literally took
Smith in his arms and hugged him; for he now felt absolutely sure of coping
with Hood, and defeating him duly," disclosed Col. James F. Rusling.[31]

To distract Hood, Thomas ordered General Steedman to lead a diversionary attack on the Rebel right. Two years younger than Smith, Steedman
was also a Pennsylvania native. Although he was not a West Point graduate
and had, in fact, no formal education, he could claim a variety of practical
experiences. As a young man, he had fought in the Mexican War before becoming a politician in Ohio. In 1849, he had rushed off to pan for gold in Cal-

ifornia. At the outbreak of the war, he was back in Ohio as editor of a Democratic newspaper. In spite of his civilian background and his Democratic connections, he had risen steadily through the ranks and at Chickamauga in September 1863 had joined Thomas in holding his position. Steedman, who insisted that reporters spell his name right (not Steadman), commanded attention; he was a large man with a pugnacious personality. He was also a notorious womanizer whose exploits enlivened camp gossip. As a political general, Steedman was not always popular among the officers, but he captured the respect of the common soldier with his acts of bravery. Yet even the average soldier raised an eyebrow when Steedman arrived from Chattanooga, for many of the men he brought with him were black.

The formation of a provisional division under Steedman set tongues wagging. Besides having three brigades composed of a variety of white units made up of men who had been unable to rejoin their commands serving with Sherman (including a brigade under future president Benjamin Harrison), he had two brigades of African Americans. The First Colored brigade, under Col. Thomas J. Morgan, included the Fourteenth, Sixteenth, Seventeenth, Eighteenth, and Forty-fourth U.S. Colored Troops. The Second Colored brigade, commanded by Col. Charles R. Thompson, was made up of the Twelfth, Thirteenth, and 100th U.S. Colored Troops and a light battery. Even Steedman, who had supported Stephen Douglas's Democratic Party in the 1860 presidential election, admitted, "I wonder what my Democratic friends . . . would think of me if they knew I was fighting . . . with 'nigger' troops?"[32]

Like Sherman, Thomas had reservations about the value of black troops, but Sherman could prevent having black units serve with his armies, Thomas had no choice. In his attempt to pull together an army out of the remnants left by Sherman, he had to take every available man he could find, and that included black troops. Like Sherman, he did not believe that blacks would make good soldiers and had preferred to use them in more traditional roles. Thomas had little use for officers who persisted in their attempt to have blacks assigned to combat units. Colonel Morgan, whom Thomas placed in that category, remarked that when he had told the Virginian that his black soldiers would fight just as well as any whites, the commanding general answered curtly that he "thought not."[33]

In truth, most of the black units had no combat experience. The Twelfth and Thirteenth USCT, composed of contrabands, had just come from west Tennessee, where they had been guarding the railroads. An officer in the Twelfth commented: "From slavery to freedom was itself a grand transition; but to become Union soldiers was a still bigger promotion, exceeding their most sanguine hopes—a privilege estimated at its full value." A man in the Thirteenth USCT noted that the troops were "the bravest set of men on the Western Continent. They think nothing of routing the guerrillas, that roam at large in the wilds of Tennessee."[34]

Some of the black soldiers had old scores to settle. The men of the Forty-fourth USCT had come a long way in hopes of avenging their comrades captured at Dalton. Their commander Lewis Johnson, who also remembered his humiliating surrender in north Georgia, had endured a harrowing trip to get his men to Nashville. The soldiers had boarded one of the last cars to head down the tracks before Forrest cut the line. They also survived a train derailment and had narrowly escaped capture when Forrest disabled the locomotive pulling the boxcars on December 2. Forrest's success forced more than two hundred of the Forty-fourth and eighty from the Fourteenth USCT to run for the safety of a nearby blockhouse. In the skirmish that followed, Johnson ran low on ammunition and, after losing one-third of his men, "resolved to abandon the stockade" and fight his way to Nashville. He was well aware of Forrest's reputation, and he could not forget the threats that the Confederates had aimed at his men at Dalton. "I knew that should the place be surrendered or taken by assault a butchery would follow," he concluded. After leaving the stockade at 3:30 A.M., Johnson and his command silently passed through the Confederate line. His black troops, Johnson noted, had "determined to die rather than be taken prisoners."[35]

The coming battle would try the mettle of the African American troops, and there was a wide range of opinion over whether they could meet the test. Men like Colonel Morgan were convinced they could. When organizing the Fourteenth USCT in late 1863, he had interviewed each prospective soldier personally. "When I told . . . one who wanted to 'fight for freedom,' that he might lose his life," Morgan reflected, the man replied "'but my people will be free.'"[36]

Not all the officers leading black units felt this confident. Capt. Job Aldrich served under his brother-in-law Col. William R. Shafter in the Seventeenth USCT, a regiment assigned to the post at Nashville. As rumors spread through the camps that Thomas intended to attack Hood, Aldrich had become convinced he would die. He entrusted his money and personal items to Shafter's wife, who was visiting Nashville, then wrote his own wife a letter: "The clock strikes one, good night. At five the dance of death begins around Nashville. Who shall be partners in the dance? God only knows. Echo alone answers who? Farewell."[37]

CHAPTER NINE

Hood and Thomas

Thomas held firm to his decision not to move until the weather improved, and it was late in the afternoon on the thirteenth before nature finally cooperated. The wind shifted, and milder breezes from the southeast made the evening feel quite warm. As a result, the ice rapidly melted. By nine o'clock, Thomas felt cautiously confident and informed Halleck that he was ready "to assume the offensive" if the weather obliged. To his chagrin, when he arose the next morning, he discovered that one problem had been replaced by another. The roads were sodden from the melting snow and ice, causing wagons to founder and become bogged down. Gluelike sludge adhered to the soldiers' boots, and a Michigan cavalryman complained that the streets in Nashville had become "a vast sea of mud."[1]

Yet Thomas knew he was at the end of his tether and dangerously close to being removed. Just days before he had humbly informed Grant, "If you should deem it necessary to relieve me I shall submit without a murmur." So throughout the day on the fourteenth, he had his men wading through the mire preparing for battle. He seemed more enthusiastic than he had been for several days; he even hoped that the thaw would prove beneficial. A rise in the river, closed because of low water, might allow the gunboats to navigate as far as Nashville. His confidence renewed, he replied to Halleck's most recent warning by promising, "The ice having melted away to-day, the enemy will be attacked to-morrow morning."[2]

Circumstances beyond Thomas's control frustrated his plans. When the soldiers rose at four on the fifteenth, thick fog covered the landscape. Since Wilson's troopers were to play a major part in his strategy, he decided to delay until visibility improved. He intended to use Smith's three divisions to hit Stewart's corps, but the cavalry had to protect Smith's exposed flank and needed sound footing. Thomas planned for the cavalry to shield Smith's right, while Wood's corps would protect Smith's left. Schofield was held in reserve to man the trenches left empty by Wood. Although unhappy with his assignment, Schofield could not persuade Thomas to change his instructions. As the morning progressed and the murky gray persisted, confusion inevitably resulted as units tried to move into position.

The organization required for a battle, shifting and arranging thousands of men, was in itself an enormous task. Even if the weather cooperated, nature still conspired against commanders; there was always a hedge, a grove of trees, or a ditch to cross. The mud magnified every obstacle a hundredfold, and each impediment disrupted the columns of moving men. So when the sun finally broke through on the morning of December 15, anxious and tense Federal soldiers worried that the long delay had cost them the advantage.

Thomas had placed his trust in James Steedman, whom he knew would follow his instructions implicitly. Steedman's provisional division was to initiate the diversionary attack intended to mislead the Rebels into believing that Cheatham's corps, on the west, would bear the brunt of the assault. Steedman explained to Colonel Morgan, who would lead the advance, that this "was to be a feint, intended to betray Hood into the belief that it was the real attack, and lead him to support his right by weakening his left, where Thomas intended to assault him." After Morgan surveyed the enemy position, he concluded that his men simply needed to silence some Rebel rifle pits.[3]

This was the opportunity that many African American soldiers had eagerly anticipated. The skirmish line consisted of the Fourteenth USCT, followed by the Seventeenth USCT under Shafter, and then the Forty-fourth USCT under Johnson. Because of the dense fog, the order to advance, scheduled for dawn, did not come until 8:00 A.M.

The Confederates, watching the preparation across the lines, had laid a trap. Shafter had no trouble pushing back the Rebels until he reached the railroad where the tracks of the Nashville & Chattanooga line ran through a manmade ravine about twenty feet long. He could not advance; he had to move either right or left down the tracks. Unfortunately for Shafter, he had encountered soldiers from Cleburne's old division. The Texans of Granbury's brigade, in a concealed lunette, had patiently watched the stream of blue approaching. The Confederates manned four cannons behind a parapet with heavy headlogs on top and a ditch in front. The defenders knew that every shot had to count, and they had waited patiently until the Federal troops reached the railroad cut before disclosing their position. A battery suddenly unmasked and opened at close range on the clusters of oncoming soldiers. The blacks, startled and frightened by the flash and roar of the cannon, raced for the safety of the ravine. Panic became chaos. Daniel Govan, an old Arkansas friend of Pat Cleburne's, quickly anchored his infantry at one end of the ravine and fired on the frightened mass.[4]

In a matter of minutes, two of Shafter's regiments disintegrated. "It was an awful battle," he divulged to his sister. Several officers and scores of soldiers died at the hands of Confederates. Shafter also had to inform his sister that her husband, Job Aldrich, a captain in the Seventeenth USCT, was among the dead. She already knew from his last letter that her husband expected to die. When Shafter found his brother-in-law's corpse the next morning, the body had been stripped. There was nothing left, he told the new widow; "all his clothes—everything" was gone.[5]

The reaction of the Rebels to the black troops and their white officers was predictable. Two days before the battle, Texan Samuel Foster had entered in his diary: "The Yanks have been fighting our picket line with negroes, for nearly a week, and we have killed several so close that they can't get them. So they remain where they fell froze as hard as a log." Arkansan Philip Stephenson left a vivid account of the racial prejudice. "This was the first time that we of the Army of Tennessee had ever met our former slaves in battle," he announced. "It excited in our men the intensest indignation, but that indignation expressed itself in a way peculiarly ominous and yet quite natural for the 'masters.'" Stephenson, who recalled this incident with extraordinary clarity, wrote: "As soon as it was found out that the men advancing upon them were Negroes, a deliberate policy was adopted. It was to let them come almost to the works before a shot was to be fired, and then the whole line was to rise up and empty their guns into them." Indeed, the Rebels used this scheme with deadly effect. "On the darkies came, slowly and wavering enough for that silence was terribly significant," continued Stephenson. "On they came, closer and closer, until, as our men said afterward, they could see the whites of their eyes. *Then* up rose the line of grey and crash went that deadly volley of lead full into the poor fellows' faces. The carnage was awful. It is doubtful if a single bullet missed."[6]

Fear had seized the black soldiers, and, afraid of capture, they ran in every direction. Most of the casualties in the fighting that followed were among men of the Fourteenth USCT, who led the advance, while the Fortyfourth USCT fled the hailstorm of shot and shell up the Murfreesboro Pike. Regular Union regiments that had tried to take the Rebel lunette met with no more success than the men in the black regiments; they also were repulsed. In fact, some of the white troops "behaved in the most cowardly and disgraceful manner," reported their commander. As a result, the assault on the east of the Confederate line sputtered and ended in failure. Around noon, Steedman reformed his scattered units, but the fighting shifted to long-range exchanges among sharpshooters.[7]

The Confederates did not know it, but some of the blacks in the advance belonged to the same regiment that had barely escaped the wrath of Texas soldiers at Dalton. Stephenson added: "Before Granburys Texans it was particularly sickening. Of course they made no fight. The survivors fled as fast [as] they could go. The whites behind them tried to rally them to another charge, but it was of no use." Stephenson claimed that the Rebels saw white officers with bayonets fixed, forcing the soldiers forward, but this apparently was hearsay and not an event he witnessed firsthand.[8]

Civilians also participated in the developing drama. When the battle began, the residents of Nashville, many of whom were Confederate sympathizers, came out to the city's edge "in droves." On the hills behind the Federal lines, silent townspeople watched. "No army on the continent ever played on any field to so large and so sullen an audience," mumbled an Illinois colonel. Even after the fighting settled into scattered exchanges along the Nolensville Pike, a Rebel artilleryman observed in astonishment as two women appeared between the lines. "Bareheaded they were," he recalled, "without wraps, without luggage or anything in their hands. They were walking along in the open, making their way to our lines, heading for the works just to our battery's left. . . . No sign of fear did they show, although their calmness was that which belongs to that supreme moment of helplessness in peril. . . . I think the women escaped injury, but I do not know." Capt. James Dinkins, in command of the escort company for General Chalmers, recalled seeing Selene Harding "standing on the stone arm of the front steps waving her handkerchief. The bullets were falling thick and fast about her, but she had no fear in her heart. She looked like a goddess. She was the gamest little human being in all the crowd. As I rode past I caught the handkerchief and urged her to go into the house, but she would not, until the boys had disappeared behind the barn."[9]

Still, the battle raged. By the time Thomas learned that the attack on Hood's right had stalled, he was already frustrated with his main assault on the Confederate left. The cavalry had waited for the order to advance, but when the troopers finally moved they accomplished little. Thomas knew that the real fighting could not begin until Smith had his soldiers in position to the west of Hood's line. It was half past noon before Wood directed his 13,500 men forward. But when they hit the Confederate breastworks, the astonished Federals discovered them abandoned except for skirmishers. To his chagrin, Thomas soon found that by the time he arrived the enemy had already withdrawn; the Rebels having pulled back in search of firewood five days earlier. So, at 2:00 P.M. on a short winter day, Thomas realized that he was still almost a mile from the actual Rebel line.

To the west, where Smith was to lead the main attack, one delay followed another, and it was 2:00 P.M. before Union troopers made contact with Rebel fortifications at Redoubt No. 5. Defended by only one hundred men, it quickly fell, leaving Redoubt No. 4 an exposed position to the Federals if they could move swiftly. But the Rebel gunners in No. 4 quickly turned their guns and fired on the Federals in No. 5. A Union soldier wrote, "To remain in our captured fort was certain death . . . to retreat promised little better, while to attempt the capture of this second fort seemed madness." Sensing disaster, General Hatch wasted no time in ordering the soldiers, both infantry and cavalry, to charge. As the men raced for No. 4, a steady fire from Spencer repeating rifles prevented the Confederates, who were frantically loading and reloading their cannon, from taking careful aim. When blue-clad soldiers reached the earthwork, the fighting became hand-to-hand, and, after realizing that resistance was futile, the remaining Rebels in Redoubt No. 4 fled. Their guns were turned, and within minutes they were firing into the confused, wavering—and now retreating—Rebel line. Hatch captured about 150 prisoners and six guns in the two redoubts.[10]

Until the redoubts fell, the battle developed just as Hood anticipated. Thomas, he thought, would hit an entrenched position just as the Confederates had at Franklin. Of course, Hood's plan would work only if Stewart held his position and he took advantage of his interior lines to move reinforcements quickly from one part of the battlefield to another. That became the problem, for no one seemed to move quickly. The reinforcements that Hood ordered to Stewart did not arrive before the two redoubts fell, and when they did appear, Federal fire pushed them back. Stewart was in real trouble, with Union soldiers pressing in on his north and west and now coming up from the south. Hood sent men from Cheatham's corps on the extreme right to support Stewart. Before help materialized, Redoubt No. 3, the last on the west side of the Hillsboro Pike, capitulated.

The Confederate line collapsed when the remaining two redoubts, Nos. 1 and 2, fell, and Union soldiers wheeled Rebel guns around to fire on the escaping defenders. Men fled south and east in the direction of the Granny

White Pike. Even the inspirational sight of Mary Bradford, who ran out of her house on the east side of the road under heavy fire, could not stay the retreat. The young woman "did all she could to induce the men to stop and fight, appealing to them and begging them," W. D. Gale told his wife, but all her entreaties were "in vain." Her action prompted Hood to say "he intended to mention her courageous conduct in his report, which," noted Gale, "will immortalize her." Indeed, Mary Bradford does appear in Hood's postwar account. Hood narrated the way she darted among the men, "regardless of the storm of bullets, and, in the name of God and of our country, implored them to re-form and face the enemy. Her name deserves to be enrolled among the heroes of the war, and it is with pride that I bear testimony to her bravery and patriotism." To the soldiers in the Army of Tennessee who read these words long after the war, it was a barbed reminder that while they had fled, a Southern woman had not. Moreover, what Mary Bradford could not do, neither could the reinforcements from Cheatham. Men continued to race south. As Hood and his staff rode up to watch the disaster, he called out to a brigade of Texas infantry who were positioned on high ground near the pike. "Texans, I want you to hold this hill regardless of what transpires around you," he exclaimed. "We will do it, General," came the reply. Texan J. J. Tunnell bragged, "Night closed the conflict with our line unmoved."[11]

As darkness enveloped the battlefield, Hood pondered what had gone wrong. He had been sure that Thomas would attack Cheatham's position, so sure that he had reinforced that sector, weakening Stewart to the west. Hood had counted on the men in the five redoubts to hold. But victories came from rigid training and iron discipline as well as faultless communications. Subordinate commanders always knew what was expected of them, and any weakness in their own line was quickly covered; any weakness in the enemy's ranks was rapidly exploited. In theory, at least, this was what a commander hoped he could do better than his opponent. For Hood, this had not happened as the Union assault unfolded, for the Army of Tennessee had displayed neither iron discipline nor faultless communications. Now Hood had to gather the pieces and reform for the next day's battle.

Hood's situation was critical. Many commanders might have considered it desperate, but he had closed his mind to suggestions of retreat. That night as he looked at the thousands of campfires of the huge Federal army sparkling in the low-lying hills, he knew that in the morning Thomas would undoubtedly attack. There is little in Hood's account of the battle to explain his state of mind that night. The disaster on the left of the line had destroyed any chance for him to be the aggressor, but as he made his plans, he believed that he must stay and fight. Hood had to stake all on the slim chance of victory. Renewing the battle was not widely supported, and men looking for omens found many in the day's events. W. D. Gale, assistant adjutant general of Stewart's corps, wrote his wife (the daughter of the dead Leonidas Polk): "The men seem utterly lethargic and without interest in the battle. I never witnessed such lack of enthusiasm, and began to fear for tomorrow, hoping that General Hood would retreat during the night . . . but he would not give it up."[12]

Hood had to be ready at first light, and, as he repositioned his troops, he needed to believe that his army could repulse an attack. During the night, the weary Confederates, hungry, muddy, and cold, prepared new entrenchments, with a front around two and a half miles long, on the Brentwood Hills. Many Rebels did not settle into their new position until the early morning, and they hurried to strengthen the line until 7:00 A.M., when Federal batteries opened, making it dangerous to continue. Stephen D. Lee held the right of the line, anchored on Overton Hill (known locally as Peach Orchard Hill). Stewart's tired troops manned the center, while Cheatham's men took a position on Hood's extreme left, joining Ector's brigade on the hill that the Texans had held at the close of the previous day's fighting. Since the Confederate line curved back to create an angle at each end (a refused flank), the distance they defended was over three miles. With only about fifteen thousand effective troops and eighty pieces of artillery, Hood manned a weak line. On the left, Cheatham had thirty-four pieces of artillery, on the right Lee had twenty-eight guns, while in the center Stewart counted only eighteen. Moreover, the men of the Army of Tennessee had little rest for they had spent almost every minute preparing for the coming day. They were too tired, both mentally and physically, for the coming battle.

"Thursday night in Nashville was an anxious one," wrote a reporter for the *New York Herald*. "Troops were moving through the city, officers and orderlies riding to and fro, and eager groups crowded the hotels and saloons, discussing the events of the day." Officers returning to town "grasp one another's hands in mute congratulation." Unionists were "wild with exultation," while Rebel sympathizers, "whose lips swear loyalty while their hearts hatch treason—grow faint hearted."[13]

Thomas savored his success, and soon after the fighting subsided, he hurried to telegraph the appropriate message to his anxious superiors back east. At the same time, he wired his wife at the New York Hotel. "We have whipped the enemy," he told his beloved Frances, and have "taken many

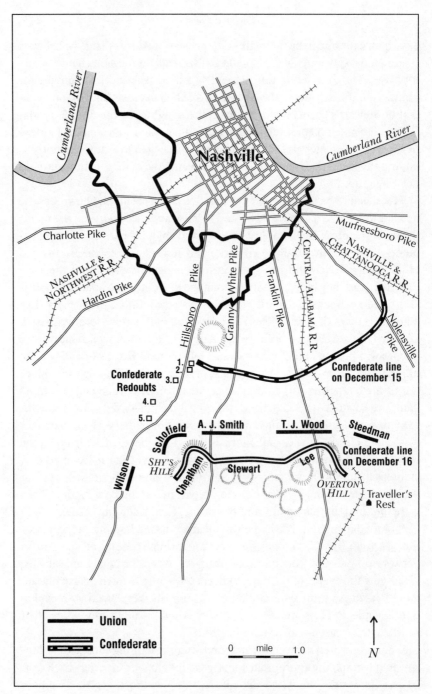

8. Nashville, the second day

prisoners and considerable artillery." His official communication with Halleck, however, presented a reserved statement of fact. It hit the wires at 9:00
P.M., but it was almost two and a half hours before the telegram reached its
destination. It took only thirty minutes for the War Department to respond
with praise for Thomas's "brilliant achievements" and promise that he and
his army would receive a one-hundred-gun salute in the morning. Even
Grant had to compliment Thomas. "I was just on my way to Nashville," he
told the Virginian, but learning of "your splendid success of to-day, I shall
go no farther. Push the enemy now," he cautioned, "and give him no rest
until he is entirely destroyed. Your army will cheerfully suffer many privations to break up Hood's army and render it useless for future operations."
In an effort to keep the methodical Thomas moving, Grant closed: "Do not
stop for trains or supplies, but take them from the country, as the enemy
have done. Much is now expected."[14]

Even Lincoln sent a warning that left no doubt that Thomas was not out
of the woods yet. "Please accept for yourself, officers, and men the nation's
thanks for your good work of yesterday," Lincoln told Thomas on December 16. "You made a magnificent beginning," he emphasized, but "a grand
consummation is within your easy reach. Do not let it slip."[15]

So as the following morning dawned warm and foggy, Thomas prepared
for the climactic finale. If all went well, he could defeat the Rebel army and
humble Hood in a great open-field battle. He planned a decisive, major action, even if it entailed some risk. He intended to outflank and turn the Confederate left, which curved back in an angle near the Granny White Pike.
He had Schofield on the extreme western end of the Federal line at the point
of the angle, with Smith to his left astride the pike. On the eastern side of the
line, Steedman held the far left, with Wood to his right covering the angle at
that end of the Rebel line. At 8:00 A.M. Thomas sent the gritty A. J. Smith
toward a steep hill on the Confederate left, but in less than an hour, Smith's
western troops stalled in the face of strong Rebel entrenchments. At the
same time, Schofield, cautious after Franklin, was not going anywhere until
he knew Hood's intentions, and the Federal cavalry, also on the Federal
right, made little headway. The morning mist turned to rain, and by noon it
was coming down hard. As it grew colder, a new storm gathered in the darkened sky, and Federal soldiers, anxious for the order to advance, felt the
temperature drop. "With our oil cloths wrapped about our shoulders we sat
in our trenches," stated a wet and miserable Union soldier, "waiting and
watching."[16]

Although Thomas wanted the main attack to come in the west, Wood thought he saw an opportunity to turn the Confederate flank in the east by hitting Overton Hill. Steedman, on his left, agreed, and the two men, both anxious for glory, ordered an assault around three o'clock. The men selected were from the 100th and Twelfth USCT, followed by the Thirteenth USCT. Lt. Col. Charles H. Grosvenor's provisional brigade of white infantry, with a small regiment of black troops, would provide support. The soldiers recognized the peril of the undertaking, for the assault, toward a strongly fortified position, would be over a plowed field, and the syrupy mud would check their forward progress. So as the soldiers silently prepared to charge, some of them asked their officers to hold their money or valuables. "This and little talk among themselves showed a settled resolution, to unflinchingly face death in the cause of freedom and nationality," commented Capt. D. E. Straight of the 100th USCT.[17]

"On they came in splendid order," a Rebel artilleryman on Overton Hill recalled. Their banners waved as the officers, with swords drawn, rode up and down in front of the lines. When the defenders opened on them, they were so close together that "every shot from Rebel muskets and cannon was telling with fearful effect," lamented Capt. Henry V. Freeman of the Twelfth USCT. When the first two regiments faltered, the men in Thirteenth struggled on; this was their first time under fire. "There were very few negroes who retreated in our front," declared an Alabamian, "and none were at their post when the firing ceased; for we fired as long as there was anything to shoot at."[18]

As the battle intensified, Hood ordered reinforcements from Cleburne's old division, Granbury's and Lowrey's men, to support Lee. Many soldiers rushed headlong into the fire of the Texans, who had taken a heavy toll on the black units just the day before. The slaughter was appalling, and Brig. Gen. James T. Holtzclaw, leading Alabama troops, watched the black soldiers being mowed down by Rebel fire. They continued forward, but, he observed, "they came only to die. I have seen most of the battle-fields of the West, but never saw dead men thicker than in front of my two right regiments." Holtzclaw had trouble preventing his men from following up the slaughter with a pursuit, but the Rebels finally settled for capturing a few regimental flags. One had inscribed upon it "Thirteenth Regiment U.S. Colored Infantry, Presented by the colored ladies of Murfreesboro." A Union surgeon who treated the wounded told his family: "Don't tell me negroes won't fight! I know better." The Thirteenth USCT suffered 220 casualties in its first battle, nearly 40 percent of the regiment's strength. Thomas had not expected the loss on that part of the line to be high, for he had planned to launch the main attack in the west. The fighting on Overton Hill, however, proved costly, exacting around one-third of the total casualties for the entire two-day battle.[19]

When the fighting finally erupted in the west, the Federal objective became a steep outcropping, known among locals as Compton's Hill, and manned by Bate's division of Cheatham's corps. Unfortunately for the defenders, Hood had previously weakened the position by sending some of the men to reinforce other units. He believed that their location, at the crest of a precipitous slope, was safe, and had stretched his defenders thin. He soon realized his mistake. Brig. Gen. John McArthur, a pugnacious Scot who commanded a division under Smith, detected a weakness in the placement of Rebel artillery. In practical terms that meant that the cannon, sitting on the crown of the hill instead of the military crest, could not be brought to bear along the entire slope. Bate, who moved into breastworks constructed the night before, realized this too. By this time it was too late to remedy the mistake, and there was no chance for reinforcements. Bate had no choice but to stay and fight, and about 4:00 P.M. McArthur ordered an assault.

The contest for the hill produced some of the most vicious hand-to-hand combat of the entire war. As McArthur's troops charged up the incline, it became a corner of hell. Infantrymen struggled to keep their formations and follow commands to load and fire, while around them writhed the shattered bodies of comrades. Men stumbled and fell, but because of its placement, the artillery did little significant damage, and when the Rebels recognized what was happening, they panicked. Lt. Col. William M. Shy of the Twentieth Tennessee, who died in the fray, would be immortalized when this hill was named for him after the war. Through the smoke and roaring and flashing of cannon, Hood's western anchor dissolved. With enemy infantry assaulting the front and flank of the hill and Wilson's cavalry closing on the rear, a Rebel private remarked, "Yankee bullets and shells were coming from all directions, passing one another in the air." Hood's mistake, obvious to all, was that the main cavalry, under Forrest, was still absent at Murfreesboro and could not deal with Wilson. When the carnage ended, Col. William McMillan reported the capture of Brig. Gen. Thomas B. Smith, along with more than fifteen hundred enlisted men, eighty-four field, staff, and line officers, four battle flags, and eight cannon and caissons.[20]

Confusion spread through the Rebel ranks, turning quickly to panic. This was not the disciplined Rebel army that had fought at Franklin only two weeks before. Instead, it was "like a flock of wild geese when they have lost their leader," declared one soldier. The mass of fleeing Rebels grew to huge proportions, and soon a dense herd of terrified soldiers, artillerymen, and wagoners stampeded to escape. Retreating was no easy matter, for each step added "two or three pounds of stiff mud." When a soldier in the Fifth Minnesota discovered he had captured Brig. Gen. Henry R. Jackson, a Yale-educated Georgian who had stopped to pull off his heavy boots, he yelled: "Captured a general, by God. I will carry you to Nashville myself."[21]

The Army of Tennessee was reduced to a confused, fleeing rabble. Edwin H. Rennolds of the Fifth Tennessee recalled that as the line broke, the men "streamed across the fields, intent only on making sure that they would not spend the winter in a Federal prison." Mounting the breastworks, Rennolds warned his captain, B. F. Peeples, "If you ever expect to get out of here, it is time you were going." As the line disintegrated, Rennolds marveled: "Now began a race for liberty between the enclosing wings of the Federals. The ground was just thawing out of a smart freeze, and the sticky mud which, with the crabgrass, adhered to our shoes and soon loaded us as with weights, and fast progress was impossible, and so ever and anon we had to stop and kick off these impediments." Although some of the "bolder Confederates" paused to fire, the army, now a mob, continued south. Col. W. D. Gale remembered that his saddle turned, forcing him to dismount as his horse tried to climb the steep, muddy hills with the bullets coming "thick and fast." As Federal soldiers neared, Gale twisted his hands into his horse's mane, whipped his mount forward, "and was borne to the top of the hill by the noble animal, more dead than alive."[22]

Words could not adequately portray the chaos. "Such a scene I never saw," Tennessean Sam Watkins declared. The entire army was routed: horses and men, wagons, cannon, and artillery all blended together in tangled confusion. Weakened mules and horses refused to pull their load, and, as wagons clogged the roads, they were abandoned. Bewilderment took hold of the men as they rushed to the rear, few heeding the cries of wounded comrades, begging not to be left behind. "Ah, that was a picture!" Watkins pronounced, "It is difficult to assess whether it bears harder on Hood for allowing us to get in such a fix or on Thomas for allowing a single man of us to escape!"[23]

Hood watched in shock. An artilleryman who saw him noted wryly, "He seemed overwhelmed by his defeat and sat on his horse, a picture of despair—his head sunk on his breast, reins dangling loosely, an oil cloth blanket draping him, the fierce rain storming on and around him, his drooping horse moving slowly along. If any one looked 'whipped' that day, our unfortunate leader certainly did." Two of his division commanders were with him, and they seemed to be directing the army. "It may be that Hood was still giving orders," the soldier concluded, "but he didn't look it. . . . His dejection was conspicuous, even exceptional." Yet another soldier claimed that the Texan tried "to rally the men, but in vain." Nonetheless, one angry Confederate later wrote: "We knew we could get no help from him. He made no attempt to rally the men who were in a mob all around him, to halt them, regulate their march, or anything! Disgusted he may have been, but that was no time for a Commander-in-Chief to be overcome by disgust."[24]

Local spectators, out for a second day to watch the fighting, were also stunned. Since the Confederates had fallen back during the night, the audience from the city was not as large. Still, some civilians hoped that Hood might reappear, and they gathered along the plateau between the Granny White and Franklin Pikes. "Here the city is shut out from your view by the hills," wrote a Northern reporter, and the dark forms of citizens gathered to follow the battle, or at least hear its roar. Back in Nashville, anxious Tennesseans crowded the cupola of the capitol building. Just before the last charge, a group of Sisters of Charity appeared along the Union line. Each woman carried a decanter of wine among the wounded, lifting bloody heads off the wet ground to offer succor to dying men.[25]

The news of the Confederate disaster quickly spread. A wounded Texan wrote from Franklin on the sixteenth: "The report is that our Army has been defeated, and are in full retreat. . . . It appears this morning that there has been a fight of some sort." Another Texan scribbled from his cell at Camp Douglas: "Saturday december the 17th. The yankey received some good new's and fired 30 shotts out of the cannon." On that same day, the *New York Herald* proudly announced, "General Thomas has achieved a magnificent victory over the Rebel army under General Hood, in front of Nashville."[26]

Who was to blame for the Confederate defeat? Hood later asserted that the campaign failed because of the "unfortunate affair" at Spring Hill, the shortness of the day at Franklin, and Edmund Kirby Smith's refusal to send reinforcements from the Trans-Mississippi. A reporter for the *Herald* had a different explanation: "It was thought that Hood's severe repulse on yesterday, had so crippled him that he would not dare to renew the conflict today, and thus risk a signal defeat and repulse of his army." More to the point and perhaps more accurate: "Hood is remarkable for his dogged pertinacity and perseverance. Men are mere machines in his hands. These are excellent military qualities in a wise general, whose plans are laid with prudence and foresight. With a general of Hood's unthinking impetuosity, they generally prove fatal." Hood may have failed, and certainly he should not have expected his demoralized army to fight a second day, but the command structure in the Army of Tennessee, never strong and weakened by Franklin, failed too.[27]

Perhaps the greatest irony of the battle came as the Rebels fled. An Arkansas Confederate turned to look at his pursuers in blue. At one point they were close enough for him to see their faces clearly, and "oh woeful humiliation," he wrote. "The faces of Negroes! Pushed on by white soldiers in their rear, but *there*, nevertheless in the front rank of those our men were running from. . . . Such was the battle of Nashville."[28]

While Hood's bewildered soldiers headed toward Franklin, some acts of heroism occurred. Brig. Gen. Daniel H. Reynolds's Arkansans and Ector's brigade under Col. David Coleman, primarily dismounted Texans, held a road open for Cheatham's men to escape, and General Stephen Lee rallied his troops to halt the Federal pursuit east of the pike. General Chalmers's cavalry also fought with determination, although Col. Ed Rucker was captured.

"General Thomas has defeated Hood near Nashville," Halleck announced on December 18, "and it is hoped that he will completely crush his army." Sherman, of course, could not contain his elation, and on Christmas Eve he told Halleck that he was very "gratified at the news from Thomas in Tennessee, because it fulfills my plan, which contemplated his being fully able to dispose of Hood in case he ventured north of the Tennessee River." Yet he knew he could not easily dismiss Hood's Rebel army and continued, "I am very anxious that Thomas should follow up his successes to the very uttermost point." He wanted Thomas to push Hood into Mississippi or Alabama, inflicting the same terror on the civilian population that Sherman had on Georgians. "I attach more importance to these deep incisions into the enemy's country, because this war differs from European wars in this particular. We are not only fighting hostile armies, but a hostile people, and must make old and young, rich and poor, feel the hard hand of war, as well as their organized armies." Although Thomas's next move remained in doubt, even Grant had to admit that Thomas had "done magnificently" once he finally started.[29]

For the Confederates, the interval between the battle and Christmas was a nightmare. As the army trudged south through intermittent rain and falling temperatures, men with tattered clothing suffered, and those without shoes covered their bare feet as best they could. Food was scarce, and as the precipitation froze, the ice covered the trees and made it impossible to build fires to dry clothing or warm cold bodies. Then came the snow, and a blustery north wind froze wet clothing. The intense cold was almost a blessing, however, for before the roads froze, the earth was a sea of mud that exhausted the animals as they tried to drag supply wagons and artillery through the mire. Weary horses and mules collapsed for lack of forage. Seeing the mass of beaten Rebels marching south, Hood, who tried to make the best of the situation, was moved to say, "Let us go out of Tennessee, singing hymns of praise." But before that could happen, he had to devise a plan to reach the safety of the other shore. Just getting out of Tennessee was not enough; he needed to put the river between his army and the pursuing Federals.[30]

On Christmas, as the first of Hood's soldiers arrived at the Tennessee River, the weather warmed, but when the snow and ice melted it became almost impossible to move wagons and artillery through muddy quagmires that had once been roads. Nonetheless, the men tried to celebrate as best they could. On Christmas Eve, a Rebel captain had noted, "Some of my men go out in the country and get some Whiskey, and we have a Jolly Christmas night." Rather than making him cheerful, the holidays had the opposite effect. As melancholy enveloped him, he told his diary: "This is Christmas 1864. Where were we last Christmas," or two years ago? "If we had counted noses then, and again today the missing would outnumber the present." In his despair, he added that Hood had "betrayed his whole Army." Still, "a wee drop" helped the soldiers forget. "Everyone seems to know that today is Christmas," he concluded, and they all wanted to make the best of it.[31]

Rebel horsemen had no time to celebrate, for they spent the holidays protecting the army's rear. Forrest rejoined Hood, but all he could do was cover the retreat. He had only about three thousand men, but he augmented their number with a hodgepodge of infantry under Edward Walthall, although nearly a quarter of the foot soldiers had no shoes. The two sides skirmished on Christmas Eve, and Forrest celebrated Christmas by routing Union cavalry near Pulaski. After suffering another defeat the next day, James Wilson decided to halt his pursuit. Forrest and Walthall protected Hood's withdrawal to the Tennessee, and the last Confederates finally arrived at the river on December 28.

The river crossing was the final trial. Fortunately for the Confederates, a Federal occupying force had abandoned fifteen pontoon boats at Decatur, Alabama, when they evacuated the town. Those boats, floated to Bainbridge, would make up for the ones Hood lost on the retreat. With torches lighting the dark waters, the Confederates spent Christmas night throwing together a makeshift bridge. The shaky structure, pushed into a crescent by the strong current, barely survived for three days. Hour by hour the weary soldiers walked in single file three paces apart. Artillery and supply wagons moved slowly and patiently with great care. Union gunboats harmlessly peppered the water with shells as the last of the Confederate army reached the southern bank. A civilian who watched the soldiers pass his home wrote in his diary that they were "the most broke down set I ever saw."[32]

Everything seemed to be going right for Thomas, although Lincoln wanted him to destroy Hood rather than let him escape. On the day after the battle, the president had wired Thomas his congratulations on a job well done but warned him not to let Hood slip away. Over the next few days, Thomas received telegrams from both Halleck and Stanton urging him to finish off Hood's army. On December 21, Halleck prodded Thomas, reminding him that a "vigorous pursuit" of Hood was important to Sherman's plans. By this time Thomas was certainly tired of hearing about Sherman's strategy, and he answered tersely that he was doing all he could to crush the Rebels, but following an army through an exhausted countryside that was nothing but mud was not "child's play." In responding to Halleck's message that he was not pushing the Rebels hard enough, Thomas retorted, "I can safely state that this army is willing to submit to any sacrifice to oust Hood's army, or to strike any other blow which would contribute to the destruction of the rebellion."[33]

Certainly the weather hampered movement. Thomas had snapped in his own defense that he could not control the elements, and the bitter cold was just as trying for the pursuers as the pursued. Union cavalryman James Wilson complained that while his men "suffered dreadfully," their mounts fared even worse. There was no grass, and jaded horses fell from hunger or foundered, crippled by hoof disease from the constantly wet weather. By the time his troopers reached the Tennessee River, Wilson estimated that only seven thousand animals were fit for service.[34]

In spite of complaints from Washington that Thomas was not moving fast enough, everyone had to agree on the political implications of his victory. Even Grant admitted that the Virginian had succeeded, and on Christmas Eve, Thomas received notification that Lincoln had approved his promotion to major general in the U.S. Army; Thomas would fill the only vacancy that existed at that level in the regular army. After Thomas read the dispatch from Stanton with the news, he turned to Surgeon George E. Cooper and asked, "What do you think of that?" When Cooper answered that it was "better late than never," Thomas retorted, "I suppose it is better late than never, but it is too late to be appreciated; I earned this at Chickamauga."[35]

The holidays seemed bright indeed for Union prospects in the west. As if to underscore the futility of the Confederacy's cause, Wilson, under a flag of truce, presented Hood with an official copy of a dispatch from Washington two days after Christmas. He did so, he smugly announced to Hood, so that the Texan could circulate the official news that Savannah had surrendered.[36]

Hood did not need Wilson to remind him that he had failed. Not only had he abandoned Tennessee in defeat, ceding the state to Union troops, but he had also sealed the fate of Georgia when he marched into Alabama in October. A Rebel officer later concluded of the failed campaign, "General Hood had been over-confident and too enthusiastic." Both politically and militarily Hood had turned out to be a disappointment to those who had counted on him to change the course of the war. That he could not have done so meant little to those Southerners who depended on him. While it might be unfair to blame Hood for not accomplishing something that perhaps no one could have done, it is appropriate to hold him accountable for the cost of his failure. While in Tennessee, he had lost touch with reality, so it was not until the army arrived in Mississippi that he could assess the human sacrifice of his ill-conceived campaign. Many soldiers had died in the five weeks Hood spent in Tennessee. The seriously wounded had been left behind, and a good number of Tennessee soldiers had deserted rather than retreat again. On December 27, army surgeon George W. Peddy told his wife that nothing was left but "a remnant of a demoralized army."[37]

The numbers seemed to substantiate Peddy's claim. When muster was taken on the last day of 1864, Hood counted 16,913 enlisted men and 1,795 officers present for duty, less than half the number he had on September 20, when he reported an effective total of 40,403. Hood probably inflated his true number; Beauregard did not think there were more than 15,000 when he arrived in the camps in mid-January. The exactness of Hood's count is inconsequential; because of leaves of absence it was impossible to assess accurately the army's strength. What was significant was that one of the Confederacy's two main armies no longer posed a significant threat. A soldier in Granbury's brigade attributed this destruction to the suicidal frontal assaults. "This thing what they call chargin brest works is not the thing it is cracked up to be," he wrote. "It is very unhealthy. It has ruined our brigade—out of nine regiment in [all] we have only about four hundred for duty. There is only about seventy-five men" in two Texas regiments. In Tennessee alone Hood had lost 13,189 men taken prisoners; more than 2,000 deserted to Federal lines, and the killed and wounded numbered about 8,600, a total of 23,789. In addition, Hood had gone into Tennessee with 124 guns; he came out with 59. On January 23, barely six months after he had replaced Johnston outside of Atlanta, Hood asked to be relieved. A Georgian, Maj. Gen. William H. T. Walker, who had died fighting one of Hood's battles, had prophetically written in the summer: "Hood has 'gone up like a rocket.' It is to be hoped . . . that he will not come down like the stick. He is brave, whether he has the capacity to command armies (for it requires a high order of talent) time will develop."[38]

Hood had come down like a stick, but Sherman took full credit for the victory in Tennessee and proudly told his wife, Ellen, that the decision he made to divide his army, "with one part to take Savannah and the other to meet Hood in Tennessee, are all clearly mine, and will survive us both in history." He was not modest about his achievements or doubtful about the future. "Thomas's success in Tennessee incurs to my advantage, as his operations there are a part of my plan." Sherman knew he was a hero, and a Northern newspaper confirmed it by announcing that Sherman had "identified his name forever with the Christmas festivities."[39]

CHAPTER TEN

Hood and Sherman

Three days before Christmas Sherman presented the city of Savannah to Lincoln. The Northern press proudly declared that no American would ever buy a gift for his child, sweetheart, or wife without remembering "the great soldier who has given this grandest of Christmas gifts to the country." The *New York Herald* even predicted that when Lee's soldiers learned that Thomas had annihilated Hood and that Sherman was in Georgia with sixty thousand men, there would be rebellion throughout the Army of Northern Virginia and the government would crumble. Hood's "wild goose chase" had failed, and the blame would fall squarely on President Davis; the "grand rebellion will collapse like a big balloon with all the gas let out at once."[1]

News of events in the West spread rapidly, sparking celebration in the North and increasing despair in the South. "We learn here of General Hood's defeat," a soldier wrote from Savannah. "He made nothing by his northern raid, but lost much." A Richmond correspondent admitted that a cloud of melancholia had settled over the capital. Savannah had fallen, Northern soldiers threatened southwestern Virginia, and Hood, "after his murderous victory at Franklin, has been whipped." Perhaps a young woman in Fort Valley, Georgia, summed it up best: "Christmas is here again," she told a relative. "A season of sadness & gloomy retrospection for us of the South, one of joy & gayety to the people of the North."[2]

No one was more pleased with the results of the twin campaigns than Lincoln, who told Sherman: "Many, many thanks for your Christmas gift, the capture of Savannah. When you were about leaving Atlanta for the Atlantic coast, I was anxious, if not fearful," but "I did not interfere. Now, the undertaking being a success, the honor is all yours; for I believe none of us went further than to acquiesce." Everything had worked out much better than Lincoln had expected, and he continued his praise. Sherman's strategy was "indeed a great success. Not only does it afford the obvious and immediate military advantages, but, in showing to the world that your army could be divided, putting the stronger part to an important new service, and yet leaving enough to vanquish the old opposing force of the whole—Hood's army—it brings those who sat in darkness to see a great light."[3]

In contrast to Hood, who celebrated Christmas on the run, Sherman enjoyed the evening at a military-style family dinner party at the mansion of Charles Green. Although the general had originally moved into quarters at the Pulaski House, an old hotel where he had stayed as a captain in antebellum days, Green, who was a British subject eager to protect his property, had offered his home to the city's military chief. Green had no grounds for his concern, for the residents quickly learned that the Federal occupation force offered no threat, nor did Sherman intend to evict civilians as he had in Atlanta. In fact, little changed for the city's twenty thousand inhabitants in the immediate wake of the surrender. On Christmas Day, several churches held services as usual, and Sherman attended St. John's, a beautiful Episcopal church by the Green residence. "I was delighted to see it filled," a Federal officer told his wife, "not only by a large number of our officers and men, but also a considerable number of Savannah people, ladies and gentlemen."[4]

Curiosity tempted many of Savannah's residents, both black and white, to try to catch a glimpse of the city's famous visitor. Hundreds of newly freed African Americans came to Madison Square, the small public park across from the Green house. There was a constant stream of former slaves, both men and women—some bashful, some talkative—but all respectful and courteous. Each one wanted to pay respects to the man they believed the Almighty had sent as an answer to their prayers. Sherman wrote his wife: "It would amuse you to see the Negroes. They flock to me, old and young; they pray and shout and mix up my name with that of Moses and Simon and other scriptural ones as well as 'Abham Linkum' the Great Messiah of 'Dis Jubilee.'"[5]

Savannah's white population remained quiescent. Nothing could or would be gained by resistance, but when Sherman visited families he had known in happier days, he found the women as "haughty and proud as ever." To Ellen he confided that although he had shown he could march through the heart of Georgia, Savannah's residents remained defiant. Over a year before, in September 1863, when Sherman had been on the banks of the Big Black River near Vicksburg, he had lectured Halleck about the nature of Southerners and the steps it would take to defeat them. "The South must be ruled or will rule," he judged. "We must fight it out, army against army and man against man." Yet Sherman avoided battle, preferring instead a strike on society itself. He intended to make the people "so sick of war that generations would pass before they would again appeal to it." Proudly he told his wife fifteen months later that he thought he had reached his objective with arrogant Southerners. "I think Thomas's whipping at Nashville, coupled with my march," he decided, "will take some conceit out of them."[6]

Sherman could afford to be benevolent now, and he offered safe passage to Charleston for about two hundred people, mostly women and children whose husbands and fathers were in the Confederate army. He took personal pleasure in knowing that among the families consigned to his care were those of Confederate commanders William Hardee, Lafayette McLaws, Gustavus Smith, and A. P. Stewart. He seemed particularly gratified that the "very elegant people" of Savannah did not seem "ashamed to call on the 'vandal chief'" to request favors. Although the parades and celebrations, along with a vast sea of tents, confirmed the military presence, Sherman did not disrupt the city's daily routine. He allowed the mayor and city council to function, and a Union officer noted that a foreigner visiting the city would not know that it was "so lately a prize of battle." The calm was deceptive. "Ladies walk the streets with perfect confidence and security, and the public squares are filled with children at play," wrote a Union soldier. The stores and theaters remained open, and the locals mingled with men in Union blue.[7]

This facade masked anger and frustration among loyal Confederates. Twenty-four-year-old Fanny Cohen confided to her diary, "This is the saddest Christmas that I have ever spent and my only pleasure during the day has been in looking forward to spending my next Christmas in the Confederacy." Throughout the city, residents felt the presence of the Union soldiers, for the Northern men went about without passes. In spite of attempts to maintain normality, makeshift housing appeared everywhere. Wooden huts covered the squares that gave Savannah its unique charm, and a Federal on a ship in the Savannah River concluded that the city suffered from the occupation. In January, he claimed it was in the "most dilapidated and miserable condition." Businesses remained closed, houses tightly shut, fences down, and sidewalks and wharves in disrepair. Savannah's ladies avoided going outside. Moreover, Sherman's dead horses were "laying about the streets by the dozen."[8]

Still, many Georgians remained defiant. Twenty-one-year-old Ellen House, a Savannah native who was living at Eatonton, confided to her diary on New Year's Day: "Our cause looks rather gloomy at present, and some of our people here are very blue. They acknowledge themselves to be whipped. They ought to be ashamed of themselves." Although Sherman marched through Eatonton, House had not been there at the time and had little sympathy for those who judged the cause lost. "What if Sherman has Savannah," she announced. "We will gain our independence yet." More realistically, Frances Howard, in her Savannah town house, recorded in her diary on New Year's Eve, "The city authorities have seen fit to declare the city once more in the Union."[9]

Sherman had southeast Georgia firmly under control. While some secessionists remained obstinate, deteriorating conditions plunged many people into a deep despair. Although Sherman was not responsible for all the trouble, his presence increased the loss of will that was slowly eroding Rebel society. A mountain woman griped that the country was "plum full of Cavalry just . . . stealing all the time." It was impossible for Joe Brown's state government to arrest all the deserters who plundered the innocent, and many predicted guerrilla warfare would result. Howell Cobb told President Davis that it was useless to ignore the intense despondency that ravaged the state and confided to his wife that he found the people "depressed, disaffected, and too many of them disloyal." Bands of armed men, claiming to be Rebel scouts, ranged through the country foraging and stealing horses and mules from innocent civilians. It was impossible to escape the predators, and Mary Mallard wrote from south of the city: "Everyone that comes has some plea for insult or robbery. Was there ever any civilized land given for such a length of time to lawless pillage and brutal inhumanities?" The unrest caused so much anxiety that calls for peace resonated across the state. Confederate money had dropped in value rapidly since the fall of Savannah, while gold had risen to over fifty dollars an ounce in Augusta. Such news increased the longing for the war to end.[10]

Sherman's march had evoked an unconscious emotional response that previously had appeared only as impotent discontent. Not long after Christmas, a group of Savannah Unionists asked Governor Brown to call a convention to discuss the merits of continuing the war, and many anxious Georgians in nearby counties concurred. One set of resolutions pointed out there were no defenders left in the state except old men and boys. "Therefore we think the time has come when our authorities should go boldly to work to negotiate a peace before we are entirely ruined." Proponents of a truce would even consider a separate peace. "We have," a Georgian sadly declared, "lost the hope." Georgians wanted an end of the fighting before the entire white male population was "butchered."[11]

Hood's defeat had an equally devastating effect on the people of Tennessee. Large numbers of soldiers who had lost hope in the Confederacy's chances of victory deserted. "The boys is very much dissatisfied. I think a good many of them will desert between now and spring," wrote a Texan; "some are leaving every knight." This apathy was apparent not only to the soldiers but to local residents. "If we judge the Confederacy by this section," wrote a resident of Clarksville, "the army must be greatly depleted." Tennessee's Union governor and the North's vice president–elect Andrew Johnson told General Thomas that the Confederate defeat had a "withering influence" on the Rebels in Tennessee and it "is more decided than anything which has transpired since the beginning of the rebellion." Even the Confederate governor, Isham G. Harris, traveling with Hood, admitted that "the unfortunate result of the battle at Nashville and immediate retreat of the army was very discouraging to our people."[12]

The military actions in Georgia and Tennessee also had a somber effect on soldiers in the Army of Northern Virginia. The sagging morale of the Georgia regiments in the trenches at Petersburg concerned General Lee. In late November a soldier had told his wife: "Our news from Georgia is meagre and entirely unsatisfactory. The newspapers publish nothing at all scarcely. . . . I have been very uneasy about you." On December 17, a vetern of Lee's campaigns wrote his father: "I am very much afraid the Yankees paid you a visit. . . . I am afraid to hear from home. I fear I shall hear some bad news perhaps that you have been visited by the Yanks and perhaps all you have destroyed by those scoundrels or perhaps you may be in the army, enduring all the hardships and privations of a soldier." Earlier in the spring, one young Georgian confided to his cousin that most Georgians wanted to come home. He had told his future wife: "I dont like this way fighting here in Virginia and letting the yankees run all over Georgia. I had rather fight for those that I love." So as word of the situation in Georgia spread, Lee had to worry about desertions depleting his ranks. To cut down on the opportunities for men to use leaves as a means to go home and not return, he curtailed furloughs to Georgia.[13]

The events in Georgia and Tennessee overwhelmed the Confederate government. Five days before Christmas, Rebel war clerk John B. Jones observed in Richmond that if the Northern papers were correct, Hood had suffered an "irretrievable disaster," resulting in the loss of both Tennessee and Georgia. On Christmas Eve he wrote that there was "something in the air that causes agitation in official circles." Christmas Day brought little news, but Jones added, "It is believed on the street that Savannah has been evacuated, some days ago." When it became clear the next day that the stories were probably true, he noted, "The Georgians in Lee's army are more or less demoralized, and a reward of a sixty day's furlough is given for shooting any deserter from our ranks." Two days after Christmas, he lamented that daybreak brought only "fog and gloom" for the loss of Savannah had been confirmed. The reaction in the Confederate capital was predictable. "Men are silent, and some dejected," Jones observed. "It is unquestionably the darkest period we have yet experienced." It did not matter whether Davis was directly responsible for the twin disasters; "the country will still fix upon him the responsibility and the odium."[14]

Indeed, December was a dark month for the Confederate president as his critics prepared a new assault on his administration. When news of Hood's defeat circulated through the capital, opponents of Davis's decision to replace Johnston with Hood five months earlier gained new life. As the crisis in Georgia had mounted, Davis had dispatched Bragg, his trusted military adviser, to Augusta, and during the critical days of December, Davis made most decisions alone. Lee was the only man he consulted for military advice, and neither of them actually knew the situation in the West. After learning of Hood's retreat, Davis's enemies claimed that even though the president might not have approved of Hood's decision to march north, neither had he objected. While Davis admitted that he had considered the Tennessee campaign "ill-advised," he had not called Hood back. True, Davis was tired and distracted and by mid-December genuinely ill, but even Lee had not invaded the North without first obtaining approval from the president and cabinet. "He is in a sea of trouble," wrote a Confederate. "Congress is turning madly against him."[15]

Two days after Christmas, the South Carolina writer and poet William Gilmore Simms told his son that the progress of Sherman coupled with the disaster of Hood verified the "criminality & stupidity" of the Confederate government. Removing Johnston, he claimed, was a great blunder, but sending Hood to Tennessee was worse. "In shutting the one door on him, we left open the other" and had virtually guaranteed that Sherman would take Savannah. This state of affairs, he concluded, had "brought the war to our doors." Simms would soon learn how true these last words were, for Sherman would visit the writer's plantation on his march through South Carolina.[16]

While Confederates looked for scapegoats, Sherman enjoyed taking all the praise for the success of the two campaigns. Yet Thomas had defeated Hood in Tennessee, allowing Sherman to bring economic and psychological warfare home to Southerners. To be sure, this was a working arrangement that suited both personalities. Sherman had come to believe that there were other ways to end the war than decisive battles, and it was that new brand of warfare that he practiced on the people of Georgia. He could have fought Hood but instead chose to make war on Southern society. Most Civil War generals, including Hood, still believed that a great decisive battle would settle everything.[17]

Sherman's march to the coast also had important secondary results. Even though Lee tried to curtail them, desertions in the Army of Northern Virginia continued. The actual number is impossible to estimate. Additionally, although Sherman was not directly responsible for the growing disaffection taking root in the Confederacy, his easy passage through Georgia indicated that the Confederate government was unable to respond to an emergency. The fall campaigns also revealed strengths in the Northern command system that were lacking in the Confederate. Grant, the new general in chief, was willing to make decisions and execute them, and Chief of Staff Halleck was, concluded his biographer Stephen Ambrose, a "brilliant administrator." Perhaps more important, after Lincoln created the new command structure, he allowed it to function for the most part without interference. The South had no such unity of command until it was too late. Finally, the North was fortunate in its commanders, for Sherman and Grant trusted each other and could work well together. That was not the case among generals in the Rebel Army of Tennessee.[18]

When Sherman marched out of Georgia in early 1865, he left behind a defeated people. "Clouds and darkness are all around us," wrote a Liberty County resident, "the hand of the Almighty is laid in sore judgement upon us; we are a desolated & smitten people." There was little encouraging news, and people throughout the state implored Governor Brown to do something to alleviate the suffering and control the lawlessness. From Chattooga County, a citizen warned that anarchy had reigned since the army left Dalton in October. There were shortages throughout the state. Deserters from both armies preyed on the helpless, and guerrillas roamed freely in the mountains. Sherman had indeed broken the will of Georgians to continue the war. Now he and his men would extend that desolation into South Carolina.[19]

The outcome of the campaigns in the autumn of 1864 defined the military careers of both Hood and Sherman. While Sherman had surpassed anything he had achieved in the Old Army and his future looked bright, Hood not only lost the respect of his soldiers and Southern civilians but also failed to claim the hand of Sally Preston. On his way to Richmond in February 1865, Hood visited Buck in South Carolina. What happened between the two or who was responsible for the breakup will never be known, but before he left, the engagement was over. How much Hood's recent debacle had on the failure of the romance will also remain a mystery. Certainly Hood had enjoyed early fame, and the liaison with the beautiful Buck Preston had blossomed, but both his career and the courtship had begun to wilt by Christmas. Sherman, however, had experienced the opposite in his wartime fortunes. He had survived charges that he was incompetent, even crazy. By January 1865, as Hood said good-bye to the remnants of the army, Sherman delighted in the realization that he was, at least for the time being, a Northern hero.

Following the failed campaign, Davis vented his anger on those he felt had let the country down, and Edmund Kirby Smith was at the top of that list. He believed that Trans-Mississippians had not kept Union troops occupied long enough and castigated Smith for consistently refusing to send reinforcements across the river. Davis blamed Smith for not doing more to prevent A. J. Smith from reaching Nashville and for not forwarding reinforcements to Hood's beleaguered army to offset the men Thomas gained from that blunder. Moreover, Davis chastised Kirby Smith for not following up the victories in the Red River and Arkansas campaigns in April, thus preventing Union troops from crossing the Mississippi. Smith, he judged, should have created an effective diversion, and by not doing so, he had not acted in the best interest of the Confederate nation. "We have one cause, one country, and the States have been confederated to unite their power for the defence of each," continued the president. Although Davis wrote this scathing letter on Christmas Eve, no reinforcements would come from west of the river for it was all Smith could do to keep his soldiers from going home. Hood, in his postwar account of events, also used this rationalization, for he emphasized several times how much he counted on Trans-Mississippi reinforcements when planning his invasion of the North. Thus both Davis and Hood believed that the responsibility for the army's defeat should be shared with their comrades across the Mississippi.[20]

There was certainly enough fault-finding to go around, although most Confederate soldiers placed the accountability directly on their commander, particularly after rumors circulated through the camps that Hood had censured the men. Soldiers grumbled when they heard that Hood believed he had overestimated their fighting spirit and questioned their devotion to the cause. But Hood had tried to do too much; he asked too much of his men. Moreover, the Army of Tennessee suffered from a weak command structure and generals who could not, or simply did not, live up to expectations. Still, one of Hood's detractors pointed out that if Hood was to be believed, then it was easy to agree that "if things had happened otherwise, the campaign would have been a success instead of a failure." What happened was "not so much criminal as unfortunate—but then his countrymen were more unfortunate still." Hood's defenders insisted that Johnston's inability to hold north Georgia was the key. Even Hardee's actions in the battles for Atlanta came into question, as did Braxton Bragg's previous failures. If Davis wanted to blame Kirby Smith for actions he did not take after the April campaigns in Arkansas and Louisiana, then the accusations and finger-pointing could go on forever, as indeed they seemed to do once the war ended. In fairness to both Hood and Johnston, it is doubtful that by the summer of 1864 either man had a realistic chance of changing the course of the war in the West. Certainly, when Hood took command ouside of Atlanta, Rebel fortunes looked dim. But while he could share the blame for the loss of Atlanta with Johnston, the failures at Franklin and Nashville were his alone.[21]

The Tennessee campaign was one of the most controversial in the western theater, and the participants continued to disagree in the decades following the Confederacy's collapse. Joseph E. Johnston attacked the Confederate president and, to a lesser degree, Hood's competence as an army commander, in a book published in 1874. A year later Sherman produced his memoirs, and although not as scathing in his criticism of Hood as Johnston's account, Sherman nevertheless had some harsh words about Hood's "rash" behavior while at the same time praising Johnston. After this postwar attack, Hood felt compelled to write his own version of events but could not find a publisher before he died in 1879. Beauregard later arranged for the manuscript's release as a way to benefit Hood's orphaned children. Not surprisingly, Beauregard had found Hood's criticism of Johnston appealing, and Hood's *Advance and Retreat* appeared in print in 1880. Not only did Hood blame Johnston for wartime failure, he included Hardee, Cheatham, and soldiers in the Army of Tennessee. Neither Johnston nor Hood composed objective accounts. Both men wrote self-serving tomes, and both tried to explain their actions based on years of reflection.[22]

Postwar feuding was not limited to former Confederates. Although the Federals had won not only both campaigns and the war, they also fell to bickering over who should receive the credit. Jacob Cox, who published several accounts of both the Georgia and Tennessee campaigns, claimed he, not Stanley, commanded the line at Franklin. This, of course, elicited a response from Stanley, and he called Cox "a reckless inventor of lies" and "a very false knave." Even John Schofield felt compelled to answer questions about the Tennessee campaign and published his own book in 1897. Thomas, who had died in 1870, was fair game, particularly for Schofield, and when Schofield acted as a pallbearer at Thomas's funeral, another general remarked, "If Thomas only knew it, he would turn in his coffin."[23]

Yet George Thomas deserves a share of the credit for the success of the Union campaigns. To him war was a science, and the battle at Nashville was not the only time he had displayed competence as a commander. It is easy to second-guess how Thomas handled matters in early December, just as it is easy to point out that Hood's shortcomings worked to Thomas's advantage. But Thomas, said Henry Halleck, was "a noble old war horse." Sherman himself admitted that it was only after Atlanta surrendered and Hood escaped that the "real trouble" began. Perhaps another Union commander could have done better, but to argue that engages in speculation and raises questions about who that man might be. Maybe the Virginian was not a brilliant battlefield commander, but there are few men cast from the mold that produces soldiers like Robert E. Lee. It could also be pointed out that Sherman was not always a brilliant battlefield commander either, for he preferred ways to end the fighting that avoided bloodshed. Sherman thought enough of Thomas to leave him to deal with Hood, while he pursued the kind of warfare he favored, which did not require the offensive except when absolutely necessary. And Thomas, in spite of constant nagging from Washington, succeeded in mounting a successful campaign. He thereby allowed Sherman to strike the final death blow to the Confederacy by marching through South Carolina and on to fame. Even Sherman admitted that if Thomas had failed, he would have had to retrace his steps and deal with Hood.[24]

Yet for all he did to give Sherman the freedom to march into history, Thomas received little praise and much criticism for failing to annihilate Hood's army, even though the days of destroying an army in the open field had become, for all practical purposes, obsolete. Thomas had much going against him. He was a Southerner in a Northern army; he had no powerful politicians from his home state lobbying for him in Washington; and he was not close to Grant, Sherman, or Schofield, all of whom became commanding generals in the U.S. Army. In fact, when he died in 1870 at age fifty-four, Thomas was in the process of responding to a piece published in the *New York Tribune* that criticized his actions in Tennessee, an article probably written by Schofield.[25]

Nor did the hard-fighting Andrew Jackson Smith receive recognition for his part in the battle at Nashville, for as soon as the fighting ended he was dispatched to Mobile. In fact, his command was moved around so much and served under so many commanders that he referred to them as the "lost tribes of Israel." To reinforce Thomas, he had marched his men across Missouri with a relentless purpose of mind. Thomas knew, as did all the soldiers in the fortifications at Nashville, that without his timely arrival the battle could have turned into a real contest.[26]

Finally, it would be remiss not to give Sherman the recognition he deserves. He conceived the strategy and sold it to his superiors. Grant's trust in his friend worked to Sherman's advantage, and even a skeptical Lincoln acquiesced to the plan in the end. Thomas's success was Sherman's success too, for as commanding general the grim-faced Sherman was ultimately responsible for the outcome of the two campaigns. Although Sherman certainly had won battles before he left on the march, had his career ended with the surrender of Atlanta, he would have made but a limited mark on history. It was the March to the Sea and beyond that was his claim to greatness, for it linked his name with the concept of total war.

Moreover, one outcome that Sherman could not have anticipated was that the Tennessee campaign brought to the forefront a controversial political issue, the value of black soldiers in the army. Hood's Nashville campaign marked the first time that many Union soldiers in the western armies had fought with African Americans and the first time that the Rebel Army of Tennessee had faced black troops. The terrible slaughter that occurred in the railroad cut at Nashville may have been motivated as much by a desire to avenge Franklin as it was by the fact that the trapped men were black. Certainly their color increased the blind rage, but with survival overshadowing reason, it was probable that the Rebels in Granbury's lunette, still mourning the loss of General Cleburne, would have mowed down anyone in Union blue with equal ferocity. Black soldiers acquitted themselves well in their first major battle in the western theater, although they paid a high price.

What about Hood's possible influence on the Northern presidential election? In reality, there was little chance that Confederates could change the outcome. The point to remember is that war-weary Southerners clung to the belief that Lincoln could be defeated. After Atlanta fell and while Lee was stalemated in Virginia, Hood was expected to produce a miracle. Yet the Texan appears to have given little thought to the consequences of his actions for the Northern presidential election, and Richmond did not encourage that as a goal in the overall Confederate strategy. Davis and Hood both believed the only option for the Confederacy was to fight its way to independence. When he commenced his campaign in September, he led Sherman away from Atlanta, and his original plan was generally well conceived and well executed, although one could argue that it netted nothing in the end. By nature, Hood could not stay on the defensive, and when he moved, he threatened the Union line of communication. But after reaching Dalton, he wavered. To his north, Federal garrisons frustrated his ability to cross the Tennessee River, but with Sherman to his south, he either had to flee or fight. Hood later insisted that he "expected that a forward movement of one hundred miles would re-inspirit the officers and men in a degree to impart to them confidence, enthusiasm, and hope of victory, if not strong faith in its achievement." Yet he knew his officers were *unanimous* in their opposition" to an offensive so Hood found himself in a "dilemma." He did not have enough men to entrench, nor did the naturally combative Hood want to go on the defensive. If he moved south through Georgia or Alabama it would appear that he was abandoning all he had gained in October. Sherman knew all this too. All he had to do was hold on to Atlanta until after the presidential election and not let Hood force him to abandon what he had fought so hard to win. [27]

The significance of Atlanta's fall on the election, and, by extension, the war's end, remains debatable. The city's surrender, asserted one historian, deprived the South of its only hope of winning by not losing. Therefore, the only question remaining was when, not if, the North would win and the South would lose. Other historians believe that Atlanta made no difference and that Lincoln would have won the election in November even if the Confederates had held on to the Georgia city. In either case, what happened in the weeks before the election would prove critical, and, unfortunately for Southerners, neither Hood nor Lee did anything that would offset the Union military victories at Mobile, Atlanta, and in the Shenandoah Valley. Twenty years later Jefferson Davis wrote that "the aspect of the peace party was quite encouraging, and it seemed that the real issue to be decided in the Presidential election of that year was the continuance or cessation of the war."[28]

One of Davis's biographers concluded that the Confederate president did not have illusions that a Lincoln defeat would aid the Confederacy, and Vice President Alexander Stephens thought that Davis believed four more years of Lincoln's unpopular policies would actually benefit the South by throwing the Northern people into despair. But even if Lincoln lost, he would remain in office until March, and there were no assurances that as president McClellan would not carry the war to a military conclusion. Davis held little hope of achieving a negotiated settlement regardless of who was in the White House. "We are fighting for existence," the Confederate president preached to Georgians in October, "and by fighting alone can independence be gained."[29]

So Hood moved west into Alabama and ultimately into Tennessee. His campaign, of course, went downhill from there, and as 1865 opened, the war was over for Hood and many soldiers in the Army of Tennessee. Although a fragment of the once powerful Confederate army would join Joseph E. Johnston in North Carolina in an effort to stop Sherman's advance (a march that included the 110th USCT), many veterans never fought another battle after the failed Tennessee campaign. Discouraged and defeated, only the most faithful chose to make that long trek to North Carolina.

Although Grant would accept the surrender of Lee and the Army of Northern Virginia in April, Sherman, Thomas, Smith, Schofield, and the other Union commanders in the western theater had done what Grant never did: they had crippled one of the Confederacy's main armies so that it never recovered. By the time Sherman left Savannah on his march through South Carolina, there was little hope left for the South. The March to the Sea would be Sherman's lasting legacy, while Hood's failures at Franklin and Nashville would haunt Southerners long after their nation had ceased to exist.[30]

Notes

ABBREVIATIONS

GDAH   Georgia Department of Archives and History, Atlanta

OR   U.S. War Department, *The War of the Rebellion: A Compilation of the Official Records of the Union and Confederate Armies*, 128 vols. Washington DC: U.S. Government Printing Office, 1880–1901.

USAMHI   United States Military History Institute, Carlisle PA

PREFACE

1. John Bell Hood, *Advance and Retreat: Personal Experiences in the United States and Confederate Armies* (1880; rpt. Lincoln: University of Nebraska Press, 1996), 278.

2. OR, 44:809; (except as otherwise noted, all volumes cited are from Series I).

3. Hood later wrote that the strategy he intended for the battle at Spring Hill was "one of those interesting and beautiful moves on the chess-board of war . . . which I had often desired an opportunity" to execute (*Advance and Retreat*, 283).

I. SHERMAN AND HOOD

1. Thomas Stokes was Gay's half-brother and her only male relative. See Mary A. H. Gay, *Life in Dixie during the War* (1897; rpt. Atlanta: Darby Printing Company, 1979), 94–99.

2. Mills Lane, ed., *"Dear Mother: Don't grieve about me. If I get killed, I'll only be dead": Letters from Georgia Soldiers in the Civil War* (Savannah: Beehive Press, 1977), 313–14, 318; Angus McDermid, "Letters from a Confederate Soldier," ed. Benjamin Rountree, *Georgia Review* 28 (Fall 1964): 290.

3. John B. Jones, *A Rebel War Clerk's Diary*, ed. Earl Schenck Miers (1958 rpt. Baton Rouge: Louisiana State University Press, 1993), 229. All references to Jones's

diary are taken from this one-volume condensed and annotated version. Although "Tenting on the Old Camp Ground" became popular in the South as well as in the North, where it was written by Walter Kittredge, no Southern publisher ever printed it. One possible reason is that it came so late in the war that economic conditions prevented publication. See Irwin Silber, ed., *Songs of the Civil War* (1960; rpt. New York: Dover Publications, 1995), 167–68.

4. James B. McPherson, *Ordeal by Fire: The Civil War and Reconstruction* (New York: Knopf, 1982), 437; James M. McPherson, *Battle Cry of Freedom: The Civil War Era* (New York: Oxford University Press, 1988), 771.

5. Larry E. Nelson, *Bullets, Ballots, and Rhetoric: Confederate Policy for the United States Presidential Contest of 1864* (University: University of Alabama Press, 1980), 100, 107, 117, 149.

6. *Augusta Chronicle and Sentinel*, March 6, 1864, quoted in Nelson, *Bullets, Ballots, and Rhetoric*, 38.

7. Richard M. McMurry, *John Bell Hood and the War for Southern Independence* (Lexington: University Press of Kentucky, 1982), 7–11. See also John M. Schofield, *Forty-Six Years in the Army* (New York: Century, 1897), 3–15.

8. Thomas B. Van Horne, *The Life of Major-General George H. Thomas* (New York: Charles Scribner's & Sons, 1882), 13. See also Richard W. Johnson, *A Soldier's Reminiscences in Peace and War* (Philadelphia: J. B. Lippincott, 1886), 133, for more on his role in the Second U.S. Cavalry. Johnson served as captain in the regiment. The regiment was organized in 1855 with men handpicked by Jefferson Davis, and ten companies, 710 men, left Jefferson Barracks for Fort Belknap, Texas, in October. Because it produced so many important figures in both the Northern and Southern armies, it is the best chronicled. See Francis F. McKinney, *Education in Violence: The Life of George H. Thomas and the History of the Army of the Cumberland* (Detroit: Wayne State University Press, 1961), 64–83. See also Harold B. Simpson, *Cry Comanche: The 2nd U.S. Cavalry in Texas, 1855–1861* (Hillsboro TX: Hill Jr. College Press, 1979), for the most complete history, and Freeman Cleaves, *Rock of Chickamauga: The Life of General George H. Thomas* (Norman: University of Oklahoma Press, 1948), and Donn Piatt, *General George H. Thomas: A Critical Biography* (Cincinnati: Robert Clarke, 1893), for more on Thomas.

9. McPherson, *Battle Cry of Freedom*, 761.

10. Jones, *Rebel War Clerk's Diary*, 421; OR, 38:pt. 5, 777.

11. John C. Waugh, *Reelecting Lincoln: The Battle for the 1864 Presidency* (New York: Crown, 1997), 297.

12. Charles P. Roland, *The American Iliad: The Story of the Civil War* (New York: McGraw-Hill, 1991), 176; Albert Castel, *Decision in the West: The Atlanta Campaign of 1864* (Lawrence: University Press of Kansas, 1992), 543; *Charleston Courier*, Sep-

tember 9, 1864, quoted in Nelson, *Bullets, Ballots, and Rhetoric*, 119–21; McPherson, *Ordeal by Fire*, 443.

13. Archer Jones, *Civil War Command and Strategy: The Process of Victory and Defeat* (New York: Free Press, 1992), 207.

14. Although *army group* is a modern term, it adequately describes Sherman's three armies. As a point of argument, one could criticize Sherman for stopping with Atlanta and not making an effort to destroy Hood's army. For the quotes, see J. M. Brannock to Sarah Caroline Brannock, September 12 and 17, 1864, Sarah Caroline (Gwin) Brannock Collection, Virginia Historical Society, Richmond.

15. Stephen W. Sears, *George B. McClellan: The Young Napoleon* (New York: Ticknor & Fields, 1988), 375–78.

16. OR, ser. 3, 4; 713; *New York Herald*, September 18, 1864; Robert Patrick, *Reluctant Rebel: The Secret Diary of Robert Patrick, 1861–1865*, ed. F. Jay Taylor (1959; rpt. Baton Rouge: Louisiana State University Press, 1996), 223.

17. Alfred Lacey Hough, *Soldiering in the West: The Civil War Letters of Alfred Lacey Hough*, ed. Robert G. Athearn (Philadelphia: University of Pennsylvania Press, 1957), 218; John Gourlie to "Dear Brother," November 3, 1864; John Gourlie, 123d New York Infantry Regiment, Letters to his family, Civil War Misc. Collection, USAMHI.

18. Albert Castel, "The Atlanta Campaign and the Presidential Election of 1864: How the South Almost Won by Not Losing," in Castel, *Winning and Losing in the Civil War: Essays and Stories* (Columbia: University of South Carolina Press, 1996), 24; Josiah H. Benton, *Voting in the Field: A Forgotten Chapter of the Civil War* (Boston: Privately printed, 1915), 291. For another point of view, see William C. Davis, "The Turning Point That Wasn't: The Confederates and the Election of 1864," in Davis, *The Cause Lost: Myths and Realities of the Confederacy* (Lawrence: University Press of Kansas, 1996), 127–47. For contrasting opinions, see Albert Castel and Larry J. Daniel, "The South Almost Won by Not Losing: A Rebuttal by Larry J. Daniel," *North and South* 3 (February 1998). 44–51.

19. Jones, *Rebel War Clerk's Diary*, 419; J. M. Brannock to Sarah Caroline Brannock, September 12 and 17, 1864, Brannock Collection.

20. J. M. Brannock to Sarah Caroline Brannock, September 12, 1864, Brannock Collection.

2. AFTER ATLANTA

1. Samuel T. Foster, *One of Cleburne's Command: The Civil War Reminiscences and Diary of Capt. Samuel T. Foster, Granbury's Texas Brigade, CSA*, ed. Norman D. Brown (Austin: Univ. of Texas Press, 1980), 135; *New York Herald*, October 19, 1864.

2. Patrick, *Reluctant Rebel*, 224.

3. James A. Connolly, *Three Years in the Army of the Cumberland: The Letters and Diary of Major James A. Connolly*, ed. Paul M. Angle (Bloomington: Indiana University Press, 1959), 257–62; John Gourlie to "Dear Brother," September 5, 1864, and to "Dear Sister Jennie," September 22, 1864, Civil War Misc. Collection.

4. John F. Marszalek, *Sherman: A Soldier's Passion for Order* (New York: Free Press, 1993), 163.

5. OR, 38:pt. 5, 839.

6. Stanley F. Horn, *The Army of Tennessee: A Military History* (Indianapolis: Bobbs-Merrill, 1941), 369; Gay, *Life in Dixie*, 181–82. See also Thomas G. Dyer, *Secret Yankees: The Union Circle in Confederate Atlanta* (Baltimore: Johns Hopkins, 1999), 205.

7. Marszalek, *Sherman*, 286; OR, 39:pt. 2, 503.

8. OR, 39:pt. 2, 396, 488.

9. Steven E. Woodworth, *Jefferson Davis and His Generals: The Failure of Confederate Command in the West* (Lawrence: University Press of Kansas, 1990), 291; Patrick, *Reluctant Rebel*, 230.

10. McMurry, *Hood*, 155; J. M. Brannock to "My Dear Wife," September 12, 1864, Brannock Collection.

11. OR, 39:pt. 2, 836.

12. Nathaniel Cheairs Hughes Jr., *General William J. Hardee: Old Reliable* (1965: rpt. Baton Rouge: Louisiana State University Press, 1992), 243–44.

13. Christopher Losson, *Tennessee's Forgotten Warriors: Frank Cheatham and His Confederate Division* (Knoxville: University of Tennessee Press, 1989), 30.

14. Richard M. McMurry, "Alexander P. Stewart," *Encyclopedia of the Confederacy*, ed. Richard N. Current, 4 vols. (New York: Simon & Schuster, 1993), 4:1545.

15. Herman Hattaway, "Stephen D. Lee," *Encyclopedia of the Confederacy*, ed. Current, 2:920–21.

16. OR, 39:pt. 2, 862, 864.

17. Sam R. Watkins, *"Co. Aytch": A Side Show of the Big Show* (1952; rpt. New York: Macmillan, 1962), 217 (all references to Watkins's book are taken from this version); Dunbar Rowland, ed., *Jefferson Davis, Constitutionalist: His Letters, Papers and Speeches*, 10 vols. (Jackson: Mississippi Department of Archives and History, 1923), 6:341.

18. Horace Porter, *Campaigning with Grant* (New York: Century, 1897), 313; William T. Sherman, *Memoirs of General William T. Sherman*, 2 vols. (1875; rpt. New York: DaCapo Press, 1984), 2:141; Rowland, ed., *Davis*, 6:353, 358; *New York Herald*, October 8, 1864.

19. Rowland, ed., *Davis*, 6:361.

20. Rowland, ed., *Davis*, 6:353, 355.

21. McMurry, *Hood*, 68–69; Mary Boykin Chesnut, *Mary Chesnut's Civil War*, ed. C. Vann Woodward (New Haven: Yale Univ. Press, 1981), 430–31, 441, 516.

22. Chesnut, *Mary Chesnut's Civil War*, 505, 516, 588.

23. Chesnut, *Mary Chesnut's Civil War*, 622.

24. McMurry, *Hood*, 83. See also Laurann Figg and Jane Farrell-Beck, "Amputation in the Civil War: Physical and Social Dimensions," *Journal of the History of Medicine and Allied Sciences* 48 (1993): 454–75; Martin S. Pernick, *A Calculus of Suffering: Pain, Professionalism, and Anesthesia in Nineteenth-Century America* (New York: Columbia University Press, 1985), 148–57; Frank R. Freemon, *Gangrene and Glory: Medical Care during the American Civil War* (Cranbury NJ: Fairleigh Dickinson University Press, 1999).

25. *Charleston Mercury*, November 7, 1864; Patrick, *Reluctant Rebel*, 231. For a good analysis of Hood's shifting plans, see Thomas Lawrence Connelly, *Autumn of Glory: The Army of Tennessee, 1862–1865* (Baton Rouge: Louisiana State University Press, 1971).

26. When Thomas Stokes had asked Mary to care for the articles, he had warned her: "Consider well the proposition before you consent. Should they be found in your possession, by the enemy, then our home might be demolished, and you perhaps imprisoned, or killed upon the spot." See Gay, *Life in Dixie*, 105–6, 183–92.

27. John Gourlie to "Dear Sister Jennie," September 22, 1864; David H. Blair to "Dear Sister," October 17, 1864, David Humphrey Blair Papers, 45th Ohio Infantry Regiment, Civil War Misc. Collection, USAMHI.

3. HOOD'S MARCH NORTH

1. *Richmond Enquirer*, October 19 [22], 1864.

2. Foster, *One of Cleburne's Command*, 136.

3. Foster, *One of Cleburne's Command*, 137; J. M. Brannock to "My dearest Wife," October 4, 1864, Brannock Collection; Charles A. Leuschner, *The Civil War Diary of Charles A. Leuschner*, ed. Charles D. Spurlin (Austin: Eakin Press, 1992), 48.

4. OR, 39:pt. 3, 3, 25–26, 64.

5. OR, 39:pt. 3, 162, 202, 222.

6. OR, 39:pt. 3, 202, 357. Horace Porter wrote that Sherman cited November 2 as the "first time General Grant ordered the march to the sea." He said that Sherman did not receive the October 11 telegram from Grant. See Porter, *Campaigning with Grant*, 317–18.

7. It is an interesting point that Davis visited the western armies only three times. Although Lincoln hinted that he might go to Atlanta, he never visited the West. For the quotes see OR, 39:pt. 2, 395, pt. 3, 203, 429.

8. OR, 39:pt. 3, 203; Henry Hitchcock, *Marching with Sherman*, ed. M. A. DeWolfe Howe (New Haven: Yale University Press, 1927), 29; Mills Lane, ed., *Marching through Georgia: William T. Sherman's Personal Narrative of His March Through Georgia* (New York: Arno Press, 1978), 136.

9. OR, 39:pt. 2, 370.

10. OR, 39:pt. 3, 135; OR, 39:pt. 2, 404.

11. OR, 47:pt. 2, 396–97. Nora Winder was Mrs. N. W. Meyer.

12. French later wrote: "Hood's physical condition should have been considered by the authorities before he was placed in command, and the question asked: 'Has he ever been thrown on his own resources to *provide for* and *direct* an independent command?'" See Samuel G. French, *Two Wars: An Autobiography of Gen. Samuel G. French* (Nashville: Confederate Veteran, 1901), 304.

13. George Ward Nichols, *The Story of the Great March* (1865; rpt. Williamstown ma: Corner House Publishers, 1972), 30; Sherman, *Memoirs*, 2:147; OR, 39:pt. 3, 78, 113.

14. OR, 39:pt. 1, 813; Connolly, *Three Years*, 269.

15. *Charleston Mercury*, October 8 and 14, 1864; J. M. Brannock to "My dearest Wife," October 5, 1864, Brannock Collection.

16. OR, 39:pt. 3, 805.

17. OR, 39:pt. 1, 753.

18. For more on the opinions of Lincoln and Sherman on the use of black soldiers, see Michael Fellman, "Lincoln and Sherman," in *Lincoln's Generals*, ed. Gabor S. Boritt (New York: Oxford University Press, 1994), 121–59.

19. The explosion in Virginia was the battle of the Crater on July 30, 1864.

20. OR, 39:pt. 1, 718; diary entry dated October 12, 1864, Charles Dennison Brandon Diary, Misc.-Brandon, Charles Dennison, Kansas State Historical Society, Topeka.

21. OR, 39:pt. 1, 718.

22. OR, 39:pt. 1, 719–20; William E. Bevens, *Reminiscences of a Private: William E. Bevens of the First Arkansas Infantry, C.S.A.*, ed. Daniel E. Sutherland (Fayetteville: University of Arkansas Press, 1992), 199.

23. Noah Andre Trudeau, *Like Men of War: Black Troops in the Civil War, 1862–1865* (New York: Little, Brown, 1998), 279.

24. OR, 39:pt. 1, 720–21; *Charleston Mercury*, November 7, 1864, reprinted from the *Cincinnati Commercial*, October 26, 1864.

25. *Charleston Mercury*, October 24, 1864; Philip Daingerfield Stephenson, *The Civil War Memoir of Philip Daingerfield Stephenson, D.D.* (Conway: University of Central Arkansas Press, 1995), 255; Bevens, *Reminiscences of a Private*, 199.

26. Trudeau, *Like Men of War*, 279; OR, 39:pt. 3, 914; *Charleston Mercury*, Octo-

ber 24, 1864; Lee Kennett, *Marching through Georgia: The Story of Soldiers and Civilians during Sherman's Campaign* (New York: Harper Collins, 1995), 220.

27. OR, 52:pt. 2, 595–96; Russell K. Brown, *To the Manner Born: The Life of General William H. T. Walker* (Athens: University of Georgia Press, 1994), 201.

28. Richard E. Beringer et al., *Why the South Lost the Civil War* (Athens: University of Georgia Press, 1986), 371.

29. OR, 39:pt. 1, 583.

30. John G. Nicolay and John Hay, eds., *Complete Works of Abraham Lincoln*, 12 vols. (1894; rpt. New York: Francis D. Tandy, 1905), 10:225–26, 241–42; Benton, *Voting in the Field*, 291–92.

31. Nicolay and Hay, eds., *Complete Works of Abraham Lincoln*, 10:225–26, 241–42; Benton, *Voting in the Field*, 291–92.

32. Nicolay and Hay, eds., *Complete Works of Abraham Lincoln*, 10:225–26, 241–42; Benton, *Voting in the Field*, 291–92, OR, 39:pt. 2, 532, 540–41; Oscar Osburn Winther, "The Soldier Vote in the Election of 1864," *New York History* 25 (October 1944): 453.

33. Jones, *Rebel War Clerk's Diary*, 434.

34. Alfred Roman, *Military Operations of General Beauregard*, 2 vols. (New York: Harper & Brothers, 1884 [1883]), 2:288; Richard Taylor, *Destruction and Reconstruction: Personal Experiences of the Late War in the United States* (Edinburgh: William Blackwood and Sons, 1879), 277.

35. Thomas B. Van Horne, *The Army of the Cumberland* (1875; rpt. New York: Konecky & Konecky, 1996), 454. All references to Van Horne are taken from this version.

36. Trudeau, *Like Men of War*, 276–77.

37. Trudeau, *Like Men of War*, 282.

38. Mauriel Phillips Joslyn, ed., *Charlotte's Boys: Civil War Letters of the Branch Family of Savannah* (Berryville VA: Rockbridge Publishing Company, 1996), 281.

39. Foster, *One of Cleburne's Command*, 142, 144, French, *Two Wars*, 289; Joslyn, ed., *Charlotte's Boys*, 285.

40. OR, 39:pt. 3, 378; Lane, ed., *Marching through Georgia*, 131, 134.

41. McMurry, *Hood*, 162.

42. OR, 39:pt. 3, 888.

43. French, *Two Wars*, 290.

44. OR, 39:pt. 3, 576, 660. The story is, of course, much more complicated than this. At the end of October, John A. Rawlins, on his way west to Missouri, stopped in Washington and shared his reservations about the march with Stanton and Lincoln. They telegraphed Grant, who then engaged in this exchange with Sherman. See Porter, *Campaigning with Grant*, 318.

45. Rowland, ed., *Davis*, 6:399.

46. French, *Two Wars*, 290.

47. OR, 39:pt. 3, 359, 378.

48. William Gilmore Simms, *The Letters of William Gilmore Simms*, ed. Mary C. Simms Oliphant, Alfred Taylor Odell, and T. C. Duncan Eaves, 5 vols. (Columbia: University of South Carolina Press, 1955), 4:471.

4. SHERMAN'S MARCH SOUTH

1. Dolly Lunt Burge, *The Diary of Dolly Lunt Burge, 1848–1879*, ed. Christine Jacobson Carter (Athens: University of Georgia Press, 1997), 156; Sherman, *Memoirs*, 2:170.

2. OR, 39:pt. 2, 412–13.

3. Jones, *Rebel War Clerk's Diary*, 446; OR, 39:pt. 3, 162.

4. OR, 39:pt. 3, 700; Hitchcock, *Marching with Sherman*, 42.

5. OR, 39:pt. 3, 711.

6. Ezra J. Warner, *Generals in Blue: Lives of the Union Commanders* (Baton Rouge: Louisiana State University Press, 1964), 267.

7. Connolly, *Three Years*, 295.

8. Connolly, *Three Years*, 288–89; Jones, *Rebel War Clerk's Diary*, 444.

9. State voting laws regarding soldiers were confusing and often changed during the war. See Nicolay and Hay, eds., *Complete Works of Abraham Lincoln*, 10:306; OR, 39:pt. 3, 603. For a state-by-state analysis of the soldiers' vote, see Benton, *Voting in the Field*. For a more modern look at politics and the American soldier, see Joseph Allan Frank, *With Ballot and Bayonet: The Political Socialization of the American Civil War Soldier* (Athens: University of Georgia Press, 1998).

10. Connolly, *Three Years*, 293; John Rath, *Left for Dixie: The Civil War Diary of John Rath*, ed. Kenneth Lyftogt (Parkersburg IA: Mid-Prairie Books, 1991), 53.

11. McPherson, *Ordeal by Fire*, 806; Rowland, ed., *Davis*, 6:386.

12. J. M. Lanning, Tenth Alabama Infantry, Microfilm Roll 49, GDAH.

13. Nichols, *Story of the Great March*, 38.

14. Sherman, *Memoirs*, 2:111; Hitchcock, *Marching with Sherman*, 35; Nichols, *Story of the Great March*, 41.

15. Marszalek, *Sherman*, 294; Bell Irvin Wiley, ed., *Letters of Warren Akin, Confederate Congressman* (Athens: University of Georgia Press, 1959), 300. Also see Mark Grimsley, *The Hard Hand of War: Union Military Policy toward Southern Civilians, 1861–1865* (Cambridge: Cambridge University Press, 1995), for more on Sherman's policy.

16. Joseph T. Glatthaar, *The March to the Sea and Beyond: Sherman's Troops in the Savannah and Carolinas Campaign* (New York: New York University Press, 1985),

16; Charles W. Wills, *Army Life of an Illinois Soldier* (1906; rpt. Carbondale: Southern Illinois University Press, 1996), 314.

17. OR, 44, 19–25.

18. Carrie V. Timberlake to "My Dear Cousin Tom," December 1, 1864, Blanton Family Papers, Virginia Historical Society, Richmond. Commas and capitalization have been added to make this excerpt readable.

19. Burge, *Diary*, 157–58.

20. OR, 39:pt. 3, 713–14; James M. McPherson, *For Cause and Comrade: Why Men Fought in the Civil War* (Oxford: Oxford University Press, 1997), 154.

21. OR, 44, 865, 867.

22. Joseph Howard Parks, *Joseph E. Brown of Georgia* (Baton Rouge: Louisiana State University Press, 1977), 306; W. F. Chancely to "Dear Cousin," June 8, 1864, typescript in possession of the author courtesy of Amma C. Crum.

23. OR, 45:pt. 1, 1218–20, 1224–25, 1242.

24. Rowland, ed., *Davis*, 6:410; Woodworth, *Davis and His Generals*, 294.

25. Kennett, *Marching through Georgia*, 253; Hitchcock, *Marching with Sherman*, 80–81.

26. OR, 39:pt. 3, 713–14; Glatthaar, *March to the Sea*, 122–23; Hitchcock, *Marching with Sherman*, 75.

27. Glatthaar, *March to the Sea*, 74–75.

28. OR, 44:14; T. Conn Bryan, *Confederate Georgia* (Athens: University of Georgia Press, 1953), 171; OR, ser. IV, 3:967–68; Hitchcock, *Marching with Sherman*, 74–75.

29. James C. Bonner, "Sherman at Milledgeville," *Journal of Southern History* 22 (August 1956): 275.

30. On January 3, 1865, the *Savannah Daily Morning News* stated: "A Mr. Patrick Cain, overseer for dr. jarrett, was killed by the Federals, for what reason we are not advised." See Anna Maria Green, *The Journal of a Milledgeville Girl, 1861–1867*, ed. James C. Bonner (Athens: University of Georgia Press, 1964), 60; James C. Bonner, *Milledgeville: Georgia's Antebellum Capital* (1978; rpt. Macon: Mercer University Press, 1985), 187; *Milledgeville Southern Recorder*, December 20, 1864; Connolly, *Three Years*, 318; Hitchcock, *Marching with Sherman*, 85.

31. Taylor, *Destruction and Reconstruction*, 280–81.

32. Wills, *Army Life*, 323–24; Theodore F. Upson, *With Sherman to the Sea: The Civil War Letters, Diaries and Reminiscences of Theodore F. Upson*, ed. Oscar Osburn Winther (Bloomington: Indiana University Press, 1958), 138; Richard M. Patchin and Deborah Jean Patchin, comps., *Letters of Jonathan Bridges: A Confederate Soldier of Stewart County, Georgia* (N.p., n.d.), 58.

33. Cass County is now Bartow County. Marcellus A. Stovall, who had left West

Point before graduating, was promoted to Confederate brigadier general in 1863. He had fought in the Atlanta campaign and was with the Army of Tennessee. Although he lived in Rome, it appears he had refugeed his family to Augusta early in the war. See Lucy Josephine Cunyus, *The History of Bartow County* ([Cartersville GA]: Tribune Publishing Co., 1933), 250–51; Connolly, *Three Years*, 334. Although the story of Cecelia (also spelled Cecilia) comes from Cunyus, it was substantiated by a man who is writing a family history (C. L. Bragg to the author, August 29, September 15, 1998). Pleasant A. Stovall, when editor of the *Augusta Chronicle*, asked Sherman specifically why he bypassed the city. In a letter written on October 21, 1888, and published in the *Confederate Veteran*, Sherman recalled his fear that the Confederates had fortified both Augusta and Macon but naturally did not mention Cecelia (*Confederate Veteran* 22 [August 1914]: 369).

34. Mills Lane, ed., *Times That Prove People's Principles: Civil War in Georgia, a Documentary History* (Savannah: Beehive Press, 1993), 152; Lawrence Huff, "'A Bitter Draught We have Had to Quaff': Sherman's March through the Eyes of Joseph Addison Turner," *Georgia Historical Quarterly* 72 (Summer 1988): 320; Glatthaar, *March to the Sea*, 128.

35. Kate Nichols later died in the mental institution. See Green, *Journal of a Milledgeville Girl*, 63. The *Savannah Daily Morning News* had taken the story from the *Augusta Register*.

36. *Savannah Daily Morning News*, December 2, 1864, quoting a letter in the *Macon Telegraph*; Paul D. Escott, "The Context of Freedom: Georgia's Slaves During the Civil War," *Georgia Historical Quarterly* 58 (Spring 1974): 93.

37. Adele Logan Alexander, *Ambiguous Lives: Free Women of Color in Rural Georgia, 1789–1879* (Fayetteville: University of Arkansas Press, 1991), 134–38.

38. Glatthaar, *March to the Sea*, 73. See also Michael Fellman, *Citizen Sherman: A Life of William Tecumseh Sherman* (New York: Random House, 1995), for more on the actions of Sherman's soldiers.

39. OR, 44:408; Connolly, *Three Years*, 335.

40. Connolly, *Three Years*, 329.

41. Trudeau, *Like Men of War*, 325, 328, 330; OR, 44:416.

42. Trudeau, *Like Men of War*, 330–31.

43. William R. Scaife, "Sherman's March to the Sea," *Blue & Gray Magazine* 7 (December 1989): 32.

44. Rowland, ed., *Davis*, 6:407, 408, 421.

45. Burge, *Diary*, 163, 165; Robert Manson Myers, ed., *The Children of Pride: A True Story of Georgia and the Civil War* (New Haven: Yale University Press, 1972), 1216.

46. Rowland, ed., *Davis*, 6:355, 413; Jones, *Rebel War Clerk's Diary*, 453; D. H. Blair to "Dear Brother," November 20 [30], 1864, Blair Papers.

5. HOOD'S ADVANCE INTO TENNESSEE

1. O. P. Bowser, "Notes on Granbury's Brigade," in Dudley G. Wooten, *A Comprehensive History of Texas, 1685 to 1897* (Dallas: William G. Scarff, 1898), 751; Foster, *One of Cleburne's Command*, 145.

2. The concept of total war is debated by historians. This term was not used during the Civil War and is subject to varying interpretations by twentieth-century students of war. It should be remembered, however, that actual destruction varied according to regions and events. Daniel E. Sutherland, who believes that John Pope tried to wage total war in Virginia in 1862, concludes: "Total war had been declared once again [in 1864], and this time, developed more fully and applied more widely than Pope had ever envisioned, it would prove deadly for the Confederacy. Yet Grant benefitted enormously from the fact that a precedent for waging war had already been set, the legal machinery erected, and the philosophy accepted" (Sutherland, "Abraham Lincoln, John Pope, and the Origins of Total War," *Journal of Military History* 56 [October 1992]: 585–86). The historian James M. McPherson agrees that in 1862 there was a "decisive turn toward total war," but not all historians concur. See McPherson, *Battle Cry of Freedom*, 490–510. For another point of view, see Mark E. Neely Jr., "Was the Civil War a Total War?" *Civil War History* 37 (March 1991): 5–28. Also see Eric T. Dean Jr., "Rethinking the Civil War: Beyond 'Revolutions,' 'Reconstructions,' and the 'New Social History,'" *Southern Historian* 15 (Spring 1994): 28–50.

3. Stephen V. Ash, *Middle Tennessee Society Transformed, 1860–1870: War and Peace in the Upper South* (Baton Rouge: Louisiana State University Press, 1988), 85–87. See also Benjamin Franklin Cooling, *Fort Donelson's Legacy: War and Society in Kentucky and Tennessee, 1862–1863* (Knoxville: University of Tennessee Press, 1997).

4. Ash, *Middle Tennessee Society*, 112–13.

5. Ash, *Middle Tennessee Society*, 89.

6. Watkins, "*Co. Aytch*," 227; Stephenson, *Civil War Memoir*, 274, 276.

7. November 16, Davis's day of prayer, was the day that Sherman left Atlanta. See Joslyn, ed., *Charlotte's Boys*, 288.

8. OR, 45:pt. 1, 1219.

9. OR, 45:pt. 2, 663; Foster, *One of Cleburne's Command*, 144; Stephenson, *Civil War Memoir*, 274, 276.

10. Stephenson, *Civil War Memoir*, 276; Joel Dyer Murphree, "Autobiography and Civil War Letters of Joel Murphree of Troy, Alabama," *Alabama Historical Quarterly* 19 (1957): 201.

11. Douglas Hale, *The Third Texas Cavalry in the Civil War* (Norman: University of Oklahoma Press, 1993), 254; George L. Griscom, *Fighting With Ross' Texas Cav-*

alry Brigade C.S.A.: The Diary of George L. Griscom, Adjutant, 9th Texas Cavalry Regiment (Hillsboro TX: Hill Junior College Press, 1976), 187.

12. OR, 45:pt. 1, 752.

13. Ash, *Middle Tennessee Society*, 86, 90–91.

14. Ash, *Middle Tennessee Society*, 135, 149; OR, 31:pt. 3, 262.

15. OR, 45:pt. 1, 356.

16. Wiley Sword, *The Confederacy's Last Hurrah: Spring Hill, Franklin, and Nashville* (1992; rpt. Lawrence: University Press of Kansas, 1993), 111.

17. OR, 39:pt. 2, 442; OR, 39:pt. 3, 64.

18. OR, 45:pt. 1, 970.

19. OR, 45:pt. 1, 970–71.

20. D. H. Blair to "Dear Sister," November 20 [30], 1864, Blair Papers.

21. Ash, *Middle Tennessee Society*, 103, 165–66.

22. OR, 45:pt. 1, 719–20, 736; R. W. Banks, *Battle of Franklin* (1908; rpt. Dayton OH: Morningside House, 1988), 24.

23. Leuschner, *Civil War Diary*, 49; Murphree, "Autobiography and Civil War Letters," 201; Stephenson, *Civil War Memoir*, 278–79.

24. Foster, *One of Cleburne's Command*, 146.

25. Charles Todd Quintard, *Doctor Quintard: Chaplain C.S.A. and Second Bishop of Tennessee*, ed. Arthur Howard Noll (Sewanee: University Press of Sewanee, Tennessee, 1905), 107–8.

26. Irving A. Buck, *Cleburne and His Command* (Jackson TN: McCowat-Mercer Press, 1959), 280. See also Craig L. Symonds, *Stonewall Jackson of the West: Patrick Cleburne and the Civil War* (Lawrence: University Press of Kansas, 1997), for a complete account.

27. Hood, *Advance and Retreat*, 283.

28. Murphree, "Autobiography and Civil War Letters," 201; OR, 45:pt. 1, 1243, 1254.

29. Watkins, *"Co. Aytch,"* 231.

30. Jessie and George Peters divorced after the war. In the divorce proceedings he complained that they had lived separately since May 1, 1863, a week before Van Dorn's death. The couple remarried some time later and were living in Memphis when he died in 1889. Jessie Peters lived until 1921, when she died in Memphis and was buried beside her husband. See Robert G. Hartje, *Van Dorn: The Life and Times of a Confederate General* (Nashville: Vanderbilt University Press, 1967), 307–20.

31. James Lee McDonough and Thomas L. Connelly, *Five Tragic Hours: The Battle of Franklin* (Knoxville: University of Tennessee Press, 1983), 42.

32. Sword, *The Confederacy's Last Hurrah*, 126.

33. John K. Shellenberger, *The Battle of Spring Hill, Tennessee, November 30, 1864* (Cleveland OH: Arthur H. Clark, 1916), 13.

34. Reminiscences of L. H. Mangum in *A Memorial and Biographical History of Johnson and Hill Counties, Texas* (Chicago: Lewis Publishing Company, 1892), 139–40.

35. Bowser, "Notes on Granbury's Brigade," 751.

36. Benjamin Franklin Cheatham, "The Lost Opportunity at Spring Hill, Tenn.—General Cheatham's Reply to Hood," *Southern Historical Society Papers* 9 (1881); 526; Sword, *The Confederacy's Last Hurrah*, 134; McDonough and Connelly, *Five Tragic Hours*, 55.

37. Sword, *The Confederacy's Last Hurrah*, 144–45.

38. McDonough and Connelly, *Five Tragic Hours*, 58; David E. Roth, "The Mysteries of Spring Hill, Tennessee," *Blue & Gray Magazine* 2 (October–November 1984): 28.

39. Sword, *The Confederacy's Last Hurrah*, 143, 152; Roth, "Mysteries of Spring Hill," 26.

40. Sword, *The Confederacy's Last Hurrah*, 152; McDonough and Connelly, *Five Tragic Hours*, 58.

41. Buck, *Cleburne and His Command*, 272–73.

42. Sword, *The Confederacy's Last Hurrah*, 155.

43. Losson, *Tennessee's Forgotten Warriors*, 210; Quintard, *Doctor Quintard*, 111.

44. Joslyn, ed., *Charlotte's Boys*, 291; Murphree, "Autobiography and Civil War Letters," 202; Stephenson, *Civil War Memoir*, 280; Jacob Cox, *The March to the Sea, Franklin and Nashville* (1882; rpt. New York: Jack Brussel, n.d.), 80.

45. Murphree, "Autobiography and Civil War Letters," 201.

6. HOOD AT FRANKLIN

1. Hitchcock, *Marching with Sherman*, 110–12.

2. Sword, *The Confederacy's Last Hurrah*, 156.

3. W. D. Gale to Kate Gale, January 14, 1865, *Confederate Veteran* 2 (January 1894): 4.

4. French, *Two Wars*, 292.

5. Van Horne, *Army of the Cumberland*, 471.

6. For a complete account of conditions in central Tennessee, see Stephen Ash's excellent analysis in *Middle Tennessee Society*.

7. Ash, *Middle Tennessee Society*, 100.

8. Grady McWhiney and Perry D. Jamieson, *Attack and Die: Civil War Military Tactics and the Southern Heritage* (Tuscaloosa: University of Alabama Press, 1982), 109.

9. "Frances," "Inside the Lines at Franklin," *Confederate Veteran* 3 (January 1895): 72; David R. Logsdon, comp. and ed., *Eyewitness at the Battle of Franklin* (1988; rpt. Nashville: Kettle Mills Press, 1991), 10; H. P. Figuers, "A Boy's Impressions of the Battle of Franklin," *Confederate Veteran* 23 (January 1915): 5.

10. Jacob D. Cox, *The Battle of Franklin, Tennessee, November 30, 1864* (1897; rpt. Dayton OH: Morningside House, 1983), 63.

11. Henry M. Field, *Bright Skies and Dark Shadows* (New York: Charles Scribner's Sons, 1890), 230–31; Losson, *Tennessee's Forgotten Warrior*, 218; Brian Steele Wills, *A Battle from the Start: The Life of Nathan Bedford Forrest* (1992; rpt. New York: Harper Perennial, 1993), 285. See also Robert Selph Henry, *"First with the Most": Forrest* (Indianapolis: Bobbs-Merrill, 1944).

12. Reminiscences of L. H. Mangum, 139; Symonds, *Stonewall Jackson of the West*, 255.

13. Hood, *Advance and Retreat*, 294; Buck, *Cleburne and His Command*, 280; *New York Herald*, December 5, 1864.

14. John M. Copley, *A Sketch of the Battle of Franklin, Tenn.; with Reminiscences of Camp Douglas* (Austin: Eugene Von Boeckmann, 1893), 42, 45–46.

15. Copley, *Sketch of the Battle of Franklin*, 46–48; Edwin H. Rennolds, *A History of the Henry County Commands* (Kennesaw GA: Continental Book Company, 1961), 104; Stephenson, *Civil War Memoir*, 281–82.

16. Estimates of the number of Confederates in the charge vary between sixteen thousand and eighteen thousand. See Foster, *One of Cleburne's Command*, 147; OR, 45:pt. 1, 737, Copley, *Sketch of the Battle of Franklin*, 48.

17. Horn, *Army of Tennessee*, 400; McMurry, *Hood*, 175; Cox, *March to the Sea, Franklin and Nashville*, 88; Cox, *Battle of Franklin*, 156.

18. Cox, *Battle of Franklin*, 156–57; *New York Herald*, December 3, 1864.

19. He did, however, return to the McEwen household several months later, after the war had ended, to hear the rest of the song (Field, *Bright Skies and Dark Shadows*, 248–49).

20. OR, 45:pt. 1, 653–54; Hood, *Advance and Retreat*, 293; Losson, *Tennessee's Forgotten Warrior*, 219; Stephenson, *Civil War Memoir*, 281; Ed. W. Smith Sr., "H. B. Granbury," in *Texans Who Wore the Gray*, ed. Sid S. Johnson (Tyler TX: Sid S. Johnson, 1907), 254; Rennolds, *Henry County Commands*, 104; Cox, *Battle of Franklin*, 119. For more on the use of Confederate artillery, see Larry J. Daniel, *Cannoneers in Gray: The Field Artillery of the Army of Tennessee, 1861–1865* (University: University of Alabama Press, 1984).

21. Figuers, "A Boy's Impressions of the Battle of Franklin," 6; Logsdon, comp. and ed., *Eyewitnesses at the Battle of Franklin*, 10, 12.

22. Cox, *Battle of Franklin*, 157; OR, 45:pt. 1, 256, 271.

23. Cox, *March to the Sea, Franklin and Nashville*, 89.

24. Cox, *March to the Sea, Franklin and Nashville*, 89–90.

25. Reminiscences of L. H. Mangum, 140–41; Cox, *Battle of Franklin*, 158.

26. Reminiscences of L. H. Mangum, 141. Granbury's brigade included three regiments of Texas infantry and five regiments of dismounted cavalry. Many of these men had been branded cowards for surrendering at Arkansas Post in early 1863, had fought hard to erase that stain on their honor, and had earned renown with the Army of Tennessee.

27. Losson, *Tennessee's Forgotten Warriors*, 221; McDonough and Connelly, *Five Tragic Hours*, 119.

28. Field, *Bright Skies and Dark Shadows*, 239, 245; S. A. Cunningham, "Battle of Franklin," *Confederate Veteran* 1 (April 1893): 102; B. T. Roberts, "Vivid Reminiscences of Franklin," *Confederate Veteran* 1 (November 1893): 339; S. A. Cunningham, "Death of Gen. Strahl," *Confederate Veteran* 1 (January 1893): 31.

29. Field, *Bright Skies and Dark Shadows*, 241.

30. "Louis Spencer Flatau," in Mamie Yeary, *Reminiscences of the Boys in Gray, 1861–1865* (1912; rpt. Dayton OH: Morningside House, 1986), 229–30.

31. Field, *Bright Skies and Dark Shadows*, 240–41.

32. Most of the fighting was done by Cheatham and Stewart. Bate's men, on Cheatham's far left, did not participate in the initial assault. Moreover, Stewart, on the right, could offer little assistance to the other Confederates because his line contracted as it moved toward an apex between the river and the railroad. Adding to the confusion, only one division of Lee's corps, that of Edward Johnson, reached the battle before it ended, but when these men joined the attack in the dark, they were repulsed. See OR, 45:pt. 1, 721; Copley, *Sketch of the Battle of Franklin*, 56.

33. John M. Payne, "Cleburne's Men at Franklin," *Confederate Veteran* 1 (June 1893): 172; "Gen. John Adams at Franklin," *Confederate Veteran* 5 (January 1897): 300; Field, *Bright Skies and Dark Shadows*, 252.

34. Figuers, "A Boy's Impressions of the Battle of Franklin," 6; "R. H. Cocke," "Louis Spencer Flatau," in Yeary, *Reminiscences of the Boys in Gray*, 142, 229–30; "Inside the Lines at Franklin," *Confederate Veteran* 3 (January 1895): 73; *New York Herald*, December 3, 1864.

35. Copley, *Battle of Franklin*, 64, 68; *New York Herald*, December 2, 1864.

36. Logsdon, comp. and ed., *Eyewitness at the Battle of Franklin*, 82; Jas. A. McCord to "Dear Brother," December 3, 1864, United Daughters of the Confederacy Collection, vol. 3, 221, GDAH.

37. OR, 45:pt. 2, 16; *New York Herald*, December 2, 1864.

38. Jones, *Rebel War Clerk's Diary*, 461.

39. OR, 45:pt. 2, 636, 639; William W. Heartsill, *Fourteen Hundred and 91 Days in*

the Confederate Army, ed. Bell Irvin Wiley (1876; rpt. Jackson TN: McCowat-Mercer Press, 1954), 216.

40. OR, 45:pt. 2, 659.

7. SHERMAN AT SAVANNAH

1. Jones, *Rebel War Clerk's Diary*, 455; OR, 45:pt. 2, 17.

2. Connolly, *Three Years*, 348.

3. Connolly, *Three Years*, 345; OR, 44:585, 601.

4. OR, 44:624.

5. Burke Davis, *Sherman's March* (1980; rpt. New York: Vintage Books, 1988), 88; Glatthaar, *March to the Sea*, 77; Nichols, *Story of the Great March*, 84; Hitchcock, *Marching with Sherman*, 150.

6. Glatthaar, *March to the Sea*, 53.

7. *New York Herald*, December 22, 1864.

8. Glatthaar, *March to the Sea*, 55.

9. Glatthaar, *March to the Sea*, 22.

10. Connolly, *Three Years*, 354–55.

11. Davis, *Sherman's March*, 92–94; James P. Jones, "General Jeff C. Davis, U.S.A. and Sherman's Georgia Campaign," *Georgia Historical Quarterly* 47 (March 1962): 243.

12. Connolly, *Three Years*, 347; Glatthaar, *March to the Sea*, 64; Davis, *Sherman's March*, 93.

13. *New York Herald*, December 22, 1864.

14. Partisans of Davis believed that it was the Nelson incident, and not anything the general did in Georgia, that prevented his promotion.

15. OR, 44:410; Kennett, *Marching Through Georgia*, 293.

16. Jones, *Rebel War Clerk's Diary*, 452–53.

17. Davis, *Sherman's March*, 89; Porter, *Campaigning with Grant*, 332–33.

18. Kennett, *Marching through Georgia*, 43.

19. Kennett, *Marching through Georgia*, 254; Hitchcock, *Marching with Sherman*, 166, 172, 176; Thomas Ward Osborn, *The Fiery Trail: A Union Officer's Account of Sherman's Last Campaigns*, ed. Richard Harwell and Philip N. Racine (Knoxville: University of Tennessee Press, 1986), 46; Rath, *Left for Dixie*, 64.

20. *New York Herald*, December 15, 1864; OR, 44:676.

21. Wills, *Army Life*, 334–35.

22. Hughes, *Hardee*, 258.

23. OR, 44:932.

24. OR, 44:940.

25. Keith P. Bohannon, "Ambrose Ransom Wright," in William C. Davis, ed.,

The Confederate General, 6 vols. (Harrisburg PA: National Historical Society, 1991), 6:161, 163.

26. Lesley Jill Gordon-Burr, "Gustavus W. Smith," *Encyclopedia of the Confederacy*, ed. Current, 4:1474.

27. Robert K. Krick, "Lafayette McLaws," *Encyclopedia of the Confederacy*, ed. Current, 3:974.

28. Hughes, *Hardee*, 261.

29. Hitchcock, ed., *Marching with Sherman*, 179–80; Nichols, *Story of the Great March*, 91; Lane, ed., *Marching through Georgia*, 173.

30. Scaife, "Sherman's March to the Sea," 40; OR, 44:122; Wills, *Army Life*, 335.

31. Connolly, *Three Years*, 362.

32. John W. Geary, *A Politician Goes to War: The Civil War Letters of John White Geary*, ed. William Alan Blair (University Park: Pennsylvania State University Press, 1995), 217.

33. Lane, ed., *Marching through Georgia*, 173; OR, 44:737; Osborn, *Fiery Trail*, 72.

34. Lane, ed., *Marching through Georgia*, 173; Geary, *Politician Goes to War*, 216, 218.

35. Charles C. Jones Jr., *The Siege of Savannah in December 1864* (Albany NY: Joel Munsell, 1874), 133–34.

36. Roger S. Durham, "Savannah: Mr. Lincoln's Christmas Present," *Blue & Gray Magazine* 8 (February 1991): 48; Henry Graves to "My Dearest Mother," December 28, 1864, United Daughters of the Confederacy Collection, vol. 6, 341, GDAH.

37. Connolly, *Three Years*, 368; Wills, *Army Life*, 335.

38. Jones, *Siege of Savannah*, 163; Geary, *Politician Goes to War*, 219.

39. Fellman, *Citizen Sherman*, 163; Glatthaar, *March to the Sea*, 57; Sherman, *Memoirs*, 2:248. The 110th USCT was organized at Pulaski in November 1863 as the Second Alabama Colored Infantry. Its designation was changed to the 110th USCT on June 25, 1864. See OR, 47:pt. 1, 48, 69, 238.

40. Fellman, *Citizen Sherman*, 166; Marszalek, *Sherman*, 315, Lane, ed., *Marching through Georgia*, 195.

8. HOOD AT NASHVILLE

1. OR, 44:702.

2. OR, 44:702.

3. OR, 44:728.

4. Before the war, Thomas owned a female slave he had purchased for his wife. When he left Texas in November 1860, he tried to free her, but she objected and he

took her with him back to Virginia (McKinney, *Education in Violence*, 82–83, 89–90).

5. McKinney, *Education in Violence*, 93.

6. OR, 44:728.

7. OR, 45:pt. 2, 17, 55, 70.

8. Thomas Connolly pointed out that fewer than 16,000 infantry had gone into battle that day. Of the 6,200 casualties, 1,570 were killed. Hood had "suffered more battle deaths than did the Union army at Fredericksburg, Chickamauga, Chancellorsville, Shiloh, or Stone's River," (Connolly, *Autumn of Glory*, 506; OR, 45:pt. 2, 643–44).

9. Thomas P. Lowry, *The Story the Soldiers Wouldn't Tell: Sex in the Civil War* (Mechanicsburg PA: Stackpole Books, 1994), 79–82.

10. Sword, *The Confederacy's Last Hurrah*, 301.

11. McMurry, *Hood*, 178.

12. OR, 45:pt. 1, 658, 663.

13. Foster, *One of Cleburne's Command*, 151.

14. OR, 45:pt. 2, 3.

15. Wiley Sword, "The Battle of Nashville: The Desperation of the Hour," *Blue & Gray Magazine* 11 (December 1993): 18.

16. Sword, *The Confederacy's Last Hurrah*, 290; OR, 45:pt. 2, 84.

17. Sword, "Battle of Nashville," 18.

18. OR, 45:pt. 2, 97, 115.

19. OR, 45:pt. 2, 15–16.

20. OR, 45:pt 2, III, II2.

21. Stephenson, *Civil War Memoir*, 315–16.

22. Foster, *One of Cleburne's Command*, 153; Rennolds, *Henry County Commands*, 110; Stanley F. Horn, comp. and ed., *Tennessee's War, 1861–1865, Described by Participants* (Nashville: Tennessee Civil War Commission, 1965), 329; Leuschner, *Civil War Diary*, 51.

23. Horn, *Tennessee's War*, 323.

24. Foster, *One of Cleburne's Command*, 151; Stephenson, *Civil War Memoir*, 292.

25. OR, 45:pt. 2, 653, 657.

26. Foster, *One of Cleburne's Command*, 151, 153; Stephenson, *Civil War Memoir*, 292.

27. F. Halsey Wigfall to "Dear Lou," December 5, 1864, Wigfall Papers, Library of Congress; Sword, "Battle of Nashville," 23; McMurry, *Hood*, 177; Chesnut, *Mary Chesnut's Civil War*, 683.

28. Robert C. Carden, whose reminiscences were published in *Independent*, a newspaper in Manchester, Tennessee, in 1921, are preserved in a scrapbook in the

possession of his namesake, Robert C. Carden, located on the Web at http:// www2.dmci.net/users/bmacd/default.htm.

29. There is disagreement over when Grant learned of the attack on Nashville. Grant left City Point on the afternoon of December 14 and arrived in Washington the next afternoon. One story claims that after turning an order removing Thomas over to the telegraph operator, he retired to the Willard Hotel to rest before departing for Nashville himself. According to this account, he did not know the wires were down and the telegraph operator could not relay the message to Thomas until service was restored. Other sources contest this story so the truth will never be known. See Bruce Catton, *Grant Takes Command* (Boston: Little, Brown, 1969), 399–400; Porter, *Campaigning with Grant*, 348–49; David Homer Bates, *Lincoln in the Telegraph Office* (New York: Century, 1907), 314–16; Sword, *The Confederacy's Last Hurrah*, 345–47.

30. "Smith's Guerrillas" is also sometimes spelled "Smith's Gorillas." For the quotes, see Sword, *The Confederacy's Last Hurrah*, 276; Ludwell H. Johnson, *Red River Campaign: Politics and Cotton in the Civil War* (1958; rpt. Kent OH: Kent State University Press, 1993), 165.

31. Smith's detachment from the Army of the Tennessee, along with a cavalry brigade, had been en route for Nashville when Price started on his Missouri raid in September. Diverted, the midwesterners followed the Rebels across Missouri and into Kansas. After helping to defeat Price in late October near the Kansas-Missouri border, Smith turned back toward St. Louis, marching hundreds of miles down muddy roads and across swollen streams. See Johnson, *Red River Campaign*, 270; Mark M. Boatner III, *Civil War Dictionary* (New York: David McKay, 1959), 290, 768; Warner, *Generals in Blue*, 454–55; Horn, *Tennessee's War*, 322.

32. Trudeau, *Like Men of War*, 340.

33. Trudeau, *Like Men of War*, 335.

34. Trudeau, *Like Men of War*, 336–37.

35. OR, 45:pt. 1, 541.

36. Trudeau, *Like Men of War*, 276–77.

37. Sword, *The Confederacy's Last Hurrah*, 40.

9. HOOD AND THOMAS

1. OR, 45:pt. 1, 154; OR, 45:pt. 2, 168.

2. OR, 45:pt 2, 115, 180; Sword, *The Confederacy's Last Hurrah*, 317.

3. Trudeau, *Like Men of War*, 340–41; OR, 45:pt. 1, 94.

4. Later gaining fame as "Pecos Bill," the thirty-year-old Michigan-born Shafter would fail to gain recognition in Civil War narratives, but he found a place in history by leading the army in Cuba during the Spanish-American War in 1898.

5. Trudeau, *Like Men of War*, 343; Sword, *The Confederacy's Last Hurrah*, 325, 357.

6. Foster, *One of Cleburne's Command*, 153; Stephenson, *Civil War Memoir*, 320.

7. OR, 45:pt. 1, 527.

8. Stephenson, *Civil War Memoir*, 320.

9. Selene Harding later married William H. Jackson, a brigadier general under Forrest. See Horn, *Tennessee's War*, 327, 344–45; Stephenson, *Civil War Memoir*, 321–22; Stanley F. Horn, *The Decisive Battle of Nashville* (1956; rpt. Baton Rouge: Louisiana State University Press, 1984), 85.

10. Sword, *The Confederacy's Last Hurrah*, 336.

11. Horn, *Tennessee's War*, 332; Hood, *Advance and Retreat*, 304.

12. Horn, *Tennessee's War*, 332.

13. *New York Herald*, December 22, 1864.

14. OR, 45:pt. 2, 194–95.

15. OR, 45:pt. 2, 210.

16. Sword, *The Confederacy's Last Hurrah*, 354.

17. Trudeau, *Like Men of War*, 345.

18. Trudeau, *Like Men of War*, 344–46.

19. OR, 45:pt. 1, 705; Sword, *The Confederacy's Last Hurrah*, 362–63.

20. Although the identity of Smith's attacker was never officially determined, it seems to have been Colonel McMillan. McMillan was one of "Smith's Guerrillas." Before joining the Union army, he had served as a surgeon with the Russians during the Crimean War. As a Union soldier, he had a checkered military record, having survived various charges in military courts, including "unsoldierlike conduct." McMillan became violent when General Tom Smith, whom he had captured at the hill, hurled angry words at him. The Ohio-born McMillan responded by hitting Smith about the head with his sword, inflicting several wounds on his twenty-six-year-old prisoner. Although the surgeons thought the young Confederate would die because of severe damage to his head, Smith survived. He even ran for Congress in 1870, but six years later the brain damage became so obvious that he was confined to the Tennessee State Hospital for the Insane, just a few miles from the Nashville battle site. He lived the last forty-six years of his life in the institution, outliving his attacker by twenty-one years. See OR, 45:pt. 1, 442; Horn, *Decisive Battle of Nashville*, 126, 141; Paul H. Stockdale, *The Death of an Army: The Battle of Nashville and Hood's Retreat* (Murfreesboro: Southern Heritage Press, 1992), 179.

21. Sword, "Battle of Nashville," 48; Horn, *Decisive Battle of Nashville*, 143.

22. Rennolds, *Henry County Commands*, 111–12; Horn, *Tennessee's War*, 346.

23. Watkins, *"Co. Aytch,"* 240; Stephenson, *Civil War Memoir*, 327, 330.

24. Stephenson, *Civil War Memoir*, 334–35; Horn, *Decisive Battle of Nashville*, 144.

25. *New York Herald*, December 22, 1864; Horn, *Tennessee's War*, 345.

26. Foster, *One of Cleburne's Command*, 154–55; Leuschner, *Civil War Diary*, 51; *New York Herald*, December 16, 1864.

27. Hood, *Advance and Retreat*, 304; *New York Herald*, December 22, 1864.

28. Stephenson, *Civil War Memoir*, 332.

29. OR, 44:740–41, 798–99.

30. Quintard, *Doctor Quintard*, 123.

31. Foster, *One of Cleburne's Command*, 158–59.

32. McMurry, *Hood*, 180.

33. OR, 45:pt. 2, 295–96.

34. OR, 45:pt. 1, 42, 170; OR, 45:pt. 2, 295; James Harrison Wilson, "The Union Cavalry in the Hood Campaign," in Robert U. Johnson and Clarence C. Buel, eds., *Battles and Leaders of the Civil War*, 4 vols. (New York: Century, 1884–1887, 1888), 4:471.

35. McKinney, *Education in Violence*, 432.

36. OR, 45:pt. 2, 382.

37. Clement A. Evans, ed., *Confederate Military History*, vol. 8, *Tennessee*, by James D. Porter (Atlanta: Confederate Publishing Co., 1899), 170; George W. Peddy, *Saddle Bag and Spinning Wheel Being the Civil War Letters of George W. Peddy, M.D. . . . and His Wife Kate Featherston Peddy*, ed. George Peddy Cuttino (Macon: Mercer University Press, 1981), 296.

38. OR, 39:pt. 2, 850–51; OR, ser. IV, 3:989; Daniel, *Cannoneers in Gray*, 180; John Q. Anderson, ed., *Campaigning with Parsons' Texas Cavalry Brigade, CSA: The War Journals and Letters of the Four Orr Brothers, 12th Texas Cavalry Regiment* (Hillsboro TX: Hill Junior College Press, 1967), 155; Sword, *The Confederacy's Last Hurrah*, 426; McMurry, *Hood*, 123; Hood, *Advance and Retreat*, 307; Brown, *To the Manner Born*, 257.

39. Lane, ed., *Marching through Georgia*, 187, 189; *New York Herald*, December 27, 1864.

IO. HOOD AND SHERMAN

1. OR, 44:783; *New York Herald*, December 22, 27, 1864.

2. Osborn, *Fiery Trail*, 75; *Charleston Mercury*, December 28, 1864; Mary E. Hopkins to Thomas W. Bartlett, December 23, 1864, Blanton Family Papers.

3. OR, 44:809.

4. Hitchcock, *Marching with Sherman*, 199.

slaves, see Edmund L. Drago, "How Sherman's March Through Georgia Affected the Slaves," *Georgia Historical Quarterly* 57 (Spring 1973): 361–75, and Escott, "Context of Freedom," 79–104.

6. Lane, ed., *Marching through Georgia*, 186; OR, 30:pt. 3, 698–99.

7. Lane, ed., *Marching through Georgia*, 190; Nichols, *Story of the Great March*, 108.

8. Spencer B. King Jr., ed., "Fanny Cohen's Journal of Sherman's Occupation of Savannah," *Georgia Historical Quarterly* 41 (December 1957): 412, 414; Jim Miles, *To the Sea: A History and Tour Guide of Sherman's March* Nashville: Rutledge Hill Press, 1989), 238.

9. Although the young writer criticized the actions of Savannah's citizens, it was their decision to acquiesce that prevented Sherman from destroying the city. See Ellen Renshaw House, *A Very Violent Rebel: The Civil War Diary of Ellen Renshaw House*, ed. Daniel E. Sutherland (Knoxville: University of Tennessee Press, 1996), 139. See also Katharine M. Jones, *When Sherman Came: Southern Women and the "Great March"* (New York: Bobbs-Merrill, 1964), 90.

10. Bryan, *Confederate Georgia*, 153–54.

11. Parks, *Joseph E. Brown*, 315.

12. Anderson, *Campaigning with Parsons' Texas Cavalry Brigade*, 155–56; Ash, *Middle Tennessee Society*, 168; OR, 45:pt. 2, 471, 732.

13. Lane, ed., "*Dear Mother*," 336, 338; fragment of letters of William F. Chancely dated June 8 and June 19, 1864, courtesy of Amma C. Crum.

14. Jones, *Rebel War Clerk's Diary*, 463, 465–68, 474.

15. William C. Davis, *Jefferson Davis: The Man and His Hour* (1991; rpt. Baton Rouge: Louisiana State University Press, 1996), 576.

16. Simms, *Letters*, 4:474.

17. Critics of Sherman take him to task for not destroying the Confederate army during the campaign for Atlanta.

18. Stephen E. Ambrose, *Halleck: Lincoln's Chief of Staff* (1962; rpt. Baton Rouge: Louisiana State University Press, 1990), 195.

19. Myers, ed., *Children of Pride*, 1244; Lane, ed., *Times That Prove People's Principles*, 235.

20. Rowland, ed., *Davis*, 6:428. Davis had been discussing with Smith the possibility of sending troops across the river and on September 29 had wired Smith that if he could not persuade Walker's infantry division to cross, he could substitute Wharton's cavalry. For more on the reluctance of the Texans to cross the Mississippi and their discontent with the army in the autumn of 1864, see Anne J. Bailey, *Between the Enemy and Texas: Parsons's Texas Cavalry in the Civil War* (Fort Worth: Texas Christian University Press, 1989), 194–202.

21. Undated clipping, probably March 1865, Wigfall Papers, Library of Congress.

22. Joseph E. Johnston, *Narrative of Military Operations, Directed, during the Late War between the States* (New York: D. Appleton, 1874); Sherman, *Memoirs*, 2:167. See also Hood, *Advance and Retreat*.

23. Cox, *March to the Sea, Franklin and Nashville*; Cox, *Battle of Franklin*; Sword, *The Confederacy's Last Hurrah*, 441.

24. OR, 38:pt. 5, 857. To argue that any competent Union commander could have achieved the same result would require deciding who that man might be. The historian Albert Castel concluded that "had Thomas's personal relationship with Grant permitted him to command in Georgia in 1864, almost surely the Union victory would have been easier, quicker, and more complete." While this may be an exaggeration, it is food for thought (Castel, *Decision in the West*, 565).

25. After his victory at Nashville, Grant soon broke up Thomas's command. Thomas may have been fortunate in dying before he could become involved in the postwar debates. Sherman followed Grant as commander in chief of the army, serving fourteen years, until 1884. Schofield held that position from 1888 until 1895.

26. Boatner, *Civil War Dictionary*, 768; Warner, *Generals in Blue*, 454–55.

27. Hood, *Advance and Retreat*, 263–64.

28. Jefferson Davis, *The Rise and Fall of the Confederate Government*, 2 vols. (New York: D. Appleton, 1881), 2:611.

29. Davis, *The Cause Lost*, 127–47; Rowland, ed., *Davis*, 6:358. For recent evaluations of the importance of the fall of Atlanta on the election as well as McClellan's chances of winning and bringing a negotiated peace, see Albert Castel's *Decision in the West* and "The Atlanta Campaign and the Presidential Election of 1864." For a rebuttal, see Daniel, "The South Almost Won by Not Losing." For additional information on the election, refer to Waugh, *Reelecting Lincoln*; David E. Long, *The Jewel of Liberty: Abraham Lincoln's Re-election and the End of Slavery* (Mechanicsburg PA: Stackpole Books, 1994); and William W. Freehling, *The Reintegration of American History, Slavery and the Civil War* (New York: Oxford University Press, 1994), and Nelson, *Bullets, Ballots, and Rhetoric*.

30. Although one could argue that Lee's surrender at Appomattox was a defeat of one of the Confederacy's main armies, it was not the kind of defeat that Hood's army suffered in Tennessee.

Bibliographical Essay

There are many fine books that deal with either Hood's Tennessee campaign or Sherman's March to the Sea, but only general narratives of the war consider both events in one volume. For a detailed background of the autumn campaigns of 1864 and the first battles between Hood and Sherman, see Albert Castel's fine volume *Decision in the West: The Atlanta Campaign of 1864* (Lawrence: University Press of Kansas, 1992). The most comprehensive description of the Tennessee campaign is Wiley Sword's excellent *The Confederacy's Last Hurrah: Spring Hill, Franklin, and Nashville* (1992; rpt. Lawrence: University Press of Kansas, 1993). For a less detailed version, see James Lee McDonough and Thomas L. Connelly, *Five Tragic Hours: The Battle of Franklin* (Knoxville: University of Tennessee Press, 1983). Older but still useful is Stanley F. Horn's *The Decisive Battle of Nashville* (1956; rpt. Baton Rouge: Louisiana State University Press, 1984). A popular but readable version is Winston Groom's *Shrouds of Glory—From Atlanta to Nashville: The Last Great Campaign of the Civil War* (New York: Atlantic Monthly Press, 1995). For Sherman's March to the Sea, see Lee Kennett, *Marching through Georgia: The Story of Soldiers and Civilians During Sherman's Campaign* (New York: Harper Collins, 1995), and Joseph T. Glatthaar's excellent work *The March to the Sea and Beyond: Sherman's Troops in the Savannah and Carolinas Campaign* (New York: New York University Press, 1985). Two older works are helpful, both by Jacob Cox, *The March to the Sea, Franklin and Nashville* (1882; rpt. New York: Jack Brussel, n.d.), and *The Battle of Franklin, Tennessee, November 30, 1864* (1897; rpt. Dayton OH: Morningside Bookshop, 1983). For a Southern firsthand account written after the war, see Charles C. Jones Jr., *The Siege of Savannah in December, 1864* (Albany NY: Joel Munsell, 1874). Although there are many popularized accounts of Sherman's march, one of the better remains Burke Davis, *Sherman's March* (1980; rpt. New York: Vintage Books, 1988).

The armies engaged in these two campaigns have also had their share of study. For the Confederate side, the classic *Autumn of Glory: The Army of Tennessee, 1862–1865* (Baton Rouge: Louisiana State University Press, 1971) by Thomas Lawrence Connelly is the place to begin. Other useful books include Stanley F. Horn's *The*

Army of Tennessee: A Military History (Indianapolis: Bobbs-Merrill, 1941); Larry J. Daniel's two fine studies, *Cannoneers in Gray: The Field Artillery of the Army of Tennessee, 1861–1865* (University: University of Alabama Press, 1984) and *Soldiering in the Army of Tennessee: A Portrait of Life in a Confederate Army* (Chapel Hill: University of North Carolina Press, 1991); Richard McMurry's engaging comparison, *Two Great Rebel Armies: An Essay in Confederate Military History* (Chapel Hill: University of North Carolina Press, 1989); and Steven E. Woodworth's fine analytical study of command relationships, *Jefferson Davis and His Generals: The Failure of Confederate Command in the West* (Lawrence: University Press of Kansas, 1990). For the Union side, see the modern version of the old but worthwhile Thomas B. Van Horne, *The Army of the Cumberland* (1875; rpt. New York: Konecky & Konecky, 1996). African American soldiers have received both comprehensive and excellent treatment in Noah Andre Trudeau's *Like Men of War: Black Troops in the Civil War, 1862–1865* (New York: Little, Brown, 1998). The cavalry is analyzed in Stephen Z. Starr's classic *The Union Cavalry in the Civil War*, vol. 3, *The War in the West, 1861–1865* (Baton Rouge: Louisiana State University Press, 1985).

Books on the commanders include works by the participants themselves. William T. Sherman's *Memoirs of General William T. Sherman*, 2 vols. (1875; rpt. New York: DaCapo Press, 1984), remains useful, but for a more balanced account see John F. Marszalek, *Sherman: A Soldier's Passion for Order* (New York: Free Press, 1993). Michael Fellman's *Citizen Sherman: A Life of William Tecumseh Sherman* (New York: Random House, 1995) provides a different point of view on this controversial commander. Another work that is helpful in understanding the psychology of the campaign to the sea is Charles Royster, *The Destructive War: William Tecumseh Sherman, Stonewall Jackson, and the Americans* (New York: Knopf, 1991). There is no modern biography of George Thomas, but one can read Thomas B. Van Horne, *The Life of Major-General George H. Thomas* (New York: Charles Scribner's & Sons, 1882); Francis F. McKinney, *Education in Violence: The Life of George H. Thomas and the History of the Army of the Cumberland* (Detroit: Wayne State University Press, 1961), or Freeman Cleaves *Rock of Chickamauga: The Life of General George H. Thomas* (Norman: University of Oklahoma Press, 1948), for an account of his career. John Schofield wrote his version of the war in *Forty-Six Years in the Army* (New York: Century, 1897), but James L. McDonough's biography, *Schofield: Union General in the Civil War and Reconstruction* (Tallahassee: Florida State University Press, 1972), is probably more accurate. John Bell Hood also told his own story in *Advance and Retreat: Personal Experiences in the United States and Confederate Armies* (1880; rpt. Lincoln: University of Nebraska Press, 1996), but Richard M. McMurry stripped away the veneer to find the real story in *John Bell Hood and the War for Southern Independence* (Lexington: University Press of Kentucky, 1982). P. G. T. Beauregard also had his biographer, although he wrote most of Alfred Roman's *Military Operations of General Beauregard*, 2 vols. (New York: Harper & Brothers, 1884 [1883]) himself. A balanced account is T. Harry Williams, *P. G. T. Beauregard: Napoleon in Gray* (1954;

rpt. Baton Rouge: Louisiana State University Press, 1995). The three Confederate corps commanders have their biographies too. Those include Marshall Wingfield's older work, *General A. P. Stewart: His Life and Letters* (Memphis: West Tennessee Historical Society, 1954) and a new biography by Sam Davis Elliot, *Soldier of Tennessee: General A. P. Stewart and the Civil War in the West* (Baton Rouge: Louisiana State University Press, 1999); Christopher Losson, *Tennessee's Forgotten Warriors: Frank Cheatham and His Confederate Division* (Knoxville: University of Tennessee Press, 1989); and Herman Hattaway, *General Stephen D. Lee* (Jackson: University Press of Mississippi, 1976). One renowned Rebel division commander is analyzed in Craig L. Symonds, *Stonewall Jackson of the West: Patrick Cleburne and the Civil War* (Lawrence: University Press of Kansas, 1997). For William Hardee's defense of Savannah, see Nathaniel Cheairs Hughes Jr. *General William J. Hardee: Old Reliable* (1965 rpt. Baton Rouge: Louisiana State University Press, 1992).

There are numerous accounts by individual soldiers. Some of the best Union books are James A. Connolly's *Three Years in the Army of the Cumberland: The Letters and Diary of Major James A. Connolly* (Bloomington: Indiana University Press, 1959); Henry Hitchcock, *Marching with Sherman*, ed. M. A. DeWolfe Howe (New Haven: Yale University Press, 1927); Charles W. Wills, *Army Life of an Illinois Soldier* (1906; rpt. Carbondale: Southern Illinois University Press, 1996); Alfred Lacey Hough, *Soldiering in the West: The Civil War Letters of Alfred Lacey Hough*, ed. Robert G. Athearn (Philadelphia: University of Pennsylvania Press, 1957); George Ward Nichols, *The Story of the Great March* (1865; rpt. Williamstown MA: Corner House Publishers, 1972); Thomas Ward Osborn, *The Fiery Trail: A Union Officer's Account of Sherman's Last Campaigns*, ed. Richard Harwell and Philip N. Racine (Knoxville: University of Tennessee Press, 1986); John W. Geary, *A Politician Goes to War: The Civil War Letters of John White Geary*, ed. William Alan Blair (University Park: Pennsylvania State University Press, 1995); Theodore F. Upson, *With Sherman to the Sea: The Civil War Letters, Diaries and Reminiscences of Theodore F. Upson*, ed. Oscar Osburn Winther (Bloomington: Indiana University Press, 1958). On the Confederate side, see the modern version of the engaging personal recollections Sam R. Watkins, *"Co. Aytch": A Side Show of the Big Show* (1952; rpt. New York: Macmillan, 1962). A useful diary is Samuel T. Foster, *One of Cleburne's Command: The Civil War Reminiscences and Diary of Capt. Samuel T. Foster, Granbury's Texas Brigade, CSA*, ed. Norman D. Brown (Austin: University of Texas Press, 1980).

The political scene has been the subject of two recent works: John C. Waugh *Reelecting Lincoln: The Battle for the 1864 Presidency* (New York: Crown, 1997), and David E. Long, *The Jewel of Liberty: Abraham Lincoln's Re-election and the End of Slavery* (Mechanicsburg PA: Stackpole Books 1994). For an older account, see Larry E. Nelson, *Bullets, Ballots, and Rhetoric: Confederate Policy for the United States Presidential Contest of 1864* (University: University of Alabama Press, 1980). All of these were invaluable in addressing the events of September through November 1864. Also see Joseph Allan Frank, *With Ballot and Bayonet: The Political Socialization of*

American Civil War Soldiers (Athens: University of Georgia Press, 1998), for how citizen soldiers were becoming politically aware. The one-volume condensed and annotated version of John B. Jones's wartime diary edited by Earl Schenck Miers (Baton Rouge: Louisiana State University Press, 1993) is a brief and readable version of the 1958 two-volume set and highly useful in gauging the political mood in Richmond.

The societal effects of the two campaigns can be found in several books. For Tennessee, see Stephen V. Ash, *Middle Tennessee Society Transformed, 1860–1870: War and Peace in the Upper South* (Baton Rouge: Louisiana State University Press, 1988), and Stanley F. Horn, comp. and ed., *Tennessee's War 1861–1865, Described by Participants* (Nashville: Tennessee Civil War Commission, 1965). For a look at Georgia, consult Mary A. DeCredico, *Patriotism for Profit: Georgia's Urban Entrepreneurs and the Confederate War Effort* (Chapel Hill: University of North Carolina Press, 1988); Joseph Howard Parks, *Joseph E. Brown of Georgia* (Baton Rouge: Louisiana State University Press, 1977); and T. Conn Bryan, *Confederate Georgia* (Athens: University of Georgia Press, 1953). Excellent firsthand accounts are found in Robert Manson Myers, ed., *Children of Pride: A True Story of Georgia and the Civil War* (New Haven: Yale University Press, 1972), and Katharine M. Jones, *When Sherman Came: Southern Women and the "Great March"* (New York: Bobbs-Merrill, 1964).

The experience of African Americans in Georgia is found in Clarence L. Mohr, *On the Threshold of Freedom: Masters and Slaves in Civil War Georgia* (Athens: University of Georgia Press, 1986); Whittington B. Johnson, *Black Savannah, 1788–1864* (Fayetteville: University of Arkansas Press, 1996); and Adele Logan Alexander, *Ambiguous Lives: Free Women of Color in Rural Georgia, 1789–1879* (Fayetteville: University of Arkansas Press, 1991.)

As with any suggested list of books, the reader needs to remember that memoirs, reminiscences, and any other accounts written by the participants after the war must be used with caution. While they often give us valuable information not found elsewhere, each one must be evaluated carefully on its own merits.

Index